THE MEANING OF LOVE

The Meaning of Love
Copyright © 2025 Johanna S. Billings

All rights reserved under the pan-american and international copyright conventions. This book may not be reproduced in whole or in part, except for brief quotations embodied in critical articles or reviews, in any form or by any means, electronic or mechanical, including photocopying, recording, or by any information storage and retrieval system now known or hereinafter invented, without written permission of the publisher.

All stories, characters, and incidents depicted in this book are products of the author's imagination. Any resemblance to actual persons, living or dead, events, or locales is entirely coincidental. The author and publisher assume no responsibility for any such similarities.

ISBN Paperback: 978-1-963271-76-8
ISBN ebook 978-1-963271-77-5

Published by Armin Lear Press, inc.
215 W Riverside Drive, #4362
Estes Park, CO 80517

A MEMOIR

JOHANNA S. BILLINGS

ACKNOWLEDGMENTS

If it weren't for healing, there would be no book. Therefore, I must acknowledge those who made my healing possible. Many of them are mentioned in the story, but I'd like to mention them here too.

First and foremost is Sean. That man is incredible. No words can really convey just how incredible he is. I've had therapists over the years tell me that it's not uncommon for a spouse to leave during a medical crisis, let alone a mental health crisis. Not only did he stay, but he also supported me, making appointments, finding me the care I needed, and just being there. I know it wasn't always easy for him.

Next would be my longtime friend Cheryl, who saved my life in April 2014. Equally importantly, she and I had a lot of good times. I remember laughing hysterically while trying to get photos of ourselves with all of my cats — none of whom was very thrilled about posing together. Back when long-distance phone calls were expensive, we used to make excuses for spending money and talking to each other, too. What wonderful memories.

And, of course, I also appreciate the cats themselves — Puff,

Big Zepp, Wee-Cat, Smokey, Kira Kat, Fred, Dexter, Sharpie, Macy, Pash, Lily, and Little Guy — and their unconditional love.

My Maine friends are also a big part of my healing, though I'm sure they don't realize it. So, thank you to my closest friends, Janice, Holly, Eric, DD, Terri, Wendy, and Cherilyn. By the time you read this, I will have a pile of goodies for each of you for our trades.

There have been other Mainers who have been good to me along the way. I thank them for the writing and photography opportunities they afforded me and, in some cases, their patience. These include but are not limited to Rick Levasseur, Cindy Wood, Stephen Fay, Letitia Baldwin, Edward French, Lora Whelan, Adrian Aveni, Stan Rintz, Sandy Malagara and the folks at the Schooner Gallery.

Although the healing process hadn't really begun by the time I was at North Allegheny, my track coaches, Mr. Cerny and Mr. Sabados, were a wonderfully positive force. It was through them and their coaching that I tasted joy and was motivated to go after more. Thanks, also, to my aunt and uncle on my dad's side, Frank and Mary Ann, for caring about me during the dark times at Redbank Valley. I also wish to acknowledge Mark and both the school nurse and guidance counselor there for caring enough to notice something wasn't right and calling child welfare services, even if it didn't work out as I'd hoped. The health suite there was one of the few havens I had at that time.

Special thanks to Dr. Anne Kaler and Dr. Carol Breslin, who were among my writing mentors at Gwynedd-Mercy College. They got me started and without them, I would not have gotten to where I am now.

And, of course, I thank my German language teacher at Penn State, along with the campus therapist there, whose names I no longer remember, for kicking off that leg of the journey. Thanks also to Jack, Mim, Carol, and Joel, who took over after Carol retired, for taking the baton and running with it in this relay called my life. I'd also be remiss if I didn't mention Ken and his parents.

The actual process of writing a book is a true collaboration. It requires many people to make it happen. Topping this list is Maryann Karinch of The Rudy Agency, who answered my query for this book back in 2016. It took a while for all the pieces to fall together, mostly on my end. She remained patient and offered suggestions that actually made it possible to tell this story. I appreciate her taking a chance on me, sticking with it, and finally bringing me to Armin Lear Press.

Thanks, also, to editor Vince Lupiano. The editing process was smooth and fast, even with the technology gremlins we encountered. I've always believed writing for publication is a collaboration, and together we make it better.

Thanks again to Sean and Cheryl for reading many versions of the manuscript. Thanks also to readers Danielle Woerner and SallyAnn Gray for their feedback.

IN LOVING MEMORY OF
ANNE KALER
FRIEND AND MENTOR
1935–2025

CONTENTS

1	Maine	1
2	A Journey Begins	9
3	The Cup of Heartache	17
4	Fear	37
5	Detours	53
6	Post Processing	67
7	A Family Dismantled	79
8	Nicole	91
9	The Wall	105
10	Cause and Effect	119
11	Hell is for Children	131
12	Security	155
13	Death and its Aftermath	165
14	The Respite of Maine Life	175
15	The Setup	183
16	Lessons from Cats	205
17	The Good Daughter	219
18	Speed	239
19	Exit Strategy	263
20	Gaining Independence	283
21	Facing the Ghosts	303
22	The Final Betrayal	319
23	The Crash	335
24	Rising from the Ashes	349
	Timeline	359

- 1 -

MAINE

There's something magical about crossing the Piscataqua River Bridge.

After miles of ordinary highway, the road turns sharply to the right, and you begin to see the greenish-gray framework of the bridge gently rising from the road. The top curves gracefully, and as you drive onto the bridge, you find yourself enveloped in a geometric framework that is both above and beside you.

Before you can fully appreciate the feeling, you're at the center of the bridge, where a sign with white lettering delivers the news that makes the long trip from Pennsylvania worthwhile.

Maine State Line.

Suddenly the sun seems brighter, the air fresher. A sign at the far end of the bridge notes that Maine is "the way life should be." Many come here to take a break from the rat race that characterizes life elsewhere. Many come back repeatedly, and quite a few stay.

Finally, after 20 years of visits, I did what I was meant to do all along — I stayed. And it changed my life.

Maine is where I learned that hope is not just an illusion. Maine is where I learned not to be afraid.

—

I was born and raised in Pennsylvania but never felt like I belonged. Maybe it's because we moved around so much when I was a kid. I went to six different public schools, and I think I learned how to mingle superficially but not how to form lasting friendships.

Sean and I were married in Pittsburgh in 1988, and except for a weekend in a hotel not far from the city, we never had a honeymoon. Our first trip to Maine two years later was also our first real vacation — a whole glorious week visiting Acadia National Park. We tent-camped to cut costs, and we didn't buy much in Bar Harbor because we couldn't afford it. Still, we were so struck by the beauty of the rugged coast and rural inland scenery that we returned again and again over the years.

We fantasized about moving to Maine, but our jobs were in Pennsylvania. Eventually, our work at those jobs enabled us to buy a house in the southeastern corner of Pennsylvania. We spent summers moving from an air-conditioned house to an air-conditioned car to an air-conditioned workplace to air-conditioned stores. The humidity was ever-present and oppressive. You couldn't even take a walk without getting soaked with sweat, and you needed a shower before bed if you wanted to sleep comfortably, even with central air conditioning. As I like to say, southeastern Pennsylvania has four seasons — almost summer, summer, more summer, and rain.

Pennsylvania has all the amenities, from shopping and restaurants to doctors and specialists, some of them well-known nationally. But Maine was a magic getaway. We could forget all the stress of life by challenging our bodies on hiking trails in the park or by climbing the Precipice, a 1,500-foot cliff featuring a nontechnical climbing trail. We returned to Maine frequently, exploring the coast from Kittery, just across the border from New Hampshire, all the way to Lubec, the easternmost point in the United States. We even went inland to places like Moosehead Lake and the site of the former Katahdin Iron Works.

On the way home from Maine more than 20 years after our first trip, Sean and I looked at each other and said the same thing: We needed a more permanent connection to the state we loved so much. For the next two years, we looked for a house. Our wish list was simple — a small place with no lawn and not in need of major repairs. In the summer of 2013, we found a place without a lawn. Everything worked, so it didn't really need to be repaired. But it did need a lot of cosmetics. We had a wonderful time fixing it up, thinking it would be a summer place and retirement home.

I was so excited about the house in Maine that I never saw the emotional crash coming. At first, I felt just a little off. I had been taking antidepressants for about 10 years, and every so often, I needed to switch drugs or adjust the dose. I thought that was the case this time. My doctor, who had been managing my medications for years, put me on a different medication, but that made it worse. At that point, he said to stop taking the new drug and see a psychiatrist. By Christmas of that year, I was despondent. I saw a well-known psychiatrist who diagnosed me with bipolar disorder and put me on medication that dulled the emotional pain, along with everything else. I was calm. But I couldn't think. My hands didn't seem to work, and I would get impatient and throw things, then fall into a bawling heap.

I was even afraid to drive. The sensation of turning one particular corner near my house — on a road I needed to travel to get pretty much anywhere — would send me into a panic. I would grip the steering wheel, panting, and then feel surprised when I made it to the end of the curve. I persisted, determined to beat this, as I thought I had beaten the demons of my past before. But, it seemed the rules had changed. Pure determination fell short. I could get around that curve, sure, but I would just be afraid again the next time.

Because of my condition, I ended up having to take six months off work. I thought my career was over and that I would never return to my job as a weekly newspaper editor. One day, however, the doctors said I was stabilized, and I could return to work and my former life. I lamented that I didn't remember what it was like to feel joy. I was told to be patient. It would come back, they said. I waited. It didn't come back.

I did my job, feeling as empty as an old milk container. I got everything done, from writing to editing to photographing community events and people. But there was no joy, no high from the creative process. I felt like I was just going through the motions without really living. The psychiatrist had upped my dose of medication, so I was no longer afraid to drive. But my legs trembled so bad I couldn't hike. When I complained, he lowered my dose. Although that meant I could hike again, I found I greatly preferred even, easy terrain over the rustic trails through the woods that Sean and I had always enjoyed. I figured it was just how it was going to be. I would avoid strenuous hiking trails. I would never again climb the Precipice. I would have to adjust and accept my new state of being.

It was in late 2014, just a few months after I returned to work, that I found out about a job opportunity in Maine. The *Bangor Daily News*, which went by the nickname BDN, was looking for a reporter to cover the area where we'd bought our house. The job was too perfect not to go for it. So I did, and I got the job. Sean's company okayed the move and his plan to work remotely from Maine. Our dream of moving to Maine was coming true. Sean and I arranged to have a local contractor finish the upstairs of the house in Maine, and we put our place in Pennsylvania up for sale. I moved during a snowstorm in mid-February 2015, and Sean stayed in Pennsylvania to wrap things up, joining me permanently mid-summer.

The job at the BDN was difficult. It shouldn't have been — I was an experienced and award-winning journalist, and I had worked for dailies before. I worked from a one-room office in my coverage area, which kept me isolated from my colleagues, and I'm sure that didn't help. Naturally, I expected some adjustment difficulties working a new beat in another state. There were differences in the structures of local government. Maine has a shoreline and issues related to fishing. Pennsylvania doesn't. I didn't know until I got to Maine that the state's sheriffs and game wardens play a much different role in law enforcement than their counterparts in Pennsylvania. Still, those were minor differences that shouldn't have been the giant obstacles they were. I remember one interview in particular. The issue was somewhat complicated but not overly so. Yet I left feeling like I didn't understand a word my source said.

"If you don't understand something, just ask," my boss would say. He was a sweetheart and it was only after I knew him a while that I could tell when he was rattled. And I rattled him. I struggled with simple instructions and wondered how I had been able to function in my previous job. I suppose I did it by rote. I knew the job well. I knew the players well. I knew the issues well. I didn't need to learn about complex local issues; I already understood them. Not so in Maine, where I found myself assigned to do a story on alewives, a species of fish I'd never heard of before. I thought alewives would drown me in my confusion.

And then, one day, I couldn't get out of bed. I remember the date, Sept. 1, 2015. Sleep was my escape. In bed, I could cocoon under the covers. As I lay on my side, my cheek touched the soft, well-worn acrylic yarn of my Bankie, which is, for all intents and purposes, my security blanket. Holding him — it was Sean who decided Bankie had gender — I could feel loved, secure, even safe. As I drifted off to sleep, I could pretend sheriffs and local governments were all the same and that everything I didn't know about alewives didn't scare me. I didn't know how long I would sleep. When I was unconscious, I didn't have to be concerned about the following day. That was the point.

Sean was concerned, however. He knew something had to be done, or I would just crash again. He woke me up at three that afternoon to make me eat something and announced he had found me a counselor. He had scheduled my first appointment with her for three weeks later.

And that's how the most important journey in my life began in a tiny little town in rural Maine. I would find here what I could never find in Pennsylvania, even with all the experts and expensive medications.

- 2 -
A JOURNEY BEGINS

The first time I saw a counselor, I was a sophomore at Penn State. At that time, I felt like I was on a high-speed train heading for the end of the line. I could see the tracks would end, forcing me to crash into a concrete barrier. There were no sidings, no station, and no way to avoid the inevitable. Seeing the crash coming was frightening, but I couldn't figure out a way to get off the tracks.

It got worse as I began to see the collision actually beginning to take shape. My grades had been good during my first year at Penn State. I even made the dean's list. In my sophomore year, however, I barely passed.

One day that spring, my German teacher took me aside.

"You seem depressed," she said, placing her hand on my shoulder. "I think you might want to get some counseling."

I was stunned. I knew I hadn't been particularly well prepared for class and had assumed that was what she wanted to talk about. Looking back, I'm amazed because this woman barely knew me, yet my pain was so obvious she felt she needed to help me. I'm especially grateful now because her concern is what started me on my healing journey.

"I've noticed a change since the beginning of the year," she continued. "How are things at home?"

I had to admit, they weren't good. I listened without a word as she explained that I could go to counseling for free through the university. I didn't think a counselor could help, but I decided I had nothing to lose by trying. So I made an appointment.

Having no idea what was really bothering me, I told the counselor that my confusion and lack of interest in school came from my major. I didn't like my classes and couldn't imagine two more years of them.

"Well, what do you think you'd like to do instead?"

I eyed the counselor, a thin woman who sat curled up in her brown leather chair, her short white-blonde hair contrasting vividly against the dark leather. The question threw me. I had no idea what I wanted. It had never been an issue before.

She asked some questions about my interests, and I admitted that the only thing that really mattered was running and that I'd like to be a coach. The only academic subject I had any interest in was foreign language, and it seemed natural that teaching language would be a perfect complement to coaching.

"Then why don't you become a foreign language teacher and a track coach?"

The answer was obvious to me. "My mother would never tolerate it."

"Why should that keep you from doing it?"

My word, this woman wouldn't let up. I had no idea how to answer her question. Not even fully understanding the connection, I told her my mother had fits of rage over seemingly minor things like hamburger condiments and ice cream. I described how my mother wanted her friends, colleagues, and neighbors to think she was rich and that she was paying my tuition, even though neither was true. I was facing severe financial woes because she refused to follow the rules of the financial aid process, thereby making me ineligible for grant money. Time after time, I took out student loans to cover the shortfall in tuition payments. My mother knew I was borrowing to cover expenses, yet she refused to do what was necessary to get my tuition paid any other way.

"This is your life. You shouldn't have to put up with that," the counselor said. I sat there, my head leaning slightly forward, my mouth open wide in astonishment. The counselor continued. "If she's not even paying for your college, why should she get any say in what you major in?"

No amount of logic could debunk the counselor's argument. But the thought that she was right terrified me almost as much as staying on the same course and crashing.

After a couple of days of mulling it over, I went ahead and changed my major to secondary education with German as my specialty. I knew that my problems with the language, not due to a lack of ability but rather to my lack of application at the crucial early stages, would eventually catch up with me. But I'd worry about that later.

In the end, however, I chose an entirely different path — I dropped out of college altogether and moved to the opposite end of the state. My mother's response was to inform me that I "no longer exist."

Her next call was blunt. "I've decided that since you've elected to move out, I shouldn't be supporting you anymore. Since I paid for your car, it's mine, and I want it back." She spoke her sentence immediately after I answered the phone, stating it simply, without emotion, and without any of the usual pleasantries that accompany a phone call.

I was equally blunt. "Well, since I paid for the fuel pump and the tires currently on it, they're mine, and I'm keeping them."

Click. Her attempts to control me from afar had only just begun.

—

After dropping out of college, I met with a new counselor, Jack. I saw him once a week for three years. His major contribution to my healing was to validate the fact that I could never please my mother. She had sent me hate mail shortly after her phone call about the car, and I showed it to him.

Well, her letters certainly verify what I've always thought about her. She changes like wind," he said, raising his eyebrows as he examined the papers before him.

"Yeah, I guess I never realized how changeable she is," I said. "She can be so nice and then suddenly, without warning, she's sarcastic and vindictive."

Jack looked up. "It appears that for some reason, she needs to put you down."

"She sure does that enough."

"It appears that many things are black and white with your mother, including you," he said. "There are no gray areas. When you don't live up to her expectations, whatever they may be, you're all bad to her."

As odd as it seemed, my mother had actually called and invited me to come to see her in Pittsburgh for Christmas that year. Others, including Ken, my boyfriend at the time, felt I should go and "make peace" with her.

"What do you think?" Jack asked.

"I don't want to go." He listened quietly as I spoke and waited while I paused. "I don't know if I'll be able to handle it if she turns on me, but I wonder if that's just an excuse to avoid going."

"I think you should do what your gut tells you to do," Jack said.

"Ken thinks I should go," I said as if that meant I really should.

"Ken doesn't have to deal with her if she gets ugly." Jack's comment startled me.

"Ken thinks I should be elated to hear from her, but I'm not," I said. "And I'm afraid there's something wrong with me. She's my mother and I'm supposed to love her and want a relationship with her."

A puff of air escaped his throat as he turned his head slightly sideways with his mouth open. "I don't think that's unusual at all. Most people who think you should love your mother and want a relationship with her think so because their mothers didn't abuse them the way your mother abused you."

Not only was Jack a professional who had studied human behavior, but also he was the only person who seemed to truly understand my relationship with my mother and what it was like to be me.

Jack had worked for an agency with a sliding scale, so, for a time, I didn't have to give up groceries or rent in order to go. As I began to work my way up from under the poverty line, however, counseling became cost-prohibitive. I wasn't able to go regularly for about 10 years.

Then, I began seeing a counselor named Mim, who offered another shocking revelation.

She was in the middle of making a point that I no longer remember when she said, "You were violently abused." At that moment, she paused and looked at me. "You do know that, don't you? That you were violently abused?"

Actually, I hadn't known. A part of me definitely believed it was wrong for my mother to call me names like "fucking bitch," or to hit me. But I had been hearing for years from my mother's friends that I should be grateful for all my mother had done for me. How could it be that no one else saw it the way I did? My mother herself used to say that if you have repeated problems of the same kind with different people, it must be you, not them. So I figured her friends must be right, that she was a wonderful mother and I was the ungrateful fucking bitch she said I was.

But here was Mim saying what I always suspected was true. And didn't Jack say it, too? And the counselor at Penn State before him? Another wow.

—

Nearly 40 years after my first counseling session at Penn State, I found myself working for the BDN from a one-room office in a small town. Somehow, I managed to get myself back to work on Sept. 2, 2015, the day after I attempted to escape the world by sleeping. And, somehow, I continued to function for the next three weeks until my first counseling session in Maine.

When appointment time finally came, I put my Bankie into a fleece drawstring bag and left my office to meet Carol.

Work with a new counselor typically begins with a session or two where the patient just relates background information.

Carol began by asking what brought me to her office.

I told her my husband recognized the need, found her, and made the appointment.

"But why did you decide to come?" she asked.

Though I don't remember exactly, I probably sighed in exasperation. I was there because I couldn't get out of bed a few weeks earlier. But, since then, I had been out of bed and functioning, so that wasn't exactly it.

I would discover that she had a propensity for precision in language, and a general answer like, "I need counseling," just wouldn't do.

She asked about my goals. I didn't have any goals beyond being able to function. She pushed for precision but it would be some time before she would get that.

So, she started asking about my past. I gave her an overview of my childhood — my parents split up when I was 11 and placed my severely handicapped sister, Nicole, in what can best be described as a nursing home. After a year or so, we stopped visiting my sister, and my mother would slug me if I even said her name. My dad knew my mother was becoming increasingly abusive and sought to get custody of me. But he was killed by a drunk driver before this could ever happen. I was 15.

After that, my mother's abuse became worse. College shielded me somewhat, but only temporarily. My efforts to build a successful adult life were interrupted 10 days before my 26th birthday when my mother shot herself. Despite that, I survived. By all outward appearances, I was fine. So why couldn't I get out of bed that day? Why had I crashed so hard before the bipolar diagnosis?

"Do you have bipolar disorder?" my counselor asked.

I didn't really understand the question. Hadn't I just told her it was my diagnosis?

We went through the symptoms of bipolar disorder, which includes extreme highs and lows, and I explained how it fits. She seemed satisfied for the moment.

As we moved on to other topics, the first real issue we tackled was recurring dreams about my mother.

In the dreams, I return to her house in Pittsburgh for some reason and go inside. I am aware that the house has been sitting empty for some time, and as I begin to look around, she suddenly appears. I am shocked because I thought she was dead. At that point, the dream generally ends.

The next thing Carol said would change everything.

"You're still afraid of her."

- 3 -
THE CUP OF HEARTACHE

Neanderthals raised my mother. At a glance, they appear civilized. They walk upright, speak words, and wear clothes.

But, in the world of the Neanderthals, love, hate, and violence tangled together to become indistinguishable, like strands of old Christmas lights stored for too long in the attic.

My mother's father was an over-the-road truck driver and an alcoholic. When he came home on Saturday nights, my mother would say, she and her siblings — two brothers and four sisters — would sit huddled by the window and watch for him. "The longer it took him to pull in the driveway, the worse the beatings would be."

Once, I asked her what her mother did about it.

"Nothing."

Even as a child, my mother knew something was dreadfully wrong at home and, as quickly as possible, set forth a path out of there. Not long after her high school graduation, she and my father eloped and moved from their native Pittsburgh neighborhoods across Pennsylvania to the Harrisburg area, eventually settling in Middletown. My mother left a world without compassion, empathy, or understanding and set out to create a world for herself that was full of those things.

For the first two years of my life, I have little doubt that she succeeded. But, when my sister was born severely handicapped, my mother's world began to unravel. She had escaped the heartache caused by her family. Now, the heartache was back in a different form.

Nicole had been born in 1966 into a world before anti-discrimination laws and handicapped parking spaces. These obstacles made it even harder for my mother to care for Nicole. And she made her feelings known to the world around her.

I remember one time when I was about 10, my mother took my sister and me out to eat. We stood in the restaurant lobby for several minutes before anyone acknowledged us. Then, the three of us were seated at a table clearly meant for two that was right beside the kitchen door. Finally, my mother got up, took Nicole by the hand, and stood in the middle of the restaurant dining room to announce that she had been slighted because she had a mentally disabled child and, therefore, we would be leaving. She said everyone there should be ashamed for letting this happen. I just stood there, a little sheepish. I was too young to understand the implications of how the restaurant had treated us. I had just wanted to eat.

My mother also got involved in advocacy, organizing a "Ride a Bike for the Retarded" event to raise money for the March of Dimes. She wrote letters to legislators. She did everything she could to educate those around her about Nicole, about mental retardation, and about the discrimination and lack of compassion that existed in the world.

But, as good as my mother was at these things, she was not good at holding her emotions in check. Her anger over the injustice she saw spilled out like the hot foam that squeezes out from under the lid of a pot of boiling potatoes. The heat of her anger grew over the years, threatening to burn her. She had to find a way to channel it.

What she needed was a target — someplace to aim all that fury and all that rage.

So she found one.

Me.

—

As a young child, I understood the word "retarded" to be merely one of a number of words used to describe the world around me. These words were neither negative nor positive. They just were.

The girl down the street was blonde. The poodle across the street was black. The people next door were Jewish. Nicole was retarded.

The fact that the full impact of the word "retarded" was lost on me infuriated my mother. In her mind, no one needed to learn about compassion, empathy, and understanding more than me.

One such lesson came during a Sunday night ritual — bath time. I was about 6 years old, and Nicole was 4.

Typically, my mother would put my sister and me in the tub together and leave us unsupervised until she decided it was time to bark at me to get washed.

I'd pick up the washrag and soap up. Sometimes, I used the washcloth to create hair for "Handy," a bird-like creature with an upper lip made of four fingers and a lower jaw made of only my thumb. Sometimes, I'd make Handy talk to Nicole, but she seldom reacted. Nicole spent her time leaning forward so that her body was nearly folded in half and mouthing the water. That's all she ever did in the tub. Except sometimes she pooped.

"M-o-o-o-m!" I'd scream as if I was about to be bitten by a scorpion. "Nicole pooped, and I'm still in the tub!"

If my dad were the one home with us, he would quickly whisk me out of the tub if I didn't already jump out on my own. But my mother certainly never came running. If she were the one to take care of the problem, she would do so in her own time and dismiss my concerns. "So she pooped," my mother would scoff. "It won't kill you."

But I was sure it would. Someday, she would find me dead in the tub, and she probably wouldn't even notice.

Usually our baths ended with my mother chasing me out of the tub and washing Nicole. Once, I dared to ask my mother why I had to wash myself and Nicole didn't. Instead of explaining to me that Nicole *couldn't*, my mother responded by unleashing her pent-up fury.

"You don't want to wash yourself?" my mother demanded, her eyes narrowed, her full lips taut in the upside-down triangle shape they took when she was angry. "You're lucky you can wash yourself!"

With one hand, she grabbed my arm just below the shoulder and yanked me to my feet. She dipped the washcloth into the water and lathered it up. My mouth was partially open, and when she brought the soapy, wet washcloth to my face, I tasted the sharp, bitter flavor of blue Camay. Holding the back of my head with one hand, she pushed the washcloth into my mouth, nose, and eyes with the other. "How do you like being washed?" she bellowed. I was unable to say anything as I fought for breath, trying to turn my head from side to side to escape the suffocating terry cloth.

When the washcloth finally left my face, I could breathe, but not without inhaling soap bubbles. I tried to use one of my hands to wipe the soap away, but my mother yanked it downward. "I'm washing that arm!" she shouted.

As she continued to manhandle me in the name of cleanliness, I began to cry.

"Knock off your goddamn crying," her angry voice snapped. "Jesus Christ, Johanna. You're *always* crying."

In shame, I swallowed hard and tried to stop.

"Get out of here," she said when she had finished washing me. "Get out of my sight."

Without a word, I stepped away and dried off just out of reach of my mother and her rage. I knew she was right about one thing. I was always crying. I didn't know how to stop.

—

Although Nicole wasn't interested in playing in the tub, she could be a lot of fun outside of it. One day, while my parents were outside, I arranged the dining room chairs into three rows of two to create the body of an imaginary covered wagon. I sat in one chair and put Nicole in the seat beside me, the remaining four chairs behind us. As the driver, I held the reins to the horses that pulled us through the frontier. Once we reached our destination, I had to take Nicole out of her seat to make camp and then put her back into the wagon when our business was done.

Nicole loved the attention. All the way across our imaginary frontier, she would laugh and scream, quickly clasping and unclasping her hands, a motion I called "flicking." The faster she flicked her hands, the more excited and happy she was. When she was happy playing with me, I was happy too.

The problem came when my mother would tell me specifically to "go play with Nicole." The dreaded command would put me in a state of awkward panic. I would go to her room with her, but then I wouldn't know what to do. I remember once I wound up her Fisher Price Ferris wheel to watch the little people go around and then removed them to watch the empty seats. Nicole sat nearby, flicking but making no sound.

My mother was quick to notice I didn't perform to her satisfaction. "I thought I told you to play with Nicole," she said after suddenly appearing in the doorway.

"I *am*," I insisted.

"It doesn't look to me like you're playing with her. It looks like you're entertaining yourself," she said, stepping into the room and squatting to pick up my sister. "Come on, Nicole. We'll go play for real."

I wasn't sure if I should be relieved to be free of this duty I couldn't perform or if I should be angry because I'd been robbed of my sister's quiet company.

—

As a young child, I believed that Nicole got more attention because she was prettier. I thought my dirty blonde hair, green eyes, and fair skin were much less interesting than her dark locks, olive skin, and bright blue eyes. The fact that my mother allowed Nicole to grow her hair long while making me keep mine short only fueled my jealousy. I tried in vain to convince her to let me grow my hair long, and when she finally relented, she made a point of repeatedly telling me how ugly it was until I gave in and let her have it cut.

In second grade, I was a witch for Halloween and wore my costume for our school parade and party. I removed my pointed black witch's cap but left the black wig on, certain it made me prettier. In the school bathroom, I looked in the mirror. I looked great with dark hair, even if the hair itself wasn't as pretty as Nicole's.

Glancing from side to side to make sure no one was looking, I raised my hands to my chest and flicked them as Nicole did. Hmmmm. Not bad, I thought.

I skipped down the hall back to class, my cap under my arm, fake dark hair bouncing with each step.

As soon as I got home, my mother told me to get rid of that awful wig.

"Mom, can I dye my hair black?" I asked later that afternoon as she was changing Nicole's diaper and singing to her.

"I love Nicole, and Nicole loves me," my mother sang. "Under the shade of the yum yum tree." My sister laughed, her long legs curled up above her in a fetal position. As always, she held her hands rigidly together, clasping and unclasping, as her long dark hair cascaded away from her face. "I love Nicole, and Nicole loves me. Yes, she do-oo-oo."

"Mo-o-o-o-o-m!" I demanded.

"You don't need dark hair," my mother said without looking up from what she was doing. She went back to singing, stopping only to order me to dunk the dirty diaper in the toilet to clean it off before putting it in the diaper pail.

I sighed and did as I was told.

—

One of the best parts of my childhood was finding a cat. When the longhaired female cat showed up at our house, she came to me without hesitation.

She was absolutely beautiful, and, as a third grader in love, I knew I had to show her to my parents in hopes that they'd let me keep her. After luring the cat to our front door, I called my mother, who was as taken with the pretty white cat as I was. No doubt this was because the cat wasn't afraid of Nicole, who was screaming, chirping, and even lunging in joy at the sight of the little creature. The only thing that changed the cat's calm, loving demeanor was the sight of our Irish setter. One look at Kelly, who had poked her head through the doorway into the foyer, and the cat literally climbed the wall. Our front door had a row of small windows on either side, and the cat used the narrow wooden ledges between them to propel herself upward and hang on.

We laughed as my mother sent the dog to the kitchen and closed the hall door. Once calmed, my new cat began to work her magic, winning over my parents with her patience and love for Nicole. She never ran from Nicole, she never hissed, and she never bared a claw.

But Puff loved me best, and we shared a special bond. I used to pick her up and hold her like a mother holds a tot. She would wrap her front paws around my neck, lay her head down on my shoulder, and purr, and I could hold her like this as long as I wanted.

I didn't play with dolls, but I enjoyed taking my favorite things, including toy horses and my football, for rides in my doll carriage. Puff patiently allowed me to wrap her up in blankets, even on a blistering summer day, and put her in the baby carriage for walks through the neighborhood.

I was disappointed when my mother announced plans to have the cat spayed. Our dog was spayed, too, and, like most kids, I wished we could have puppies or kittens. But my parents wanted nothing to do with finding homes for baby animals. Although I disliked having it done at the time, I now know this was the responsible thing to do. I still got my wish, though, because Puff was already pregnant by the time I'd found her and so we let her have her kittens.

One evening, when I'd been playing in the finished basement with her, Puff kept wanting to go into the game room, where our pool table was, and she led me to a box near the freezer. The next morning, there were five babies in the box with her — three white, one orange-striped, and one gray-striped.

Puff allowed me to handle her newborns, which I did with my parents' help and supervision. Puff even allowed Nicole to be close and probably would have let her hold a kitten. But we knew

Nicole didn't have the hand-eye coordination necessary to handle something so fragile. Maybe Puff knew that, too, but she also knew she could trust our judgment.

One of the white kittens died within the first week of birth. The remaining four, who came to be known as Spot, Skitters, Gray Job, and Orange Job (the last two names courtesy of my father), were the source of the most fun I ever had as a child. Spot was the chief instigator and had been named because he was white, except for a brown spot on the top of his head. He would often wait for his two brothers or one sister to come by so he could ambush them. My parents, Nicole, and I would all sit roaring with laughter as the kittens held each other down, kicking their back feet in each other's faces.

One morning, we came down to the game room to find no kittens. With questioning expressions, the four of us looked around, wondering where they could have gone. Then, a tiny head popped up out of one of the pockets of the pool table and then back down again almost immediately. Another head popped up from another pocket and then back down again. Even Nicole couldn't resist joining the laughter as fuzzy little pool balls moved from pocket to pocket, sticking up their heads like Punxsutawney Phil, the famous weather-predicting groundhog.

Once, we were late taking them to the vet for a checkup after my mother, and I faced the dubious task of removing them from inside the winter tires of my parent's cars. We'd reach for a kitten who would scurry around on the inside of the tire. Trying to catch them was delightful but losing battle. We probably could have caught them more quickly than we did, but we were too busy laughing.

When the kittens were old enough, they all went to homes in the neighborhood. Puff, who was spayed after all the kittens had been adopted, remained my faithful companion for the next three years.

—

As I grew older, I began to see the differences in my parents.

My mother was definitely more easily angered, and, at times, she seemed to even enjoy punishing me. When I was in second or third grade, she asked me who I would prefer to have punished me — her or my dad. When I said my dad, her response was, "Well, now I know that I should be the one to punish you."

My mother was very careful not to get too abusive when my dad was around. I also learned many years later that she'd actually convinced all our neighbors that she didn't believe in spanking. Not only did she use spanking as a form of punishment, but we also had at least one wooden paddle set aside specifically for this job. Known as "the baby bopper," it had come from a paddle ball set; the ball and string had been removed. When I was really young, my mother could scare me into submission by saying, "Do you want me to go get the baby bopper?"

I remember one spanking in particular. I had not been allowed to play with the girl across the street as punishment for some wrongdoing I no longer recall. My mother told me that she would hit me 20 times with the baby bopper if I so much as said "hello" to her.

Sitting on the carport watching this girl in her yard across the street, I couldn't resist calling her name and relaying an important piece of information: "I have seven red bugs." These were red milkweed beetles that we caught nearly every day in July and August, and, to us, the awe-inspiring red bugs were status symbols. The more red bugs you could get, the more worthy you became.

"Seven, oh," she answered, standing in her front yard near the curb and looking my way.

Before I could even consider saying another word, my mother was on me like a swarm of mosquitoes. I got my 20 whacks, though years later, she would try to convince me it had been only seven.

My mother had said she wanted to be known as the disciplinarian, and she certainly got her wish.

I was much more comfortable with my dad. He was the one who would take long walks with me and buy me soda or candy. He was the one who would answer my questions about Nicole without getting mad at me, and he could always make me laugh.

I loved to ride with him in the car. Once, while in the car, my dad suddenly beeped his horn and enthusiastically waved at the person in an oncoming car.

"Who was that?" I asked.

"I don't know," he said with a shrug, his face full of seriousness.

"Then why'd you beep and wave?"

"So he'd wonder for the next seven days who the guy was in the blue Maverick."

I started laughing at the thought of this guy driving home, trying to figure out who we were and how we knew him.

Another car approached. Once again, my dad beeped his horn and threw his hand out the window in an eager wave. I laughed until I could barely breathe.

The next time, I joined in, waving my hands wildly and smiling like I knew the other driver intimately.

"You can get people walking the same way," said my dad, beeping the horn and waving to a jogger who turned around with a confused look.

"And you can always point," he said, beeping the horn with his right hand and then shoving his left arm out the window to point at a person out working in his yard. The man stared as we passed, and I continued laughing. Soon, we were both pointing at virtually everyone we saw. Though I couldn't contain my laughter, my dad's expression remained serious, as if what we were doing was the most natural thing in the world. For him, the silliness was natural.

He listened to me, too. After I mentioned that I liked the orange daylilies that we saw growing wild along the Pennsylvania roadside in late June, my dad began stopping to pick some for me on his way home from work.

Even today, long after his death, I still think of him whenever I see the orange flowers reaching for the sky in bunches alongside the road. They represent the mixture of joy and sadness — joy because the flower represents something special that my dad and I shared without my mother and Nicole — and sadness because I would eventually lose them all.

—

My mother liked to point out to others that Nicole knew when people were talking about her. As my parents and several neighborhood couples sat together around our dining room table discussing Nicole, she was joyful. She cruised around the living and dining rooms, flicking and screaming with a big smile on her face. She didn't walk by putting one foot in front of the other but rather by shifting her weight from one straight, stiff leg to the other in a kind of shuffle. Despite her inability to move like the rest of us, she had a certain amount of grace, and I liked watching her walk, especially when she was happy. Though I still resented that my mother failed to notice my existence, I didn't hold that against Nicole.

When the topic of conversation changed, Nicole's screams rose and took on an irritated quality. As she screamed, her head appeared to vibrate slightly from side to side.

"See?" my mother said. "She knows we stopped talking about her." The others at the table agreed that Nicole understood far more than anyone realized.

—

When I was in about fourth grade, Nicole enrolled in a program called the Aurora Club. Held in a downtown Harrisburg row house, the program was an early organized gathering for disabled children. I don't remember anything about it except the challenge of finding a parking space and the walk, sometimes a rather long one, to our destination.

My job was to hold one of Nicole's hands while my mother held the other to assist her in walking. Her choppy gait never was particularly fast and we were sometimes further slowed when her narrow feet would literally walk out of her shoes. This was especially troublesome when we didn't notice right away because one of us would have to wait with Nicole while the other retraced our steps to fetch the missing shoe. Then, my mother would have to put it back on Nicole's foot before we could proceed.

Sometimes, Nicole would tire and simply decide she was done walking. Her legs would go limp under her, and we would realize this when our arms were nearly ripped from their sockets by the sudden dead weight. At the count of three, we would lift her back to her feet, and, with any luck, she would walk at least a few more steps before refusing again to continue.

We often encountered cold stares from others who didn't think we were giving them their fair share of the sidewalk. Sometimes, people were even rude enough to comment.

"Oh, drop dead," my mother would shout. "Can't you see this little girl is handicapped?"

Once, a gray-haired man pushed us aside because we were taking up too much room. My mother shouted at him, but he ignored us.

Depending on the distance and Nicole's level of cooperation, my mother might end up having to carry her. Helplessly, I would follow along, wishing I could ease my mother's obvious physical strain because making things better for my mother made her less likely to lash out at me.

—

The summer before sixth grade, I learned that Nicole would be starting school in the fall. I was ecstatic. I spent the afternoon on my swing set, soaring through the air, fantasizing about the new person my sister was to become. She would learn to talk, read, write, add and subtract. I didn't know how she was supposed to learn these things or how school would transform her. But I knew that "normal" kids went to school, and I reasoned that if she were going, she would become normal too.

My parents explained that she would not be attending the same school that I did. They agreed to drive me to my school on the first day, even if it made me late, so that I could see my sister off. Instead of the big yellow school bus that I'd expected, Nicole was picked up by a blue station wagon that carried three or four other kids, all of whom were more or less like her.

My parents had warned me not to expect great changes in my sister. Watching the station wagon back out of the driveway, I began to understand their warning that things would never be the way I had hoped.

I never did visit her school. I don't even know where it was. Seeing her classmates and what I considered to be a poor substitute for a school bus was enough to mark the beginning of the long, slow process of coming to terms with the fact that my sister would never be like the other kids.

It broke my heart.

—

Just as Nicole had understood when she was the center of attention, she also understood when things weren't going well. By the time I was in sixth grade, I could sense a growing tension in the house. Nicole noticed it, too.

One time, Nicole and I were seated for dinner, Nicole next to my mother's chair so she could be fed. I was seated on the other side of the table. My parents were in the kitchen when they began to quarrel. Though I couldn't make out the words, I could hear the sharp tones of their bickering. Nicole sat with her head down, her left hand on her temple, slowly tapping. Her right arm remained in her lap. The only time she could keep her hands apart was when she was upset.

Suddenly, my parents burst through the saloon-style doors into the dining room. My mother was holding a butcher knife, and my dad was trying to take it from her. My memory has an almost surreal quality. I watched the shadows on the white walls rather than my parents' struggling bodies. It was easier that way because I didn't have to see the gleam of the knife. I cried as Nicole just sat there, tapping her temple, her long dark hair hanging down so you couldn't see her face.

Another time, I came inside for dinner to find only two places set, one for me and the other for my mother and Nicole to share. Just as I had come into the dining room to sit down, my father exited the kitchen with a slam of the door. The louvered windows rattled.

"Isn't Dad eating with us?" I asked.

My mother's head jolted upward as if someone had pulled her hair. I could see her eyes were on fire, even though the dining room drapes were closed and the light in the dining room was off. "Your father's no good!" my mother barked. "I'm leaving him. And I'm taking you with me!"

A week or so later, I got off the school bus to see a "for sale" sign in front of our house. When the other kids asked about it, I pretended I had known all along, even though I'd actually had no idea that the sign would be there. But I knew it meant my parents were separating.

—

During our early sessions, as I told Carol about my past, she asked me a number of what I considered to be philosophical questions. One was whether I believed complete healing was possible.

"No."

"Why?"

I presented my theory of the cup of heartache. Heartache is like liquid poured into a cup that is your soul. It can hold only so much. Over time, some of the liquid heartache will evaporate. But, another traumatic experience will fill up the cup again. If too much heartache is poured in too fast, the cup overflows. That's when you've reached your breaking point. Even if all the liquid evaporates, a black residue is left, like a stain from burnt coffee. The cup is never pure again. It happened to my mother, and it happened to me.

"I'm damaged goods," I declared.

"Why would you say that?" she asked.

"I'm broken," I said. The cup wasn't overflowing at that moment, but it was full. If I were to experience more trauma, the cup would overflow. Even a little thing could make it overflow. In fact, that's what happened the day I couldn't get out of bed.

Carol was silent for a moment. Then she asked more questions as if she didn't quite understand my analogy. I tried another tack. I told her I'm like a crate that's been weakened. A crate can only hold so much weight — heartache — before it breaks.

She asked me how I was damaged. I told her about my emotional outbursts and how they always managed to ruin a good thing.

She asked if the outbursts actually ruined anything.

Well, of course, they did. The fact that I was inferior, damaged, and broken had been drilled into my head by my mother and then, later, by members of Sean's family. No one wanted to hear about my pain. My mother failed to understand the husband she lost was my father; the daughter she lost was my sister. She had no sympathy, and no matter how hard I tried to hide the pain, it would burst out of me like the figure that comes out of a jack-in-the-box. I failed to hide my pain; therefore, I failed as a person. And I knew I had failed because it wasn't only my mother who repeatedly told me so.

Carol said she does believe complete healing is possible. It can be difficult because you have to take off the bandages and expose the wounded flesh, but it can be done. There will always be a scar. You can touch the scar and remember but be essentially healed.

I wasn't convinced, but I agreed to give it a try. What did I have to lose?

- 4 -
FEAR

I've spent most of my life in fear. It's not a conscious thing, like when you look over your shoulder because someone is following you. It's more like persistent anxiety that peaks suddenly, without warning, as if you've just been shot by a rubber band at close range.

I didn't know what it was. I just accepted that this was my state of being. I had to avoid situations in which I was likely to get upset because the fear manifested itself as anger. And, if I did get angry, I had to try not to ruin whatever good I had going for me at that moment. Most times, though, I had to do damage control after the inevitable outburst. I couldn't control my emotions. I cried when I was angry and yelled when I was sad. Behind it all was fear. But I didn't understand that. I just thought it was a character flaw.

Sean was the first person who seemed to be able to handle all that. Our first date was a disaster — complete with what I felt was the inevitable outburst. A coworker invited me to a party. I pictured about 25 people, beer, chips, and soda. It was her, her fiance, me and Sean. I had met him only once before, briefly, in the company parking lot.

Our very small party began with a case of beer. I had one, my coworker had two and the guys had the rest. We ended up at the home of one of the other couple's relatives, where everyone was drunk but me. For some reason, I still don't understand, they all thought it would be funny to tie me to the bed with Sean.

I freaked.

I imagine most people would freak out if they wound up in a room full of strangers who wanted to shackle them, but, at the time, I thought it was just another example of my character flaw.

I don't remember what came next, only that eventually, I found myself in the back seat of my coworker's boyfriend's car, crying in Sean's arms. I felt like he didn't blame me, like he would take care of me, like maybe, just maybe, it would all be okay.

When the car reached my apartment, the other couple unabashedly dumped Sean off with me. He asked if he could stay and was surprised when I said yes. I wasn't in any state to drive him home anyway. He didn't try to take advantage of me, though he did persistently try to convince me to take advantage of him. He was disappointed. But he persisted in getting me to go out with him again.

Despite how he had protected and nurtured me in that frightening situation, I blew him off, and I continued to do so. He kept coming back. You'd think I'd figure it out, that this one was staying. But, in my broken psyche, the number of times one had to come back in order for me to believe it was forever was the number of times it had already happened, plus at least one. He even said to me once, "I'm not going to abandon you like everyone else has." It was a lovely thing for him to say, and I understood the words but I didn't really understand their meaning.

Less than two years after that disastrous first date, we were married in a small church in the Pittsburgh area. On the surface, life was normal. Inside, I was just waiting for the inevitable. Sooner or later, I figured, I wouldn't measure up somehow, and I'd be thrown away again.

But the day I feared never came, despite my best efforts at times to fuck it all up. He stood by me, for better, for worse, in sickness and in health. And, a few years after we moved to Maine, I would finally understand why.

—

I first heard about PTSD in the context of Vietnam veterans who had experienced trauma during combat and were somehow triggered by that trauma back home. At the time, I was surprised this had happened only with Vietnam veterans. I learned later that it actually has happened to veterans from previous wars, but no one ever talked about it. How painful it must have been for all of them.

I didn't encounter evidence that PTSD affected those outside the military until about 2009, when a 12-year-old boy was run over by a school bus in front of the local middle school in Pennsylvania. One of the paramedics who tried to save the boy's life spoke out about his experiences and began teaching classes about PTSD to first responders. I covered one of his classes for the newspaper as I had covered the boy's death. It made sense that first responders would be vulnerable to post-traumatic stress, considering the heartbreaking life-and-death situations they deal with in their work.

I was no veteran, nor was I an emergency responder. Still, Carol gently introduced the idea that what I was dealing with — fear — was actually PTSD. I had been, at least metaphorically, treated like a caged animal, subject to the whim of my master, and it often got violent. There were similarities.

I was surprised, yet I wasn't. Some 20 years earlier, Mim had suggested the same thing. Still, it took a while for the idea to sink in. But when it did, I felt a sense of relief. If PTSD was what was causing my emotional outbursts, then it was possible that my losing control wasn't due to a character flaw. The idea was freeing.

Still, an idea isn't worth much until you put it to use. I had to learn how to recognize when I'd been triggered and figure out a way to cope. But, the fact that it was actually possible was something I was joyful to consider.

Triggers are borne out of repeated frightening or traumatic experiences. When living with my mother, I never knew what to expect or what would set her off. I found that it helped to have fresh coffee ready and waiting when she got home from work. This required getting water and coffee grounds in a clean filter and then pacing around the kitchen, waiting to see her car's headlights or hear the garage door opening. Then, I would hit the switch to get the coffee brewing. But even this did not guarantee I wouldn't get smacked or punched because she could — and often did — find fault with something else I had done or not done. The rules changed daily. Maybe she had wanted me to wash the ashtrays and come home to find them dirty. Maybe she had wanted something for dinner other than what I made. Maybe she thought I had too many lights on in the house, wasting electricity. It could be literally anything. She rarely bothered to tell me what she wanted, and I imagine she might not even have known herself. Without even realizing it, she expected me to take care of her and was angry when I didn't know to do whatever it was that she equated with love that day.

Sometimes, I just said the wrong thing, like my sister's name. She would react quickly with a stinging slap to the face. I'd see it coming and flinch.

"How dare you flinch!" she'd growl and hit me again and again until I could take the hit without flinching.

Once, she told me to make her some frozen French fries, and when I didn't find them in the freezer quickly enough, she shoved me aside and threw everything in the freezer at me. I dodged frozen meat, bags of vegetables, containers of leftovers, and ice cube trays. Some things hit me, and they hurt. When the freezer was empty, and she saw there actually were no French fries in there, she told me to clean up what she said was my mess. I hid my bruises from others as I had always done.

Another time, she threw a fit because I didn't answer the phone. She was sure whoever was calling was going to change her life for the better somehow, and she missed this golden opportunity because of me. The next time the phone rang, I answered it and got in trouble because, apparently, she hadn't wanted to talk to the person who had called that time.

She'd been reported to child welfare authorities but always played the poor widow trying to raise a belligerent child. The authorities never knew about any of the scenarios I just described, and none of them ever asked me what life was like with her. The only sympathetic ear I'd ever found was the nurse at the school I'd attended in ninth and tenth grade. I flipped out at school one day, kicking my locker and throwing my books across the floor, and then I dissolved into a puddle of tears. The nurse, who had seen and asked about the bruises, called child welfare, not that it did any good.

By the time I was 16, I concluded that there was no sense in asking anyone for help. My cries always fell on deaf ears, whether I was reaching out to a teacher, a neighbor, or the authorities. I started my junior year at a new school and I told no one what it was really like for me at home behind closed doors. I told no one about the names she called me, about how she hit me, criticized me, and threw things at me, all the while telling her friends what a proud and doting mother she was. And when she bought a fancy car — a 1979 Corvette customized by her brother — I played along. Sure, I loved the car. It was one hell of an experience to drive a Corvette at age 17. But, like all things in my life, it came with a price. She lorded it over my head, offering it as proof that she was a great mother. She regularly pointed out that I could drive the car as long as I followed the rules, whatever they were. A few years later, she decided to sell the Corvette, without any input from me, and buy herself a Mercedes. So, it was never really my car. Or maybe I just missed one of the rules. I don't know.

What I did know during my last two years in high school was that I could not count on anyone but myself. I had to find a way to survive under her roof until I was of legal age. Then, I would stand up to her.

And I did.

I was 18 and a college student home on break when my

mother was having trouble putting together a you-assemble shelving unit. Without leaving the room on the first floor where she was working, she bellowed for me to "come here." As always, I was expected to be able to hear her, no matter where I was in the house, and to immediately drop whatever I was doing to do her bidding. As I reached the doorway, I could see her on her knees, wooden parts, and hardware scattered about all around her.

"Get that!" she shouted, pointing in the general direction of several items. I didn't know what she wanted and asked for clarification.

"THAAAT!" She screamed so loud her whole body shook.

"I don't know what 'that' is," I said, shaking my head slightly.

"That's because you're *stupid*!" she shouted. "Now, hand that to me!"

I took a deep breath.

"I am not stupid, and I'm not going to put up with this," I announced, surprising even myself. "Call me when you can talk calmly." And with that, I turned and left.

"GET BACK HERE!" I heard her scream, but I kept going up the stairs to my bedroom on the third floor of the townhouse.

She followed. "How dare you walk away from me!" she shouted. "How dare you treat me that way!"

As I reached the third-floor landing, I could hear her approaching. I turned to see what she would do next.

As she reached the landing behind me, she lifted her right arm to take a swing towards my face. I blocked it by raising my left arm. Her other fist flew towards me from the other direction. I blocked that one, too, and gave her a little push backward away from me.

Stunned, she stepped back and caught her balance, her mouth hanging open like the door of a decrepit mailbox. I was a high school and collegiate athlete. She often bragged about this to colleagues, friends, and neighbors, saying I was deceptively strong and fast. In contrast, she was a smoker who never exercised. If the altercation were to escalate, she was clearly outgunned and she knew it.

Instead of continuing her physical attack, she tried to push my guilt buttons. "I can't believe you raised your hand to me," she said, her jaw still hanging, her eyes remaining wide with surprise.

I said nothing. But I would not turn my back until she retreated, and I knew for sure that the fistfight was over. "I can't believe you raised your hand to me," she said, again and again, before finally turning to go slowly back downstairs. "I can't believe you raised your hand to me."

"I don't know why the hell not," I finally said. "You've been raising your hand to me for years."

She turned abruptly toward me and stared for a moment but said nothing. I held my ground with both my feet and my eyes until she turned again to continue her retreat.

My mother never hit me again.

Carol agreed that standing up to her took guts. But, she insisted, I was still afraid.

At first, I didn't buy it. But then I remembered how sometimes, long after she died, I would think I heard my mother's voice in the wind, bellowing my name.

"Johanna!"

In that instant, between whatever I heard and my realization that she was dead and couldn't be calling for me, I would literally stop breathing. I could feel my body tense up, and my eyes widened.

Yes, I was still afraid of her.

—

Carol and I began to assess exactly what was happening when I would get upset. I reacted with what appeared to be anger, but she was sure there was something else behind it.

"Anger has served me well," I said one day during a session. "It's kept me from becoming more of a victim."

A previous counselor, Mim, had actually said that to me, and it helped me to understand myself.

Carol agreed I had found many creative ways to survive. Anger was one of them. But she said I didn't need it anymore. She had taught anger management classes, and the first thing her clients would learn was to stop and do nothing.

I had done that. When I knew I was starting to get upset, my tactic was to remove myself from the situation whenever possible until I calmed down.

Carol agreed this was good, but she wanted to help get me to the point where I could still handle my emotions even if flight weren't an immediate option.

Whoa! Wait! Let's go back a minute. Was she saying I need anger management?

She was.

Carol acknowledged I could function in society without my anger causing me trouble with the law. However, she believed figuring it out anyway would be healing and helpful in my relationships.

She told me she'd had combat veterans as clients, and when one of them would hear the sound of a helicopter flying overhead, he'd be under the desk in a split second. In this case, the sound of the helicopter was a trigger that made him feel like he was back in combat.

Carol taught him how to hear the noise and separate the fear he felt during the previous situation — combat — from the current situation, whatever it was, that took place in the relative safety of civilian life. What she would teach me would be similar. I would learn to separate the fear that came from my mother's abuse by first recognizing that I was safe from her in the current situation.

It was shocking to gradually realize I could not remember ever feeling safe, even as an adult. I had escaped the actual abuse, but everyday situations in the present included triggers that made me feel a need to protect myself. Carol again likened it to a cornered and wounded animal striking out in defense. I would claw, snarl, growl, and strike out to protect myself from an attack or a perceived attack. The wounds were my pain, the sadness behind the anger. But I didn't understand that. I had to discover for myself that I could be safe.

—

At one time or another, we've all been in a situation where a coworker, neighbor, or family member just pushes our buttons. I eventually left the BDN, taking a part-time job that I thought would be rewarding but also give me time for freelance projects. It didn't take me long to identify the person who would trigger me again and again and again. We mixed like oil and water.

She was an equal in the company hierarchy, and she worked in another office, so I didn't have to deal with her on a daily basis. Still, what she did or didn't do, as the case often was, affected me and my ability to get my job done. To make matters worse, the boss had asked me to mentor her since I actually had more experience than she did. She wanted none of this, and it strained an already difficult relationship.

Finally, in addition to withholding the information I needed for several assignments, my coworker took credit for my work. Carol had permitted me to call in an emergency outside of our appointments, and when I found out my coworker did this, I finally felt compelled to do so. What I saw as my coworker's lack of respect and professionalism had me rattled. I came home, took an hour's walk, and still hadn't calmed down. In Pennsylvania, a four-mile walk would calm me down from any work stressors. Sean would say he could see the tension leaving my body by the halfway point. I could feel it, too. This time, however, it didn't work at all.

Carol probably spent an hour on the phone with me that day. I had gotten the first part of the process right. I didn't say anything to my coworker or the boss. I started by trying to calm myself down with a walk, which had worked in the past. And, when it didn't work, she said, I was right to seek her help.

I found myself on that August day pacing our driveway with my cell phone to my ear. Carol asked me what I was feeling. All I knew was I was agitated and angry. She asked me to look beyond that. It was probably one of what she called "the big four" — anger, pain, sadness, or fear.

I was too restless to sit or even stand still. Walking around helped control the excess energy as I tried to figure out what I was feeling — fear. Carol asked me what I feared. The question stumped me. She kept pressing until I recognized that I feared not getting proper credit for my work and being misunderstood.

She asked who needed to give me credit and understand me. I told her I needed this from my coworker and the boss. She asked why.

Stumped again.

Carol pressed. I took a deep breath and pondered the question as I paced, listening for a moment to the fine gravel in the driveway crunching under my shoes. I looked up at the trees surrounding our wooded lot and appreciated what felt like the safety buffer I needed. The only line of sight to the outside world was the sky. This is one of the things I love about being in Maine. It was reassuring.

I finally answered the question. If I'm not understood and I don't get proper credit, then they will think less of me.

Carol asked why what they think matters.

I was silent. But Carol knew I was still on the line, thinking, as I made another circle around the driveway in front of the garage. Finally, I said my boss's opinion matters because I want to keep my job.

I anticipated her next question. Why does it matter what your coworker thinks?

"I don't know," I said. "I suppose it really doesn't."

"But it does," she said, "or you wouldn't need to be on the phone with me."

It took a while, but I figured it out. It mattered because I wanted my mother's approval and could never get it. Because her disapproval came with violence, I felt afraid when I didn't have someone else's approval.

Yep. Carol had been right. Even then, 25 years after her death, I was still afraid of my mother.

I called Carol a number of times over the next couple of months. She'd help me calm myself, identify what I feared, and then the trigger. Next, we would, as she liked to say, "tease it apart" from the reality of the current situation. My coworker and my boss were not my mother. They were not likely to hurt me physically. Winning their approval would not make me a better person or bring me the mother's love that I desperately craved.

During our sessions, Carol would take me the whole way through the worst-case scenario, asking me over and over again, "Then what?" I began to realize that the worst thing that could happen in these situations wouldn't necessarily be the end of the world as I had dreaded.

—

The work situation came to a head a couple of months later at a company Christmas party. My coworker literally snubbed me when I arrived at the restaurant, warmly greeting other employees who had come in with me. I wasn't surprised and hoped that I could just make it through the event, enjoying the company of those I did like.

But it wasn't to be. My coworker took every opportunity to continue to do her best to make me feel uncomfortable. And she succeeded. Seated at the table, I stared at the menu but could not comprehend the words on the page. I put the menu down and then tried again. Same thing. My brain simply refused to compute. In an effort to hide the rising anxiety, I took a sip of my drink and opened the menu again. Still, I had no idea what kind of food this place served.

When I looked up, it was as if I was in a bubble. I could see what was going on around me, but I couldn't comprehend it. I heard noises, but nothing registered as voices or words. The only thing that registered was my fear.

Run!

I wanted to flee, but I could not move. The fear was paralyzing like quicksand slowly making its way up to my neck. I feared I had to get out of there before I was swallowed.

I told Sean what I was feeling, and he said we should leave and I announced our departure to my friends. I don't know exactly what I said, only that I told them I needed to leave and I needed to leave *now*.

At that moment, the boss stood up to make a speech. I hoped this would distract me from my fear and bring me back to the same plane as everyone else. But he announced that my nemesis would be taking photos of the party. I felt disrespected because I'm a national award-winning photographer with a quality camera that I carry with me. Yet he chose to have her take snapshots for our two publications with a cellphone. He knew I was an accomplished photographer. And he knew how I felt about her and that she was vindictive and unprofessional in her dealings with me. He had even told me on several occasions that he knew she was wrong. So why would he do this? I heard him call my name, something about the photos, but I couldn't comprehend what he said. I wondered if I was supposed to respond. I didn't want my picture taken, least of all by her. And I didn't want her photos in my publication or have her name in any way connected to mine. The panic grew.

The boss finished his speech and sat down. Sean tried to reassure me, telling me he loved me and that the boss was behaving like an ass, reinforcing my coworker's negative behavior toward me. Despite his kind words, I still felt the need to flee. Seeing I could not be calmed or reassured, he said simply, "Let's go." We stood, gathered our coats, and left the room.

As we were about to exit the building, I heard someone calling my name. It was my boss. Standing in the doorway, I turned to face him, and he asked where I was going.

I tried to avoid answering in any detail. I simply needed to leave so that I didn't have a breakdown in front of everyone. But he didn't accept the simple answer of "I just need to leave" or "I just need to get out of here."

He persisted with the questions. Why? What happened? Flustered, I said, "I don't feel safe." He asked why. I avoided the question once or twice, but he persisted. Backed into a corner, I took a chance with the truth. After all, he seemed concerned.

"It's PTSD," I said. "I don't feel safe. I need to leave."

He stared for a moment, his mouth hanging open ever so slightly, but he continued to look concerned. Still, I figured he would turn on me eventually. They always do. That's how this works. They all want to know what's wrong and how they can help but then when you tell them, they see you as just another lunatic. I felt not only fear but also shame.

I turned and stepped outside, and Sean followed, allowing the door to close behind us. Then we got into my car, where the tears began to flow freely, and I called Carol. Sean sat in the seat beside me quietly, offering tissues and his calming presence. It took a couple of minutes through my sobs for Carol to understand what had happened.

"What do you want to do now?" she asked.

"I want to quit," I said. "I'm not saying I'm going to. But right now, I want to."

Most people would have encouraged me not to quit because I liked the job, yada yada. But Carol accepted what I said. I could quit if I wanted. The trick was to make sure I really wanted to quit before I actually did so.

We were on the phone for about an hour, and it took another couple of days for me to feel like I was back to normal. In our next session, Carol and I dissected the events of that night, and I realized what was going on.

My mother loved to show off. She loved to have other kids in the neighborhood over for games or makeovers. As the judge in our little contests, she always picked the other kids over me. As the authority figure at that party, my boss represented my mother, and he had done the same thing to me that she did, showing what I perceived as favoritism to another person, especially one whose skills were no match for mine. Only in this case, the other person was also one who treated me badly. At least I had liked the other kids whom my mother had chosen over me.

I quit that job a month later and never looked back. Two jobs in Maine hadn't worked out as I had hoped. But I wasn't afraid that I had made a mistake. I saw it as a sign that I should follow my dreams. Over the course of the next year, I decided to do something I had always wanted to do, something I'd always been afraid to do. I set my sites on becoming a professional photographer.

- 5 -
DETOURS

The first time I held a 35mm camera, it was magic. At least, it was after I asked the inevitable question: What button do I push?

At the time, I had been working at a small semi-weekly newspaper in Wyoming County, Pennsylvania. The editor asked me to take a photo of something I no longer remember. I had never before even seen a 35mm camera up close, let alone held one.

I was nervous, of course, but once I got out there and started shooting, I discovered a passion for recording images and started shooting everything I could. The newspaper was supportive and allowed me to borrow the camera. Many of my shots were published as stand-alone photos — a single photo with a caption, without an accompanying story.

And so, on that day, I entered the world of photography much like I had entered the world of journalism — without a college degree or any formal training.

But let me back up a bit. I went to college not because I wanted to but rather because it was expected of me. I was an honor student at high school that was highly ranked in both academics and athletics. Back then, especially, people didn't ask honor students at those kinds of schools whether they planned to attend college; they just assumed we would.

Like many 16-year-olds, both then and now, I chose a college and a career path without any real idea of what I wanted to do with my life. All I knew was that I wanted to run track.

When I was about 10, I ran a race against a neighborhood boy riding a bicycle — and won. In seventh grade, one of my friends invited me to join her and a neighborhood couple in their twenties who were going jogging. My friend dropped out after about a half mile, as did everyone else who had joined us. But I kept going, keeping pace with these experienced runners for their full two-mile workout. Every time I saw them after that, they called me "the jogger." I just smiled, certain that anyone could run two miles without any training. It would be another four years before I'd realize that wasn't so.

By that time, my parents had split up, and I was living alone with my mother. We moved several times between when we left Middletown at the end of sixth grade in 1976 and when I started my freshman year in high school in 1978. The latest move was to a small, isolated coal mining town in northwestern Pennsylvania that put me in what I have since dubbed The School From Hell. I went out for track. But my mother made me quit the team. She wasn't entirely unjustified, either. The coach didn't approve of girls and boys interacting during practice, and he made that fact known in an ugly way.

"Hey!" he shouted in front of everyone within earshot whenever a handful of girls were brave enough to warm up with the boys. "What are you sluts doing? Get over there and do your own damn warm-ups. This isn't a dating service. It's practice."

My mother's motives were rarely as simple as protecting her child. Had she really wanted to protect me from a negative influence, she could have taken up the matter with the principal or school board. Instead, about six months later, when she didn't want me to have a boyfriend, she actually said to me, "What the track coach said was true. You are a little slut!"

We moved again before the start of my junior year, and with no boys in the picture, she had no objection to my going out for track at the new school, North Allegheny.

I ran two seasons of track and one season of cross country, earning a district medal during my senior year — and second season — of track. In April or May of my senior year, a recruiter from the University of Pittsburgh, who had actually come to see my competitors in the mile and two-mile, was impressed enough with my performance against them that he asked if I was interested in a track scholarship.

But track scholarships weren't good enough for my mother. Like an idiot, I turned down more than one in an attempt to please her. I thought if I just made the right decisions, she would love me. But there were no right decisions. Ever. I know that now.

Ironically, my mother claimed not to have the money to send me to college. She wanted me to rectify that by getting an academic scholarship. I would learn after her death that my mother had received $65,000 in insurance and legal settlements after a drunk driver killed my dad. This money was supposed to pay for my college education. However, I never saw a dime of it beyond the $200 she gave me for books at the start of my first year. At that time, a semester of college tuition, along with room and board, was $2,500. She could have paid cash for my college education, including my books and any other expenses, and walked away with $40,000 for herself. But she wanted more. She had to have all of it.

Left with no other means of paying college tuition, I applied for financial aid. Since I hadn't been offered a scholarship that she deemed acceptable, my mother made things miserable for me. Whenever aid forms came in the mail, I would enter a state of panic. I knew I was expected to go to college, and I needed to get these forms completed in order to fulfill that expectation. But I also knew that asking my mother to fill them out was inviting trouble.

"What the hell is this?" she would snarl upon seeing the envelope or the forms themselves if I had removed them from the envelope and set them on the kitchen bar for her to find them.

"Financial aid forms," I would say, resisting the urge to run away.

"What do those goddamn people want now?"

Sometimes, I would remain quiet, hoping the storm would blow over before engulfing me. Other times, I would attempt to answer, usually with "I don't know." Sometimes, I played it right. Other times, I didn't.

"What do you mean you don't know?" she would snarl if I chose the latter route. Her forehead would be wrinkled in anger, and her lips pursed in an indignant inverted triangle. "You're the one going to college. You're supposed to know these things!"

"But I can't fill them out," I would plead. "They have to be filled out by a parent."

She would shout something degrading, usually calling me a foul name, and then punctuate her anger with a comment like, "If you'd get a scholarship, we wouldn't have to go through this."

But that wasn't the end of her lofty expectations for me. She wanted me to attend an Ivy League school. She was disappointed when I enrolled at Penn State, a choice I made based heavily on my desire to run track at the collegiate level. She filled out some of the financial aid forms during my senior year in high school, but once I was at Penn State, she refused to cooperate further with any aspect of the financial aid application process. She claimed the required information was no one else's business. I understood that and even agreed to a point. I could not seem to get her to understand, though, that bucking the system would not change it. At the time, I thought she simply didn't grasp the consequences of her actions. But now I believe she knew exactly what she was doing. She was hiding money.

Politics was another factor. The economic policies of the Reagan administration meant the end of the Social Security benefits my mother was receiving due to my dad's death — and this was over and above the $65,000 she already had in her pocket. The parents of students graduating high school in 1982, as I did, would be cut off completely. Parents of those already enrolled in college by May 1982 would continue to receive benefits, although they would see a 25-percent decrease each year until the payments were phased out altogether.

News of this impending reduction sent my mother into a tizzy. She saw dollar signs — and they were marching out of her life.

"You've got to enroll in college early," she announced after learning that area colleges had begun special programs designed to keep Social Security payments coming. Eligible high school seniors simply needed to enroll in college before the date of their anticipated high school graduation.

"But what about track?" I asked as I stood in the hallway, facing where she sat in one of the living room rocking chairs. I had been on the school team and doing well. I had big dreams I wasn't ready to give up.

"Well, sometimes you have to make sacrifices," she snapped. "Otherwise, you won't be able to go to college."

I decided I had to know more before I accepted my mother's plan. At my high school guidance office, I called the financial aid departments of every college I applied to in order to find out the real story. Each one said the money would be made up in other ways by the financial aid departments. One representative even went so far as to say that enrolling in college early wasn't necessary. "No qualified applicant will be denied the opportunity to attend class just because of a cut in Social Security," the college representative had said. That settled it for me.

When I told my mother what I'd learned, she stared at me silently for what seemed like a long time as she sat in her usual spot in the living room. Of course, I hadn't yet realized that the cuts in Social Security meant only a reduction in income for her. "How can you be so sure of yourself?" she finally asked.

"I talked to financial aid officers. They said I won't lose the chance to go to college." I was in my usual spot, standing in the hallway facing her through the doorway.

"What if they're wrong?" She was eerily calm.

"I don't think they are." When she said nothing, I took a

big risk and said what was really on my mind. "I need a chance at a normal senior year. I know you don't think track is important, but I do. And then there's the prom. And graduation ceremonies, not to mention finishing the Advanced Placement classes I'm taking. I just need to be normal, like everyone else." I swallowed nervously but stood my ground, waiting for the storm I was certain would come.

Surprisingly, it never did. She simply sighed and said, "all right," in a tone of voice that made it sound as if I had asked her to do something immoral. But I didn't care. I had won the right to stay in high school and start college that fall, just like everyone else.

—

The trouble with college is if you don't go to class, you tend not to do well. The passion I had for distance running did not transfer to the classroom. My mother had chosen my major for me — business with a minor in computer science. My freshman year went reasonably well. During my sophomore year, however, I crashed and burned with a D average. I got through two semesters of accounting, hated another pair of required classes in quantitative business analysis, and actively despised economics.

And so began my pattern of avoidance. If I didn't go to class, I didn't have to think about how unhappy I was doing somebody else's bidding. Avoidance allowed me to keep it together, at least on the surface.

To the outside world, I'm sure I appeared fine, except for when my frustration and fear spilled out through my fists. It did so as early as my freshman year when three girls attending a party on the dorm floor above ours came down to our floor. They had themselves a good time walking through our hall, vandalizing whatever was in reach. Standing at one end of the hall, I watched them walk away from me and my dorm mates, ripping several dry-erase memo boards and other decorations off the doors of several rooms, including mine. Those with me were angry, and someone even yelled at them, but they ignored us.

I was angry not only at them but also at the others who clearly disapproved but would not take action. Finally, I'd had enough. As I saw the three vandals enter the bathroom at the opposite end of the hall, I trotted toward them. When I reached the bathroom, each of the girls was in a different stall. I waited. When the first one emerged, I stepped toward her and smacked her across the side of the head with a powerful sideways swing of my arm.

"Oh, my God!" she yelled as I continued to pound her, her long dark hair flying around as she wildly tried to step back and avoid the onslaught. "Hurry, you guys! I need help!"

I knew that her two friends would come to her rescue, but it didn't matter. I knew I could take on all three of them, and I did. I don't even remember what they looked like, only that the other two emerged from their stalls and simultaneously tried to attack me. When that immediately failed — I moved too fast for them to get close enough to hit me — they began trying to defend their friend and themselves. Like a group of boxers, we danced around our bathroom ring, arms shooting out towards each other. I successfully managed to block punches from six different arms as I pushed them with dancing little hops back away from the door leading into the hall and around the center island that had four sinks on each side.

The fight lasted for what felt like 10 or 20 minutes, with me driving them back away from the door each time one of them tried to flee. They got ahold of me and lifted me above their heads as they tried several times, unsuccessfully, to eject me head-first from the bathroom. Finally, I decided to just end it, thrusting my body forward to release myself from their grips and get me through the door. They quickly slammed it behind me.

I don't know if the three girls ever knew why I attacked them. I do know that they reported it to campus security, and our dorm resident assistant was able to identify me as the attacker. Several days after the fight, he called me to his room to reprimand me. As we sat alone opposite each other in his room, he said all the things I anticipated — that fighting was wrong and that these girls, all of whom had minor injuries, could elect to file charges.

"You could get kicked off the track team!" he said.

I had been merely going through the motions of listening to his lecture, but that statement caught my attention. I was too angry to care what he thought, nor did I care about the opinions of those who had been too afraid to intervene. Looking back and reflecting, though, it was more like I was too afraid to acknowledge my fear, so I lashed out in order to protect myself from both real and perceived attacks. I tried to tell the RA that although I may have been wrong to fight, it didn't excuse their behavior. He didn't care, and that just made me angrier. But I let him think he had lectured me into submission so that I could leave.

Although I didn't always get into fistfights, the pressure continued to cause my emotions to spill out. It was around this time that my German language teacher was concerned enough by my behavior and affect to call me aside and suggest I see a counselor.

Those counseling sessions empowered me to the point that I changed my major from business and computer science to secondary education. During spring break, my mother and I were having dinner at a restaurant on the top floor of one of Pittsburgh's department stores when I broke the news.

"You changed your major without consulting me?" she snarled, her eyes boring into me like drill bits into a piece of wood.

I sat still and said nothing.

"Teaching isn't a profession for capable people. It's for losers," she ranted. "Well, you'll have to contend with the consequences, not me!"

The words of the university counselor kept ringing in my ears. I should consider what *I* wanted. And I wasn't sure college had anything to do with what I wanted, whatever that was. Couldn't I do something else? If I had to go to college, couldn't I find a way to live on my own for two years so I could qualify for financial aid as an independent, free of my mother's sabotage? Only one thing seemed certain. I couldn't continue on this same path. My mother, despite her best efforts to pressure me into going to college and doing well, was making it impossible for me to continue.

During my junior year in college, I began to get more and more nervous. I dreaded going to my mother's, and I knew I couldn't stay on the path she'd laid out for me. And what good would it do me, ultimately, to continue on her chosen path anyway? I despised school, and I wanted out. But where would I go?

―

I met Ken at a frat party my freshman year and we were a couple for the next three years. Although he held out hope that all this was just a misunderstanding and that my mother and I could eventually reconcile, he realized I needed more than just sympathy and encouragement. If I was going to drop out of college and buck my mother, I needed a place to stay. Ken talked his parents into allowing me to stay with them temporarily in Tunkhannock, located in the northeastern corner of Pennsylvania. I would get Ken's room, and he would sleep on a cot in another room. This solidified my decision to quit school.

I don't know what Ken said to his parents to convince them that they should do this for me. But I was grateful. Without them, I would have stayed in school on my collision course, or I would have ended up in a shelter somewhere. But I was not going home. I could not.

I had met Ken's family a number of times. I liked them, and they liked me, but we didn't know each other well. Surely, it was an imposition to have a stranger living with them. I resolved to do my part and consider myself a boarder. I would pay rent and pitch in around the house and outside with chores on their 200-acre farm.

My Penn State track coach was supportive, though she warned me that it might not be as easy as I expected. I knew that, but I also knew it was impossible to convey to someone else that I truly had no other choice.

No longer doomed, I set out to make a life for myself.

I stayed with Ken's family for the summer and got my own apartment — a three-room hovel above a bar — that fall. It came furnished, with decorations covering holes in the wall. If nothing unexpected came up and I didn't succumb to the urge to grab an order of fast food French fries too many times, my three part-time jobs covered my expenses. Once winter came, I had to turn the heat up all the way to bring the inside temperature up to 60 degrees. The apartment was chilly, but it was mine.

Within a year, I had gotten my first full-time job at the local newspaper and, with it, my introduction to photography. But I was still struggling to free myself of my mother's disapproval, abuse, and control.

Over the years, I'd kept in touch with Dot, who had been our neighbor in Middletown when I was in grade school. She also kept in touch with my mother.

"So why did you write your mother off?" she asked after I answered her phone call. Irritation was evident in her voice. I'm not even sure she said "hello" before lashing out at me.

"I didn't write my mother off. She wrote me off." I responded with just as much irritation.

"Well, what happened? Why did you drop out of school?"

I gave her an abbreviated version of the story, and she softened her tone somewhat. But I could still feel the heaviness of her judgment creeping through the phone line.

"Your mother has a lot of pride, and you're all she has."

"Well, she's going to have to break through the pride," I announced with enough conviction that I actually surprised myself. "I have to live my own life, control my destiny. I can't live for another person's dreams no matter how much they mean to that person or how much that person means to me."

Dot's tone softened again as she attempted to explain the things parents feel when faced with letting go of their kids. Her point was clear. My mother, not me, was suffering.

I kept pushing in an attempt to be heard. "I understand how she probably feels. But that's no excuse. She's got to change her ways. It's a two-way street now."

"Well, you've forced an issue," Dot replied with obvious resignation. I could almost see her face as she exhaled slowly and dragged out her words. "It will take time but she'll come around."

Then the conversation wound back around to college. "Why did you give up?" Dot asked. "You started out in what you should've stayed in."

I was confused. What major did she think I had started in? Apparently, Dot thought I had entered college with the intention of studying foreign languages and, possibly, becoming an interpreter or linguist.

"No," I said, explaining how my mother had pushed me toward business. I hated business courses, but my mother hated all my other career ideas.

"Well, she probably feels betrayed because she paid all that money for you to go to school and you—"

Whoa! I was shocked by what I had just heard, and, as always, my anger covered for me. As the wounded animal, I had to strike out to defend myself from her attacks. And so I cut her off.

"She didn't pay for shit!" I shouted as if I were pounding a gavel on a desk.

"I thought she paid for it through your dad's insurance settlement or Social Security or something?" Dot said.

"No," I said again, the word coming out with a thud. "She not only didn't pay, she refused to cooperate with the financial aid application process and in a few months, I'll have to start paying back nearly $10,000 in student loans. So don't you ever let her say she paid my way!"

I don't know if Dot was fully able to comprehend the gravity of my feelings or the significance of my mother's abuse. Although I felt we came to an understanding toward the end of our conversation, I still felt betrayed because she had initially judged me based solely on what she'd heard from my mother. Just like the people from social services, she never asked me anything before drawing conclusions.

—

After I dropped out of college and began my career as a journalist, I was able to pay my way, even if only barely. That meant I didn't have to ask my mother for anything. By that time, I had a camera in my hand and my life was going in an exciting new direction.

- 6 -
POST PROCESSING

My introduction to photography came long before the digital age. In 1986, when I shot my first few frames, images were recorded on film that had to be developed in a darkroom. You had to be in total darkness to remove the film from the camera and insert it into a canister for development. Once the film was developed, you made prints with the aid of a dim red light. Using a piece of equipment designed to hold everything in place, you would shine white light through the negative onto photographic paper and then put the paper into a series of chemical baths to make the actual print.

These days, photographers and their cameras create digital images, which the photographer then edits on the computer or even in the camera itself, an activity known as post-processing. You take the image from the camera and, in essence, develop it without chemicals. Some purists still argue this is cheating, but, for me, digital photography opened doors because I could more quickly and easily see the results of the camera settings on the image I'd shot. Then, I can take that image and decide how to help it better convey what I want. I don't manipulate images to create what isn't there — my photojournalism background precludes going in that direction — but I can make subtle changes that make the image better reflect what is really there, even if the adjustment is only subtle. And so it has been with my life as I've truly begun to heal here in Maine.

Photography was a bit like track. I fell in love quickly and completely. But I really didn't know what to do with it. Opportunities, especially in Pennsylvania, are limited. Good photographers are quite common. And, even if you find a way to stand out, what are you going to do? Shoot weddings and school portraits? Sell framed photos as art? I just didn't know.

I loved my work at that first newspaper in Tunkhannock. But, not long after I took the job, I faced a tough choice — I could afford to pay for rent, groceries, and utilities, or I could make my student loan payments, but not both. In an attempt to improve my financial situation, I took another job at a small paper in southern New York state. I didn't realize until after I started working there that this paper sent out all its film for developing. It had no darkroom.

Before the move, I had somehow managed to scrape together enough money to buy my own 35mm camera. I tried to maintain my photography skills in New York, but it was frustrating because I could not do my own film developing and printing. Commercial developing had considerable limitations, the most noteworthy being color failure, which causes a print to come out looking green or pink. This is usually because either the machine did not allow the operator to make the required adjustments or the operator chose not to. In New York, I got a part-time job in a photo processing shop where I learned how to develop color film — on a machine, yes, but one that allowed the operator to make adjustments. In fact, the owner encouraged it. Knowing how the problems I experienced with commercial developing could have been corrected just fueled my frustration.

At this time in history, photo processors were becoming less and less willing to develop black-and-white film. When I finally left the New York newspaper — and the photo processing lab where I had worked — I moved back to Pennsylvania. I found myself continuing to be saddled with the limitations of commercial processing.

Since newspaper jobs didn't pay very well, I ventured into picture framing. I loved that, too, but it also did not pay well. Fortunately, by that time, Sean and I were married, so the burden of paying bills didn't fall only on me.

Whether or not I liked the results of commercial film processing, the fact was it was expensive. Together, Sean and I could pay all the bills when we were first married, but we barely had enough money left over at the end of the month to order a pizza, let alone pay $5 for a roll of film and another $7 per roll for processing and prints.

It was like a love affair that had to end, not because of incompatibility, but rather because we were from such vastly different socio-economic backgrounds that we could not overcome our differences. I didn't have the money to run in the same circles as photography, and photography could not change its very nature to allow me to keep up. And so, we drifted apart, gradually seeing less and less of each other.

By that time, digital photography had become a thing. I was working as the editor of several weekly newspapers near Allentown, Pennsylvania. I couldn't help but notice my attractive former love in a new role. Although I let myself get sucked in again, it was not all the way, at least not initially. Believing that I was no longer interested in the technical aspects of photography, I bought one of the better point-and-shoot cameras. I thought it would be convenient not only for work but also for documenting life at home.

It was, not coincidentally, a trip to Maine with that little point-and-shoot that reawakened the passion. I was in love again, and before long, I had outgrown the point-and-shoot and invested in a digital version of the 35mm camera, known as a digital single lens reflex, or DSLR.

Sean also enjoys photography, though he's not as passionate about it. Still, we enjoy shooting the scenery and wildlife together on hikes, as well as shooting out the windows when turkeys or bears visit our little house in the Maine woods. Back in Pennsylvania, as I restarted my photography adventure, I entered contests. I won a few, too. I shot for newspapers and magazines, and while I made money, it was always secondary to the real jobs that paid the bills.

Maine has a vibrant arts community. In Pennsylvania, the only thriving arts community is in the town of New Hope. If there are any artsy towns elsewhere in the state, I certainly never found them. I spent 20 years in the Lehigh Valley in east central Pennsylvania. There are a couple of art museums that hold programs but art is not a part of mainstream life there the way it is in Maine. During our many trips to Maine, especially when we first started coming here, we would drive Route 1 north from the New Hampshire border. The landscape was laden with art galleries and shops run by entrepreneurs who were, somehow, able to actually make money from their work, and how I envied them. But the only successful photographers I knew in Pennsylvania worked for newspapers or shot weddings or portraits. I would have welcomed the chance to be a full-time photojournalist, but I wasn't really interested in the kinds of work I saw local portrait photographers do. In fact, back in New York, I worked for a short time at a portrait studio and hated it. I did not understand the appeal of pulling down screens with different backgrounds and shooting the same five poses over and over with different people.

    I toyed with the idea of pursuing a position as a photographer at the BDN, where I first worked when I moved to Maine. There weren't any openings, and, to be perfectly blunt, their photographers were a lot better than me. But every once in a while, I'd toy with the concept of "what if." I never pursued it, though. I could barely do my job as a reporter and writer. If I wanted to pursue photography or even continue working successfully as a journalist, I had to find a way to get out of the stupor induced by the medication prescribed for my bipolar diagnosis.

—

    I once described my life to Carol as being like the allergy drug commercial, where they say there's an ordinary clear, and then they pull away a film to reveal an even clearer, brighter picture. On the medication prescribed to treat bipolar disorder, I was unable to see the bright colors behind the film. The images my eyes took in were dull, like a dusty piece of chrome or an unpolished piece of brass.

The folks at the BDN had been impressed with my photography skills, saying they set me "way ahead" of the average reporter. My duties involved not only reporting and writing stories but also taking still photographs and videos. While I found the joy had come creeping back, the love I had felt when I handled that first 35mm camera, and then again when I bought my first DSLR, was gone. It was like being in a marriage where you take the other person for granted and just go through the motions. I enjoyed it, yes, but I was still stuck behind the hazy film, and that kept me from experiencing that joy to the fullest.

In order to get out of the stupor, I had to look at the events leading up to my diagnosis and try to figure out the cause. Carol suggested that what happened might be physical as well as mental. Many times in American medicine, conditions are compartmentalized and treated separately from one another with little regard for interplay. Mental health issues are seen as totally separate from foot pain, and foot pain is seen as totally different from gastric issues. And so on. Carol thought my overall medical history may have played a role as well as the stressors of my life at that time.

She was actually the first person who ever explained to me that it's necessary to wean off antidepressants before switching to another drug. I had heard the term "wean" tossed about by doctors in Pennsylvania, but, usually, they likened the process of weaning to lowering doses over about two weeks, and then you're done.

Carol was quite distressed to learn that, just before the crash,

I had changed antidepressants suddenly. When the new drug seemed to make matters worse instead of better, I stopped that one abruptly, too.

Three years later, I had a documentary on TV while I framed photos in my living room. I heard a doctor say that abruptly stopping antidepressants can bring on a type of psychosis, which, at the very least, is worse than the depression the drugs were intended to treat. Suddenly, it all made sense! This is part of what happened to me.

It was, ironically, like a scene in another drug commercial where a figure rushes through some kind of barrier to experience a better state of being.

Throughout the first year I worked with Carol, I began to question what I had once thought was a fact — my bipolar diagnosis. Finally, one day, I casually mentioned this.

"I'm not sure I have bipolar disorder," I said.

Her response was immediate.

"I don't think you do either."

I got the sense she had been waiting for me to figure out what to her had been quite obvious. She probably wanted to tell me, to convince me of what she already knew. But she realized I had to figure it out for myself. At last, I had.

Carol tossed out the idea of weaning off the medication, saying I should take my time and consider it. If, at any time, I felt uncomfortable with the results or thought I was having a relapse, I could go back to my previous dose at any time. Before we did anything, however, she wanted me to consult with my psychiatrist.

Looking back, it's interesting to note that my psychiatrist, a petite woman working out of an office in a nearby town, once said to me, "If you do have bipolar disorder…." I don't remember the context, just that she spoke as if the diagnosis wasn't a given and that had surprised me. She was supportive of the idea of weaning off the medication and agreed with Carol's statement that I could always reverse direction if it didn't work out.

I was on board, but Sean was reluctant. He feared I needed the medication to keep me from crashing again. Life during what I have since dubbed the Great Bipolar Incident had been hell for him, and he didn't want a relapse.

I explained the discussions I'd had both with Carol and the psychiatrist. I also brought him into sessions so he could take part in the discussions. I promised him that if I began to backslide, I would reverse course and go back on the full dose. No one wanted to avoid a relapse more than me.

And so began the great experiment. It took months to wean off the drugs, but as I did, I noticed the world around me coming into greater focus. The film was being lifted, and I could feel joy again.

Of course, that was not the end of the healing journey, not by far. But it did get me once again fully engaged in a love affair with the camera.

—

Maine is absolutely beautiful. It's difficult to take a bad picture. As I weaned off the medication, my balance returned, and Sean and I began hiking again on more difficult terrain. We would carry our cameras and shoot everything from the wide open scenery to close-ups of insects or lobster buoys that had washed up on shoreline hiking trails.

My increasing level of coherence was certainly a factor in my development as a photographer, but Maine's beauty didn't hurt.

I picked up some regular freelance writing assignments with two community newspapers as well as some magazines covering the state. This was a good start, especially since these assignments required accompanying photographs, but the work was based on my skills as a writer rather than a photographer. The pictures were secondary. How would I make photography a bigger part of my work?

I was asked to shoot a wedding back in Pennsylvania, and I had a great time. I was also asked to shoot senior portraits. These were great starts, but I still wanted something regular.

While enjoying a meal at a nearby restaurant, I noticed that the walls were looking rather bare. Only a few photographs remained for sale. I asked the owners if they would be interested in showing my work, and they were! I brought them several framed photos and some photo notecards.

Next, I approached two different galleries. Both agreed to display and sell my work. Even better than having these outlets accept my work was when my pieces sold and I got paid. I picked up some other photography clients in the meantime. I was off to a good start.

—

Sean and I had always been collectors, something we thought we thought we would have to give up living in Maine because our house here is considerably smaller than the house we had in Pennsylvania.

We'd actually started downsizing long before we moved. We

knew all our collections just weren't going to fit into the house in Maine. We sold off and liquidated a lot, but kept a few of our most important collections, most notably Victorian art glass. We'd surf online sites on occasion, and we'd stop every now and then at an antiques place. But, we tried to keep such activities to a minimum in order to avoid succumbing to the collecting temptation that would build up the level of clutter in the limited space.

Despite our efforts to downsize, we were unable to get rid of a number of things we considered to be too valuable to donate but not important enough to display. Having these things stored in boxes in the garage was, in our opinion, stupid. So, when a new antique and artisan mall opened just a few miles from our house in Maine, we decided this would be a good avenue for selling off those remaining treasures.

We got ourselves a space and began selling. In order to keep things fresh, we tried to move our inventory around regularly. And then we allowed ourselves to go to an auction.

We had loved auctions in Pennsylvania, especially estate auctions. You never knew what you were going to find, and you had the opportunity to be a little nosey, looking around the home and at all the contents. It was good to be going to auctions again in Maine.

We noticed that bringing in new items made everything sell better so we began actively buying for resale but trying to keep the amounts small. For our second season, we rented a bigger space and let our collecting genes run wild again, hitting auctions, flea markets, thrift stores and even other antique shops. It was fun to be able to buy something, enjoy it for a while, and then sell it off when something new came along.

The secondary market was a big help with my photography. For the first few pieces I prepared for sale, I bought frames at retail stores. This was challenging because I had to be careful to keep costs low. I didn't want to price my pieces out of the market because I had to pay for expensive frames.

So, I turned to thrift stores and yard sales. A few frames came from auction box lots. My work tends to be rustic, so older frames, even those with some wear, work well.

While scouring thrift stores and other outlets, I began to find other interesting and unusual ways to present my images. I found jewelry and trinket boxes, serving trays, wall hooks, paperweights, and even snow globes, all designed to hold and showcase photographs. I did two local photography shows, and the usable items sold at least as well as, if not better than, the framed and unframed prints. I had found my niche — photography you can use. Part of my space at the co-op would be devoted to photography displays and sales.

—

I'd started weaning off the medication after I left the job at the BDN, and I often wondered if my experience would have been different if I had been off the medication then. Of course, it would have. I wanted to tell my old boss I could think again now, although I didn't contact him to say so. I was continuing to learn that I didn't have to explain or defend myself all the time.

I learned that through a process Carol called "self-soothing." She explained that the part of me that was afraid was like a little child, reacting to things the way a child would. The frightened inner child was reacting to current events much as she did to my childhood experiences, when I was afraid of what my mother would do.

I had to learn that I was safe, that I would, in fact, be OK. I was a good person, intelligent and accomplished, she said, even if my former boss never had the chance to see me at my best. Even if he thought badly of me, she said, I was still a good person and I would still be OK.

This was a difficult concept. I began to see that my self esteem had always been performance based — I believed I was a good person only if I performed well. If I made mistakes or disappointed someone, then I equated that incidental failure with my being a failure as a person.

I remember one conversation in particular. I had told Carol that I was proud of myself because I had realized a person I had recently been working with wanted to break for lunch even though he hadn't said so. I had told him I was flexible and I would be happy to either break for lunch or continue working. He decided to break for lunch.

"I'm getting good at reading him," I said.

"Is it your job to read him?" Carol asked. "If he is hungry, can't he just tell you he wants to break for lunch?"

I had never before considered that it wasn't my job to read other people and figure out what they really wanted. After all, that had been my job with my mother. I had to try to read her and read the situation in order to determine what I should do. Any mistake I made would be met with at least harsh words and, more often than not, physical violence. It was a confusing but interesting concept to think it wasn't my responsibility after all.

- 7 -
A FAMILY DISMANTLED

Not long after my mother announced she was leaving my father, the four of us took a trip to Pittsburgh. Instead of visiting relatives, we drove outside the city to the town of Butler. My parents maintained the level of civility necessary to navigate to the unfamiliar location. As my dad turned the car down a small back road, we came to a secluded tree-lined driveway that curved along before revealing a smart brick facade with large windows and white shutters. A white sign on the small lawn declared the name of the place — Children's Rehabilitation Center. We parked the car and got out.

    A tall, thin woman with very short hair greeted us in the spacious foyer that was decorated simply with white walls and red carpet. A few chairs sat along the walls and a Dutch door opened into the hall. The woman gave us a tour through long white corridors, our heels clicking on linoleum floors that seemed unusually bright because of light reflected off more white walls.

We passed any number of kids who could have passed for Nicole's school mates.

Her name came up often.

I didn't want to be there, but I had to be, so I retreated into myself and pretended I was home catching bugs or riding my imaginary horse. I hadn't paid attention to Nicole's demeanor while we were there. Now, I wonder how she felt. No one told her directly what was happening, probably assuming she didn't understand. Now, I bet she understood exactly what was going on.

In the car making our way back down the curving driveway as we left Children's Rehab, my mother turned in her seat to face me and said, "Well, what did you think?"

"It was okay," I said.

"Good enough for Nicole to live there?"

I knew this was a trick question. Nicole would be living there. Soon. I had figured out that much. What could I possibly say that would be acceptable? I took a chance with "I guess" and waited nervously for my mother's voice to crash like thunder with her next comment.

It did.

"Well, would you want to live there?" My mother's eyes were narrowed. She was clearly waiting for a chance to attack.

"No."

"Oh, so it's good enough for Nicole, but not for you!" she barked.

"Leave her alone," my dad snapped. "What is she supposed to say?"

My mother shook her head, threw her arms up and turned to look out the front window for the silent ride home. I looked out my window and retreated into my fantasy world, a place where I could deny my frightening emotions. Nicole rode next to me in the back seat with her head down, her left hand slowly tapping her temple.

—

After Nicole moved out, my parents' sold her bedroom furniture. My mother was upset the day the buyer came and loaded it into his van. She said she felt like Nicole had died.

I remember watching the buyers load the furniture. It was a sunny day and I was standing along the side of the driveway, facing the van. I could see the front door of the house, and my mother's sad face poking out momentarily before retreating back inside. I knew it was best to remain outside, out of my mother's way, where I was relatively safe from punishment for feeling the wrong things or not feeling the right things strongly enough.

—

The next family member to depart was our dog. I stood in the back of the carport, watching as my mother loaded the Irish setter into the back of the green station wagon and drove away. It was the last time I would see Kelly. I'm not exactly sure what happened to her, but I assume my mother took her to the pound. I watched stoically. I said nothing and didn't cry about the loss for 10 years.

—

When school was out for the summer, my mother returned to the Pittsburgh area and the world of the Neanderthals. And she brought me with her. A marked change took place in her once she and I moved in with her mother, and she re-established ties with her siblings.

Weekends at the house were noisy. A constant parade of my mother's sisters, brothers, nieces, and nephews — all of them virtual strangers to me — came and went. They'd arrive, entering the house through the kitchen door without knocking, and then the adults would sit at the big rectangular kitchen table, trying to be heard by talking louder than everyone else. They all drank coffee and smoked cigarettes, the smoke rising above their heads and creating a gray-blue haze that shimmered in the light.

Most of my cousins were younger boys with whom I had little in common. But the family regarded me as one of them — a child — and that meant I was to be excluded from the adult table ritual. Now and then, my mother would call my name, and I'd jump up with anticipation at the prospect of joining the adults.

"Go get me an ashtray," my mother would say without looking at me. I'd obey, as cheerfully as possible and then hang around for a moment, hoping to be invited to stay. When the invitation failed to come, I'd hang my head to trudge across the gray and white kitchen floor back to the other room.

"Johanna!" I'd jump up again upon hearing my name, feeling the same sense of anticipation.

"Get me a cup of coffee." Without looking at me, my mother would hold up her cup and jerk her head quickly to the side towards the coffee pot on the kitchen counter no more than five feet away — a fraction of the distance I had to walk to get into the room to find out what she wanted.

Doing as I was told, I would bring the cup back as politely

as possible, as if it were my pleasure to be her servant, and set it down in front of her. Without a word of thanks, she would bring it to her lips and take a sip, never looking at me as I stood there waiting — hoping — for an acknowledgement before making the disappointing trudge back to the other room.

"Johanna!" Sometimes, my name was called even when I was upstairs or outside. Neither my mother nor her relatives would ever get up to look for me; my mother would just keep screaming my name until I showed up.

"Get your aunt a pack of cigarettes."

"Get me another cup of coffee."

"Get your grandmother her lighter."

"Get me my purse."

In the Neanderthal world, I didn't matter beyond my ability to fetch coffee, cigarettes or whatever item was desired at a given moment. No one ever said "please" or "thank you." My mother's relatives treated me with as much disdain as my mother did.

—

Whenever I saw my dad, I made sure to vent about life with the Neanderthals and their table rituals, causing him to half smile and shake his head in disgust. His reaction was strongest to my description of how my mother called me from other places to do her bidding.

"Whenever your mother did that to me, I'd pop my head in the room and say, 'What'd you bellow?'"

I laughed, enjoying the chance to connect with him.

I memorized his description of their kitchen ritual. "They all sit around the table and try to out-talk each other. And if someone wants something, that person can't go get it, even if it's only two feet away." He'd pause to punctuate that statement for dramatic effect. "They have to bellow for someone in another room" pause "to walk all the way into the kitchen," pause "go over and get the thing," pause "and hand it to them." Another pause. "And if they need something else, they wait till you leave the room and then bellow for you again." He threw his arms out to the side in a mock surrender.

"Yeah!" I said, my laughter growing louder all the while he spoke. "And it's always the kids they bellow for!"

"Get me a cup of coffee. Get me a pack of cigarettes," he'd say, throwing his head to the side as if using it to point to an imaginary coffee pot or cigarette carton. I'd laugh till my sides ached and beg him to imitate them again.

His humor always gave me a drop of comfort in my otherwise dull gray existence.

Unfortunately, though, my visits with my dad were infrequent and irregular. Arguments over child support came up often. In the fall of 1977, my dad planned to take me to dinner for my 13th birthday. When he showed up, my mother claimed he didn't pay enough and, so, he did not have the right to visit me. I was literally all dressed up with nowhere to go.

—

When school started in the fall of 1976, I was sent to live with one of my mother's two brothers. My mother had wanted me to start seventh grade in the Norwin School District, where he and his family lived. She planned to find a job and then find an apartment in the same school district so I wouldn't have to switch schools again.

Her brother, who was a couple of years younger than my mother, had short dark hair and dark eyes. He had been a state champion wrestler back in high school and still looked like a body builder. My mother adored him.

He had a wife and two sons, one in fifth grade and one in third. They lived in a large development full of kids my age, and I made friends by the end of my first week of school. Walking home from the bus stop that Friday, I was disappointed to see my mother already at my uncle's house, smiling at me through the living room window as I approached. She was ready to take me back to my grandmother's for the weekend.

So much for weekend plans.

Every Friday it was the same story — my mother was waiting for me by the time I got off the bus. Every Sunday evening, my uncle would show up at my grandmother's and take me back to his house. I spent weekends cut off from the other kids in my uncle's neighborhood and at school. My mother felt that she saw me so seldom that I should spend each weekend with her and the family, not "out gallivanting" with my friends. I hated it, especially since "spending time" with me usually just meant bellowing for me to fetch her things while she gave all her attention to whoever was sitting around the kitchen table.

Arriving back at my uncle's house one Sunday, I began unpacking my weekend bag when I looked up to see him standing silently in the doorway. He was leaning against the door frame. I smiled and continued unpacking.

"You didn't hug your grandmother," he suddenly bellowed.

"Huh?"

"When you left. You didn't hug your grandmother." His voice was loud and angry.

"Yes, I did." I honestly couldn't remember if I did or not, but this seemed the best defense.

"You will not treat your grandmother like that! She was hurt. I will not tolerate it!" He continued to shout as he shifted his weight evenly to both feet, making his posture more threatening. I stood helpless, looking at him as he ranted on, but without listening to the actual words. I was glad the twin bed was between us and suspected it was the only reason he didn't hit me. "Do you understand me?" I knew that was my cue to respond.

"Yes," I said meekly. I could play the game.

"Good." Without a word, he turned and left. I stayed in that room for the rest of the evening. I made certain to give him a wide berth in the future and to make sure he saw me hugging my grandmother the following week.

I never told my mother about this or his other unpredictable fits, and now I wonder what she would have done, if anything. Ironically, we were all blissfully unaware that 14 years later, when my mother died, this same uncle would threaten to punch me on the stairs of my mother's house when she died because he feared I'd get my hands on her valuables before he did.

—

While I started junior high 200 miles away, my dad remained in our old house with Puff. He had been looking for a job and an apartment in Pittsburgh, and we hoped that he would be able to keep the cat.

"Puff is just as sweet as pie to me," Dad told me the weekend in October 1976 when I visited my former home and saw her for the last time. "But only after she walks through the whole house hollering to make sure you're not here."

I smiled, secure in the love of my cat who was sitting in my lap, her body gently vibrating with the rumbling sounds coming from her throat.

My dad told me he would try his best to keep Puff after our house in Middletown was sold, but ultimately, it would depend on whether he could find an apartment in Pittsburgh that allowed cats. Unfortunately, timing was not on our side. The house sold before he had a place. Our apartment didn't allow cats, and my mother wasn't willing to go out on a limb to keep Puff, even temporarily.

"I realized I had no choice but to take her to the pound," my dad told me a few months later.

I clenched my jaw to deny my emotions.

"But when I got there, I couldn't go in. I sat there in the car with her for a long time." He paused. "Then a lady in a Cadillac pulled up. She got out and saw Puff as she walked past the car." He described how the woman swooned when my dad let her reach through the car window to pet the cat. When he got out of the car and handed Puff to her, the cat immediately started purring, obviously happy to be in her arms. After a brief discussion with my dad, she took Puff home without even going inside to see the other animals.

"After she left," my dad said, looking off into space. "I got back in my car and cried."

I would cry, too, but not for another 20 years. I believed I had to keep my emotions locked deep inside. It was the only way I knew how to cope.

—

My mother found a job in late October 1976 and rented a two-bedroom townhouse starting Nov. 15. It was in the Norwin School District but too far east for me to remain at the same junior high I'd attended for the previous three months. I had to switch schools anyway.

Moving into our own place meant we could have Nicole home with us for a weekend. My mother had visited her and even brought her to my grandmother's house for a few days at a time, but it had never felt like home before. With a home of our own, we thought it would be different.

But our townhouse was not our old house. We had only two bedrooms and neither had a door that locked from the outside the way Nicole's bedroom in Middletown had. That meant our sleeping eyes weren't safe from her inquisitive, prying, flicking fingers first thing in the morning. My mother also feared Nicole wasn't safe because of the stairs. By Christmas, home visits stopped altogether. I remained silent, aware that anything I said could — and probably would — be used against me, whether I tried to sympathize with my mother's difficulties or share my sadness at losing Nicole.

For a while, we continued to visit Nicole at Children's Rehab.

Nicole would emerge from a corridor of strangers. She was almost unrecognizable at first and then became only vaguely familiar. Her long, dark hair had been cut in a bob. Her gait had become increasingly choppy. Her once cheerful eyes had darkened. Instead of the laughter they once expressed, I saw only emptiness. Even when she saw us, her expression was blank. No anger. No joy. No nothing.

I found these visits almost unbearable. Today, I suspect the changes in Nicole were due to pain, the same pain I had refused to let myself feel. At age 9 she suddenly lost her entire family. We came to visit just often enough to keep her hope alive but not often enough to calm her fear that she had been abandoned.

In the late spring of 1978, only about two years since Nicole had been placed, my mother and I stopped at Children's Rehab. We entered the lobby and my mother asked the receptionist to bring Nicole out to us. When Nicole appeared in the doorway with her blank expression, my mother started to cry. Brushing away her tears, she knelt and began to talk to her youngest daughter. "I love you, Baby. Always remember that," she said as she stroked Nicole's face and hair. When she pulled Nicole close for a hug, she had to pull away momentarily to pick up Nicole's arms to put them around her neck.

As I stood there, thinking how beautiful the two of them looked entwined in an embrace, I tried not to feel the pain emanating from them. I wasn't truly aware of my own pain because I pushed it down so hard I could deny its existence.

As far as I know, this was the last time my mother ever saw Nicole.

—

"So, how did that make you feel?" Carol asked after I explained how my family had been dismantled.

I didn't really know what to say. Naturally, it felt pretty lousy. I didn't think that would be news to her. It wasn't. She reassured me that everything that happened was pretty lousy. I didn't deserve to be shoved aside. But, she was after something else, another topic I had only reluctantly ever discussed with anyone — my sister.

Although I believed that I had done a good job of overcoming my past before moving to Maine, I acknowledged that I had never come to terms with my feelings regarding Nicole. And I told Carol what I truly believed — that it was just another one of my failures.

Carol would challenge that just as she had challenged just about everything else I had believed to be true about myself.

- 8 -

NICOLE

I kept my frightening feelings about my sister stuffed down deep where I thought they couldn't hurt me. I knew I had been practicing avoidance, but I didn't know any other way. Facing these feelings scared the hell out of me.

An important part of my healing journey was learning that I could face these feelings and still be OK. It was difficult because, just like my anger, I saw my relationship with Nicole as a failure that reflected my character flaws. I had to learn to see things differently.

After I dropped out of college, I visited Nicole against my mother's wishes. I had been visiting my friend Cheryl and called my mother, who had been after me to get the rest of my things. She was cold but said she would be glad to see me get my winter coats. I told her I would be bringing Cheryl and probably someone with a bigger vehicle than mine. We ended up bringing two other people.

However, when we arrived, my mother was furious. "You can come in, but those people aren't welcome," she snapped as she stood in the doorway of the townhouse. She refused to let Cheryl in, even to use the bathroom.

"I'm not here to fight with you," I said as I stood facing her on the concrete stoop. "Since any kind of pleasant small talk seems to be out of the question, how 'bout I get the rest of my stuff?"

"Just come in and get what you came for," she snapped.

Once inside, my mother escorted me upstairs to my old room and supervised me, making sure I didn't take anything she didn't feel was rightfully mine. "What's that?" she'd say whenever I picked up something that she couldn't immediately identify. I had to justify taking every item.

My mother went downstairs ahead of me, and as I descended the stairs, I could see her sitting at the kitchen bar crying. Perhaps it was another attempt to manipulate me. Perhaps it was even real. I could feel her pain in the empathetic way someone who's known pain can. But I also knew I could not let it change anything because allowing her to regain control would ultimately destroy me.

My mother barked some insults about how rude and cold I was for coming only to get my stuff.

"I'm sorry you feel that way," I said. "But you need to learn to accept me for who I am instead of trying to make me into something I'm not."

"Oh, I know what you are!" she snapped and went into a laundry list of names as she wiped the tears away.

I wanted to comfort her but feared putting myself in harm's

way. Certain we were getting nowhere, I changed the subject. "I'm going to see Nicole," I announced.

Startled, my mother turned her head, and her eyes bored into me. "NO! You are *not!* I forbid it!" She screamed so loud her body shook. "You will *not* take those people to see Nicole!"

"Those people," I said, "are my friends."

"They're nothing but a no-good bunch of —" I'm sure she finished the sentence with a long list of put-downs. But I refused to listen. I turned and walked out the door, determined never to return to Pittsburgh again.

—

It had been years since I'd seen Nicole. My friends and I made our way up the long tree-lined driveway to the smart brick facade. "Children's Rehabilitation Center," the sign declared, although, by this time, Nicole was no child. In fact, my mother lamented, on one of the rare occasions she spoke of Nicole, that on my sister's 18th birthday, the state "confiscated" more than $21,000 in Social Security benefits Nicole had received over the years. My mother believed that if anyone should get that money, she should.

I kept my feelings numb as we entered the front door. I remembered the white walls and the Dutch door that allowed visitors to see into the corridors without allowing them to walk down them. I also remembered the smell of antiseptic that told me this was not a home in any real sense but rather a hospital. I saw a few patients, most of them sitting around or walking aimlessly, some moaning. The whole thing made me feel uncomfortable, and, for emotional safety, I stuffed my discomfort.

Instead, I turned my thoughts to something more intellectual and, therefore, safe — the question of why my 19-year-old sister could still live at a place for children. I figured it had to be because she was so small. I stood just under 5 feet tall and Nicole always had been and still was quite a bit smaller.

I asked to see her, and our group was led through the halls, all of which looked the same as they always had, with white walls and gray tile floors. We waited in a visiting area with indoor potted trees making it look a lot like a greenhouse showroom. I had never seen this room before and had no idea any such place existed here since my mother and I had always visited with Nicole only in the foyer or took her out.

My friends and I sat at one of the benches surrounding an indoor tree and waited. When a nurse led Nicole into the room, I was stunned. I expected to see the petite and lean girl with rapidly flicking hands that I remembered. This person was hunched over like she was about to pick up something on the floor. Her hands were held tightly together, but there was no motion. Her gait was stiff, and she was wearing a protective helmet so I couldn't make out what her hair actually looked like. I could see only its dark color sticking out above and below the rubber circle that went around the top of her head. Some loose strands of hair stuck out around the protective squares that covered her ears, and I thought the helmet made her look like a wrestler.

Nicole studied me with her brown eyes, and I was surprised because I remembered her eyes being blue. Her body shook ever so slightly as her eyes peered at me from underneath her black eyebrows and above lips that now jutted out in a sort of frown.

I had come looking for the sister I remembered from childhood and instead found a stranger whose signals I couldn't read. My discomfort frightened me, and I could not hold back the sobs.

Cheryl put her arm around me as the tears began to roll down my face.

The image of Nicole, her body so rigid she could not stand straight, and that helmet would stick with me for a long time.

—

It was not until my mother died in 1990 that I was emotionally and mentally able to reconnect with Nicole in a more meaningful way. When tracking her down, I learned that Children's Rehabilitation Center was closing, and Nicole was in the process of moving to a group home. This was good news to me. I remembered that my parents had always wanted her to live in a group home, but none were available back in 1976 when they placed her.

Through a series of phone calls, I got in touch with her case manager, who was thrilled to hear from me. He said he had heard there was a sister, but no one had any records of where to find me or even my name. Sean and I traveled to Pittsburgh from our home near Allentown, on the other side of the state, and met with him to find out what had been going on with Nicole and what to expect with the upcoming move.

My sister was to be moved to a group home in a residential neighborhood. One of many run by Passavant Memorial Homes, the house looked like any other house in the neighborhood, except it was a little longer and had a large garage. These houses served as homes for six to eight adults, and, in Nicole's case, her housemates included several people with whom she had lived at Children's Rehab.

I learned that Nicole, who was 26, had a pending diagnosis of Rett Syndrome, a neurological disorder that causes loss of purposeful hand use and communication skills. She had spent most of her life with a diagnosis only of profound mental retardation. Rett was discovered in 1966, the year of Nicole's birth, but nothing had been written about it in English language medical journals until 1983. At that time, Rett Syndrome was believed to cause mental disabilities. Since then, however, researchers have come to believe that someone with Rett Syndrome may not be mentally disabled at all! How tragic for Nicole. My mother had been right about one thing — Nicole knew far more than most people realized. She had often argued that it was impossible to measure Nicole's IQ because she couldn't speak or respond to questions in a way that the test administrator could understand.

"You're intellectualizing."

It was Carol interrupting what could best be described as journalism — I was telling the facts and explaining the terms without emotion.

I thought, however, that I was expressing emotion when I said that I was amazed by what I found when researching Rett — that the literature read like Nicole's case file. It had actually been comforting to me to see pictures of Rett girls who held their hands together exactly as Nicole did. That was exciting.

"You're still intellectualizing."

I didn't know how not to intellectualize. Carol wanted to know how it felt to find someone I didn't recognize. I didn't know and I was afraid to look inside to find out. The best I could do was to tell her that I found it comforting to learn about Rett because it proved my family wasn't alone in what we experienced, even though we had believed we were.

—

At that time, Nicole didn't seem to have such emotional difficulties regarding our reunion. She was glad to see me whenever I visited. She was obviously happier in the group home than she had been at the rehabilitation center. I enjoyed hearing her vocalize once again, though her sounds were, well, more adult. She was vocalizing now specifically to try to communicate where, as a child, sometimes she vocalized just for fun, the way healthy children sing or babble.

During my early visits to my sister's group home, I tried to bring along familiar things like my Bankie and Raggedy Ann dolls. Nicole had always loved Raggedy Ann. When my parents placed her at Children's Rehab, she had a well-worn talking Raggedy Ann that was to her what my Bankie is to me — her favorite possession, one that obviously brought her comfort and joy. The doll was dirty, no longer talked, and all its clothes were gone. But Nicole still loved it. My mother begged the people at Children's Rehab to let her keep it, but they did not.

I bought her Raggedy Ann dolls in stores, at yard sales, and at flea markets. I brought some to her and mailed others. I understood that she had also lost her parents, her sister, her home, her pets, and her Raggedy Ann, and no one ever explained to her why. Her losses were as profound as mine, more so in many ways.

I made sure to bring other things I thought she might enjoy. I had a collection of stuffed soccer balls — picture a soccer ball that is plush like a stuffed animal but otherwise looks exactly like the ball used in the actual game. The "furry" soccer balls, as I liked to call them, have no faces or limbs and come in a multitude of colors and sizes ranging from two inches to two feet in diameter.

During one visit, I brought one of my favorite soccer balls to show Nicole. I held it out toward her, and she laughed as her hands started moving. It was not the familiar flicking motion but rather something else. Her hand rose in the air, her fingers gracefully swaying, and then fell. It rose again and fell again several times before it came to rest on my hand. Once her hand rested on mine, it continued to twitch involuntarily but without losing contact with mine.

I had thought she was reaching for the ball but she actually just wanted to hold my hand. I had felt embarrassed because I often didn't know what to say to her. She knew what to say, and it required no words.

—

"So why don't you think you're a good sister?" Carol asked.

I didn't visit Nicole often enough, I said. I didn't find ways to better connect with her. I felt like I wanted to get to know her again slowly, but trips to Pittsburgh made that impossible. I couldn't just stop by for 20 minutes once a week.

"Do you have to visit once a week for 20 minutes to be a good sister?" Carol asked.

I didn't know. I knew only that I didn't feel like I had been there for her, that my discomfort was a sign of failure.

I told Carol that Sean and I had attempted to live in Pittsburgh after we were married but gave up after we were both unable to find full-time jobs there. Sean had been offered a good job in the Philadelphia suburbs, and we moved in order to pay our bills.

I had wanted to have Nicole move closer to me and discuss with those managing her case how this might come about. But, I never went through with pushing for it.

"How come?" Carol asked.

I felt that she should be near me because I was her only remaining family. Yet, I struggled with the idea that such a move would have taken her away from familiar surroundings and the people she'd lived with since she wanine. Her roommate was her best friend. The two of them enjoyed each other's company and would often hoot together as they watched TV or attempt to holler the word "baby" for Nicole's Raggedy Ann dolls. My sister's roommate also loved balls, and I made sure to bring her a furry soccer ball of her own.

"That doesn't sound like you didn't care," Carol said, adding that although Nicole was not living with blood relatives, her housemates had become her family. She had been with them longer than she had been with me.

I pondered that as Carol continued to pull out of me stories that demonstrated that we were two sisters who loved each other. I told her about events when we were kids and after we were reunited as adults.

One of my favorite stories was when I found the Flintstone vitamins in the bathroom medicine cabinet. I always liked the taste of them and stole one, then another and then another. Reveling in the good fortune of my thievery as I sat on the bathroom sink, I looked down to see Nicole standing there looking up at me, her hands flicking as they always did.

Well, it just wasn't fair not to share, so I gave her one, then another and another.

She laughed as she chewed, and we enjoyed sharing our little secret — until my mother started down the hall.

I quickly put the lid back on the vitamins and stuck them in the medicine chest. But my mother knew what I had done. I expected to be punished, and rightfully so. My mother didn't punish me. She found the situation amusing and liked that I had included Nicole in my escapades.

Another time, my family hosted a neighborhood picnic. My parents left a watermelon sitting in a tub of ice, and Nicole found it. Those flicking hands may not have been able to hold a crayon properly, but they could dig through a watermelon rind. Nicole also was blessed with the patience to keep digging until she reached the sweet, red fruit inside.

I saw her as I was walking by, and she looked up at me, startled, with a face that said, "You're not going to tell, are you?"

I smiled and kept walking. She smiled back, realizing I would be keeping the secret, and I left her to her work. My mother discovered Nicole and the literal fruits of her labors sometime later. Nicole and I shared a smile as my mother showed off Nicole's handiwork to the neighbors.

After our adult reunion, I learned that Nicole was allowed to have only so much money, or she would lose funding. Instead of disposing of the cash through what they called a "spend down" for items she didn't really need or putting more in her burial fund, I suggested Nicole's money be used to pay for a trip to the eastern part of the state to visit us in our home. Her funds paid a staff person to drive her out to us, where she was able to spend time with us and meet our cats. We went shopping and listened to music, and I learned more about her pain.

We showed Nicole old family photos, which she enjoyed seeing. We decided to buy her picture frames so she could display some of these in her room. While out in the van, we also tossed around the idea of going to see our dad's grave when we returned to the Pittsburgh area.

At the mention of this, Nicole became very upset, vocalizing and crying. She wasn't upset with our mother, just our dad.

"He died," the staff person told her.

It hit me like a hard, icy snowball in the chest. Apparently, no one had ever told Nicole our father had died. She knew only that he stopped going to see her not long after she moved to Children's Rehab. I don't know what, if anything, had ever been said to her about our mother, but she didn't express any anger at her, only at our dad.

Nicole was upset enough that we decided not to go. It was just too much for her to process all at once something that I'd had 20 years to think about — and all the facts.

"That sounds like you loved her," Carol said.

Yes, if I looked deep inside and allowed myself access to my emotions, I could feel that I did love her. Yet, still, I ached with guilt and shame for not connecting with her sooner, for not fighting to discuss her with my mother, and then for moving 800 miles away to Maine.

"Do you regret moving to Maine?" Carol asked.

"No," I said. "It was the best thing for me."

"So you didn't do the wrong thing?"

"I guess not," I said, but the words still rang hollow.

—

Carol and I talked about the different ways I had kept in touch with Nicole over the years. At one point, we tried monthly phone calls. During one such call, a bat had managed to get into my house and was flying around the room. As I narrated what was going on, squealed and ducked, Nicole laughed heartily. I have fond memories of this call.

Other times, Nicole seemed to be bored with the one-sided conversations. We tried email and snail mail. I would often send packages with letters that included a note asking staff to read her the letters. Every year, I sent a big box of presents for Christmas and her birthday, which was Dec. 21. I always felt bad that we were never together at Christmas, though I did know that she and other residents usually went home with staff for the holidays.

As I became more and more comfortable with my feelings regarding my sister, I began to come up with ways I could become more involved. I looked up the latest on Rett Syndrome and found an advocacy webpage that advised teachers and parents not to include activities that required hand use in the educational plans of those with the condition. They cannot use their hands, and forcing them to try only frustrates them, according to advocacy group literature.

Many of Nicole's programming plans had passed through my fingers over the years and I had noticed all included some kind of hand-over-hand instruction. They would use physical prompts to try to teach Nicole to pick up a fork or identify colors by pointing. I told Carol I intended to research this further and then make some formal recommendations for her programming based on my research. I was excited and eager to take a bigger role in my sister's life and to feel comfortable doing what I could instead of berating myself for what I couldn't.

But, it was never to be. A couple of weeks later, I received a phone call in the middle of the night. Nicole was having breathing issues and had been rushed to the hospital. While in transit, she went into cardiac arrest. Paramedics revived her, and medical personnel wanted to know whether to revive her again if necessary.

After I got off the phone, I crawled back into bed and lay there in silence for a moment. Seeing Sean was awake, I said, "Nicole's dying."

I was in a state of shock and had no idea what to do next.

"I guess we're going to Pittsburgh," Sean said, getting up and gathering clothing and other items to pack. I was grateful for his assistance and gentle, caring guidance. We left the house shortly before 7 a.m., beginning our 16-hour car ride.

I had asked that, if possible, Nicole be revived until I could get there. I received another call at 8:30 while we were on the road. She was once again in cardiac arrest.

"Let her pass," I said. I had wanted to see her, to reassure her by holding her hand as she once held mine. I didn't want her to die alone.

I learned, however, that she did not die alone. She died with her second family surrounding her. People who had worked with Nicole either at the group home or Children's Rehab came to the viewing and told us how much they loved Nicole, how she was sweet and sunny, and how she loved me and Sean.

The most telling thing, however, was that quite a few of those who attended the viewing had not worked for either Children's Rehab or the group home for years. They no longer were formally connected with Nicole through their employment, yet they had connected with her emotionally enough to give up their time and come to the viewing. They did so even though no one expected it, and no one would have thought a thing of their absence.

Even if I had not been there as much as I would have liked, Nicole was surrounded by people who loved her.

- 9 -
THE WALL

Surviving trauma brings with it a profound sense of loneliness. I had unsuccessfully tried to get help many times growing up. As an adult in the digital age, I'm constantly bombarded with trite social media platitudes extolling the virtues of positive thinking and leaving the past behind.

If only it were that simple.

Frustration comes tied to loneliness, and it has many times caused me to try to explain to others why such things are so maddening. A person who has never lived through trauma has no idea what it feels like or how to overcome it. You can't just think positively and get past it by magic. You have to face your past, and your pain in order to grow and overcome the obstacles past traumas cause. It's just maddening that society believes putting on a brave face without doing any real work toward healing is the right way to handle trauma — and people are pushy about it, especially on social media. I'm never going to convince society otherwise, much as I wish I could. What makes it especially hard is there are few resources available for overcoming trauma, and often, those that do exist are cost-prohibitive.

At least one person was there with me through much of my trauma, however. Carol helped me see this.

My mother was careful not to be abusive around my father. She would yell and spank me when he was there, but she never called me names or threw things at me.

Carol asked if Nicole ever witnessed the abuse.

Yes, I said. My sister was there.

"Do you think she knew what was going on?"

I pondered the question. I had just made an argument that Nicole did, in fact, understand what was going on around her and probably was not mentally disabled. It would be difficult to argue, then, that she had been oblivious.

"But she never seemed angry at my mother," I said.

"Your mother was her caretaker," Carol said, adding that Nicole needed my mother's care to survive. She no doubt also loved my mother. Loving and needing someone doesn't necessarily mean liking everything the person does, however.

My mind drifted back to the day I'd been told to play with Nicole, and my mother came into the room, announced that I had been only entertaining myself, and swept Nicole away. I tried to remember Nicole's expression, but it had been so long ago. Was it possible she wasn't happy about being taken from my company either? I honestly don't know. But it's possible.

I wasn't angry with Nicole for still loving my mother despite how I had been treated. I had simply never thought about it in that context before.

It gave me an odd sense of comfort to realize that Nicole not only witnessed my mother's behavior toward me but also that she may not have liked it.

Nicole also suffered, especially after our parents split up. She could not do anything proactive to recover from her wounds. She couldn't even ask someone what was going on or why her family stopped visiting.

This was another issue Carol and I discussed — that no two traumas are the same. So, those of us who experience trauma are all alone in a very real way. That's not to say we can't form good relationships or find support from those we love. It just means that no one else will truly understand, even when they try. That's sad. But, I learned that understanding from others on that deepest level, like that those of us who have lived trauma desperately want to share, is not necessary for healing or forming good relationships.

Carol said numerous clients told her the same thing as I did — that they wished their loved ones understood, that they were tired of going through it all alone. But their loved ones couldn't understand, even when they wanted to, because they hadn't lived it. Even when two people live through the same difficulties, their experiences are different. Nicole and I lived together until I was 11 and she was 9. Yet the way we experienced those years is very different. Even if she had been able to talk, she would not necessarily have the same pain as I did.

All our loved ones can do is be the best they can be and try to be supportive. What that really means in terms of specifics is going to be different for everyone.

I am alone in my story. But I am not alone in dealing with trauma.

―

Although my sister witnessed some of my mother's poor treatment of me when we were young kids, she didn't see the worst of it. After my parents split up and, especially after my dad died, my mother had no reason to hold back. No one, not even Nicole, could see what she was doing.

I feel the need to acknowledge that my mother certainly must have had a difficult time controlling and understanding her own emotions, especially those surrounding Nicole's placement. If it were me, I would feel like a failure as a mother if I couldn't care for my child, even if that wasn't necessarily true.

My mother had come from an abusive background herself and, no doubt, never learned healthy coping skills. She coped the only way she knew how — with anger, much as I had. Anger had kept her from becoming more of a victim. But she never learned she didn't need it anymore.

My two years in junior high were filled with outbursts from my mother over almost anything. Once, she made me pay for a nonstick skillet she said I ruined with a metal spatula. Another time, while making apple pie, I told her what one of my teachers had said in home economics class. My mother freaked out, screaming, how dare I push what the teacher had said. Another time, I was cutting a chocolate Easter basket with a knife and accidentally sliced the end of my finger. Instead of showing concern, my mother barked, "It's your own damn fault," and left me to tend to the bleeding myself, despite the fact that I wasn't even a teenager yet.

Things got worse yet by the time I was a freshman in high school. My mother accepted a job running a garment factory in

New Bethlehem, a town of about 1,100 people isolated in the Allegheny Mountains. We moved two hours northeast of where we had been living in Pittsburgh and two hours away from my dad.

My mother's good fortune did not last long. Less than a year later, the company was sold, and she found herself unemployed. No other suitable employment opportunities existed locally, and my mother spent the next year searching for a job back in Pittsburgh. She continued to use me as the target for her anger.

—

Before she lost her job, my mother brought home a stray orange and white tabby cat. I remember coming in the door to see a cat about six months old curled up on a black director's chair in our kitchen. A cat? My mother wouldn't want a cat. Or would she? Why would this cat be here otherwise? I was ecstatic to learn the cat was staying.

I spent many wonderful hours playing with the cat, named Carissa, and helping her to vent her boundless youthful energy. Her uncomplicated love helped fill the emptiness of my family's destruction, my mother's abuse and the loss of my sister.

My mother and I waited too long to have Carissa spayed and she darted out one day in the rain. I could hear her meows, letting me know she was outside close by, but I couldn't see her. When she came back inside, she was pregnant, though we didn't realize it at first. Later that summer, my mother and I went on a short trip. When we returned, I immediately headed downstairs to look for my cat. My mother followed. We found Carissa nesting in among some boxes piled under a counter in the basement. Her five kittens were still wet from birth.

"Johanna, I think she just had these kittens!" my mother exclaimed as Carissa purred and rubbed her head against my hand.

Carissa was pleased to see me and wanted me nearby. When I went upstairs, she would jump out of the nest and follow, hollering at me. When I'd turn around to look at her, she'd dart back down the stairs and then stop and look at me as if to say, "You coming?" She felt I should be there to welcome her new family, and she didn't want that welcome to be short. Overjoyed at this poignant show of affection, I wanted to spend the entire evening downstairs with her.

But my mother ordered me upstairs. "You need to leave the cat alone now," she said simply as she opened up one of her romance novels.

Carissa stood just inside the kitchen looking into the dining room where I stood in front of my mother's chair. "Rrrrrrooooowwww."

"I don't think she wants me to leave her alone," I said quietly.

"Just go upstairs."

I turned and sadly looked into the questioning green eyes of my beloved cat and walked towards the stairs to my room.

—

Carissa's litter consisted of two orange tabbies, a black and white one, a calico and a tortie — mostly black, with a few orange hairs mixed throughout her coat and an orange line down her face. I named this one "Mouthy" because she'd meow to get me to do things for her. When all the other kittens climbed out of the box that served as their nest, for example, Mouthy would sit there and look up at me, hollering, until I picked her up and took her out myself.

I named the black and white one "Bear," and one of the orange tabbies got the name "BJ" in honor of a popular TV series of the time that I had heard of but never watched. The other orange tabby was "Tubby" since he was the largest. The calico was "Cara Mia," which is Italian for "my dear."

My mother constantly complained that Carissa wasn't nearly as good a mother as Puff had been. "Puff cleaned up after her kittens. And she litter trained them," my mother whined as if litter training kittens were a moral issue. "Carissa just has no interest in mothering this litter."

I tried to clean up and litter train the kittens myself. But I was 14 and I didn't know how. At that time I had no idea that, if given time, the kittens would learn to use the box. I simply internalized my mother's disappointment with my cat, seeing it as some kind of reflection of my own failures.

—

A few months after we moved to the little town in the mountains, a junior at Redbank Valley High School asked me out. Mark was well-muscled with sandy blonde hair, gentle brown eyes, and a mustache. "You should see this kid," I overheard my mother say on the phone with one of her sisters. "He's built like a brick shithouse."

My mother claimed to like Mark but refused to let us go out, saying I was just a freshman and she was concerned about the difference in our ages. He was old for his grade and I was young for mine, so there was a four-year age difference. At first, my mother allowed him to come over to the house when she was home. "You have to follow the rules," she warned us both, "or that will be the end." I went along with her conditions believing she created them out of concern for me.

Two months later, my mother suddenly changed her mind and decided Mark and I should break up. Although we had followed her rules to the letter, she still accused me of deserving this as a punishment, though she gave me no specifics. Then, she said he and I had become "too involved." She never really explained what she meant by that, except to say that she thought our feelings were "too intense."

My mother wasn't satisfied with simply breaking our hearts, however. She had to taunt me about it too. "I saw Mark today," she said when arriving home a few days after she broke us up. Her singsong tone was almost as bad as the slight smile on her face that told me she actually enjoyed my pain.

As the days passed, she came up with more taunts, always with a singsong mocking tone of voice I came to despise. "The girl who gets involved with Mark will get married early, live in a dump and be unhappy," she declared one day as she set down her briefcase on a chair.

She paused, waiting for a response from me. I clenched my jaw just a little, determined not to let her see my anger. "Mercenary, aren't I?" she continued, her smile becoming even larger despite her obvious efforts to hide it.

The more she mocked me, the more certain I became that she really didn't like me, let alone love me, so I clung even more tightly to Mark. He was always there to listen or to just hold me.

And he always went out of his way to be with me, even when he knew his abusive father would get on him for it.

When summer came, taking away the opportunity for Mark and me to see each other in school, we began meeting at the site of an old building foundation in the woods. I also called him every day, either before my mother got home, and sometimes even after, when I was sure she was too absorbed in one of her romance novels to notice.

My dad didn't object to Mark. In fact, during visits, he allowed Mark and me to see each other openly. It wasn't unusual for my dad to visit for the day, take me out for dinner or ice cream, and invite Mark to come along. My mother never found out.

—

Exasperated that I continued to see Mark despite her objections, my mother frequently went off in a rage. During one of these fits, she announced that she was going to send me to live with my father and then called him, demanding he come get me.

"Get packing!" she shouted while standing in my bedroom doorway after throwing a large cardboard box into the center of the room. My hands shaking, I quickly began to gather up whatever was closest and put it into the box.

"You're not taking that!" she bellowed as I attempted to put a black AM/FM radio into the box. "That's mine!"

"Well, what should I pack?" I said, allowing a little impatience to be audible in my voice.

"Only things that belong to you," she yelled back. By this time, she had gotten a stool from the room across the hall and she was sitting on it, a cigarette in her hand.

"Why isn't this mine?" I asked, holding the radio over the box.

"I paid for that," she shouted. "You can take only the things that you bought and paid for. Everything else is mine." The radio had been a gift from her. Apparently, those gifts had been rescinded without notice. I began gathering up a few items of clothing, being careful to include only items I had purchased with my own money.

She said nothing and continued to watch me. But not more than five minutes passed before she did a complete reversal.

"Forget it! Unpack! You're not going!" she yelled, getting to her feet and waving her arms to get me to take stuff out of the box as quickly as possible.

"Why?" I asked, my voice barely audible.

"Because you actually *want* to go!" she said. I did, but I said nothing. "I can't believe you actually want to go!" She paused. "Call your father and tell him not to come!"

As she left the room, I began to cry. Picking up the phone with shaking hands, I called my dad. When he answered, I found myself crying harder, unable to speak. At last, I gained my composure enough to speak through my sobs. "She says not to come now, but please come anyway because I'm so scared. I know she's gonna be really mad at you, but I'm scared," I cried.

"Ok, you hang in there, Johanna. I'll be there as quick as I can," he said.

I hung up the phone, shaking, not sure what would happen over the next two hours until my dad arrived.

"Did you call him?" I heard my mother scream from down the hall.

"Yes," I said, after swallowing hard to make my voice sound as normal as possible.

"Did you tell him not to come?"

"Yes." I huddled on my bed with my Bankie, hugging him to seek the comfort I could get nowhere else.

My mother stayed downstairs and didn't say another word to me.

When my dad got to the house, he and my mother engaged in a long screaming match. I could hear their voices but could not make out the words. My mother had forbidden me to come downstairs, and she refused to let my dad in the house. After a good hour of fighting, I watched from my bedroom window in quiet desperation as my father left. At the end of the driveway, he turned and looked up at my bedroom window and mouthed something, but I don't know what. I knew he was trying to reassure me, and I felt a little bit better knowing that he cared. But it was not enough to overcome the anguish of being left behind with a crazy woman who seemed to hate me.

—

That summer, when my dad arrived at the house to take me for a two-week visit, we played with Carissa and her kittens before we left.

"You like those kittens; why don't you take them with you?" my mother said.

"I can't. I'm not allowed to have cats in my apartment," my dad answered flatly.

But she continued. "Aw, C'mon, George, it's only for a couple of weeks."

"I can't."

And so the nagging continued. I wanted to bring the cats because I loved them, but I understood why my dad wasn't able to take them. At last, despite my mother's nagging, my dad and I left without my cat and her babies.

When I returned two weeks later, the house was empty. Even my beloved Carissa was missing. I asked where the cats were.

"They're gone," my mother said in her mocking sing-song tone.

"What about Carissa?" I asked.

"They're gone," she repeated as if the second question was no different than the first. "And it's justified." That was all she would say.

I'm not sure what she meant by "justified," and I didn't bother asking. I was furious. I ran out of the house cursing, not knowing where I would go or how I would avoid coming home later. I was not about to share the same space with the woman who had betrayed me so cruelly. My dad found me several hours later at a newsstand/snack shop in town, where I worked delivering papers and doing odd jobs. He had apparently also called Mark, who was with him.

"I hate her!" I told them, my body so full of rage it literally shook. "I'm never going back there! *Never!*"

My dad had his hands full trying to convince me I had other options besides becoming a street bum. He listened patiently to me, acknowledging my feelings and sympathizing.

"Yes, I know what she's like," he said. "I've lived it."

"Why can't I live with you?" I sobbed.

"Look," he said. "I'm trying to get custody of you. But it's not that simple. It takes time. You're going to have to promise me to go home and stick it out until I can get things finalized."

"But I'm afraid of her sometimes."

"I know. But at least if you go home, you'll have a roof over your head. If I take you home with me now, she can make it hell for us later on."

Mark agreed. He knew his house wasn't any safer than mine, thanks to an abusive father, and, besides, my mother would know to go there looking for me.

Reluctantly, and still crying, I stood up on weak legs and allowed my dad and Mark to lead me out the door and into my dad's car. My mother refused to discuss the incident even weeks later after she had calmed down. As far as I was concerned she had proven that my feelings were inconsequential, and that her relationship with me was nothing more to her than a destructive game of conquest.

I never forgave her.

- 10 -
CAUSE AND EFFECT

Remembering how my mother got rid of my cat behind my back has always filled me with pain. It was, apparently, evident when I related the story to Carol.

"It is the one thing I never forgave her for," I announced, intending for my words to emphasize just how heinous my mother's crime was.

Carol asked me my opinions on forgiveness. What does it mean? What is its value?

I expounded on another one of my theories. "Forgiveness is not a chore to be done like the laundry. It's a process that begins with allowing yourself to be angry."

I no longer remember if she reacted. I do know I continued to expound. "I get annoyed when I see people on TV who announce immediately after they or their loved ones are victims of horrible crimes that they forgive the perpetrator. That's nonsense. You can't forgive that quickly. What they're really doing is stuffing their emotions."

Carol agreed on that count — immediate forgiveness without working through one's emotions isn't real. But, she wanted to know whether I saw purpose in forgiving, even if it takes a while.

"I suppose it can bring you peace," I said. "I forgave the guy who killed my father."

As Carol listened, I explained that my dad had been on his way to work at a new job when a 21-year-old drunk driver lost control of his car coming down a hill on a rainy afternoon. His car jumped the barrier and crashed head-on into — or, actually, nearly on top of — my dad's car. My dad was killed instantly, but the other driver was not pronounced dead until he reached the hospital. At the tender age of 15, I felt some satisfaction about that, thinking at least he lived long enough to know what he had done.

Nine years later, shortly after Sean and I were married, I reflected on how much I missed my dad. I wished he had known Sean. They shared the same wacky humor and would have certainly gotten along. When I was about to get married, my mother asked if I wanted my dad's brother to walk me down the aisle. I opted instead to walk alone in order to say without words that no one could take my dad's place.

My mind drifted to the person responsible for his death. I could not confront him or tell him how much he hurt me, how he not only took my father but also my only safe haven in the world. I could tell his parents, though, and so I imagined myself finding out where they lived and walking up some steps to knock on their door.

I imagined them opening the door and hearing myself tell them who I was. Even in my fantasy, I couldn't get the angry words out. I was, instead, struck by the fact that they had not caused this. Whatever their son had done, it was not their fault. More importantly, they suffered a loss as great as mine.

"I'm so sorry for your loss," I say in the fantasy.

I don't remember what happened next. I probably just dropped the imaginary scenario so I could let the tears fall. While they did, I realized I was no longer angry with him. I had forgiven him.

"And how did that feel?" Carol asked as I wiped away tears again in our session.

It was freeing and sad at the same time because I fully realized the crash had taken two lives, not just one. The resulting pain was greater than my own.

"So, do you think you will ever forgive your mother?" Carol asked.

My answer was swift, deliberate, and angry. "Not about the cat," I said.

"Ok, well, what about other things? Do you forgive her for the way she treated you?"

"Sometimes," I said. "I guess it depends on the day."

As always, she asked me to explain in more detail. I told her I had accomplished a lot in life. I enjoyed my marriage, my cats, my work, and my hobbies. What my mother had done to me was still painful, but the pain was less important to my life than it had been when I was a child or young adult.

"Is that so?" I don't know if Carol actually said that or if I only imagined it. Regardless, I'm sure she pushed me further into my analysis. "Is the pain no longer important?"

"It's important," I said, "just not the most important thing all the time."

"When is it important?"

Like the day I couldn't get out of bed, the day that prompted Sean to call her and make an appointment for me.

"How so?" Eventually these questions became routine enough that I could anticipate them. However, I wasn't there yet.

On days when I get overwhelmed by some sort of difficulty, I start to feel like I never get a break, I said. Whenever another difficulty appears, I think how I've suffered so much that I don't understand why I don't get to have it easy. It's not fair.

"Do you think life is fair?" she asked.

"Hell no."

"So, can you reasonably expect things to be fair?"

No, I couldn't. And that made me angry. Carol asked me to look behind the anger. What was I really feeling?

It took me a couple of tries before I figured out it was fear. She would then ask what scared me and what was the worst that could happen.

At that time, I feared the worst was that I could slip back into the grips of whatever it was that I could describe only as the Great Bipolar Incident.

We had talked about the events leading up to it, but it was still unclear to me how I had gone from being a stable, functioning adult to enough of a mess that I had to take six months off work.

We began exploring the scenario leading up to the crash that precipitated it. She asked questions about everything — my health, my personal life, my work life. She believed the crash was caused by a perfect combination of things that began with gastric bypass surgery I'd had less than a year earlier. I literally walked into the hospital with diabetes, high blood pressure, and sleep apnea and walked out the next day without those conditions. Overnight, I went from having to take two medications for diabetes to taking none. In addition, I no longer needed a CPAP machine or medications for high blood pressure. These further added to the drastic changes.

"Wow!" Carol said. "That's a huge change in your body. It's a good one, but it's huge."

The changes continued. Throughout the next six to nine months, I lost 75 pounds. This joyous accomplishment further added to changes in body chemistry.

It was the following fall — not quite a year later — that I noticed the antidepressants I had been taking didn't seem to be working as well as before. It was then that I switched abruptly to another drug, and then, when that one made things worse, I abruptly stopped.

The process of getting gastric bypass surgery is not a simple or easy one, at least not through St. Luke's Hospital in Bethlehem, Pennsylvania, where Sean and I had ours. Their program, considered the best in the nation, includes a myriad of medical tests, counseling, and regular checkups.

I noted to Carol that one of the things we learned was that after the surgery, we were not to take certain types of medications because our post-surgical bodies wouldn't be able to process them.

The obvious question seemed to be whether my body had been properly absorbing the antidepressants when I believed they had stopped working. No one really knew the answer. In addition, I hadn't known I was supposed to wean off them or wean off other medications either, and this no doubt created further chemical shock to my system.

Carol and I had these conversations several times over three years. Initially, it made sense to me, and yet it didn't. It would take a while before it would feel like I really understood.

—

During subsequent sessions, Carol and I continued on the subject of forgiveness. We didn't attack it for a full session. Instead, we would delve into it and then back off as my emotional state required. Sometimes, I would just get overwhelmed, and I would have to say so, and we would change the subject.

"Do you think your mother loved you?" Carol asked on more than one occasion.

My answers varied from "absolutely not" to "yes, in her own way" and included many different degrees in between. Carol's and my conversations on the topic gave me a chance to explore my sometimes contradictory feelings regarding my mother, her motivations, and whether she was even capable of love.

The times I said my mother loved me "in her own way," especially, opened up an avenue for discussion. Carol would start by asking what to me had become the obvious next question: how so?

I remember my mother once telling a friend that a child who grows up with love learns love. A child who grows up with violence learns violence.

Before I could explain further, Carol picked up on where this was going.

"Was she talking about herself?"

I don't know. I never saw my mother as being insightful

enough to realize why she felt and behaved the way she did. Yet the description fits perfectly.

My mother did not grow up with nurturing. Although I had not witnessed how she was treated as a child, I did see firsthand how her family treated her as an adult. Each year, my mother's immediate family would gather for Thanksgiving, Christmas Eve, Christmas Day, New Year's Eve, and New Year's Day celebrations at the home of a different sibling. Neither my mother nor I ever questioned their not driving four hours to our house in Middletown. But, after my parents split up and we moved back to the Pittsburgh area, my mother repeatedly invited them to hold one of the celebrations at our house. They never did.

"Do you think that's right?" my mother would ask me.

I would answer truthfully. "No." It seemed to me, just as it seemed to her, that there was something more to this.

Years later, when I was a student at Penn State, my grandmother developed cancer. My mother told me several times that her mother asked her to pay for her treatments. At the time, I didn't understand that the question had been asked because my mother received all that money after my dad died. I just thought they saw her as being wealthy because she had a good job. Regardless, the hospital bills were not my mother's responsibility. Yet she paid them anyway or, at least, that's what she told me.

My mother claimed that she had been cut out of her own mother's will. A search of wills on file in that county turned up nothing, so it would appear there had never been an official will. Still, it's quite possible her mother left behind some kind of letter or that her siblings told lies. In any event, my mother told me the will — or whatever document it was — said that everything was to go to my grandmother's six children — and named my mother's siblings. To my mother, listed only by first and last name with no relationship provided, the will left $25. Each of the grandchildren received some kind of special memento, except for Nicole and me.

"How did that make you feel?"

"Angry!" I said. Yes, I felt angry on my mother's behalf. How dare they treat her like that!

"What do you suppose that was like for her?" Carol would ask.

This was a feeling I could describe well. She must have felt abandoned, unloved, unworthy, fearful, sad, angry. She did not deserve to be treated like that.

"How does it feel to talk about her like that?" Carol asked. "Is it ok?"

"It feels ok," I said.

"You know, it's ok to empathize with her, to understand what she went through and acknowledge her pain," Carol said. "But please know that it does not make it ok what she did to you."

I was beginning to understand. It was like differentiating between the person and the behavior. I could feel empathy for what she had gone through, for the events that led to her lashing out at me, without ever relieving her of responsibility for her actions.

—

Carol and I also devoted a number of sessions to exploring my mother's life and my feelings of empathy.

I found it ironic that I could be mad as hell at my mother and still defend her when I thought someone else was bashing her. This was especially true when it came to her decision to place Nicole at Children's Rehab.

In the mid-1970s, disabled people weren't really treated as people. Nicole had gotten the right to attend school for the first time only a year or two before my parents split up. No other accommodations were made for people with disabilities out in the general public. There were no early intervention programs, no special education programs, no daycare, no ramps, and no special seating, showers or other amenities for those traveling. Families whose members included someone with a disability were totally on their own with no help from the outside world. If modifications to the home were necessary, they had to figure out how to pay for them on their own.

Yet, people would be quick to admonish those who had children with handicaps and "put them away." Such comments would make me angry. I even remember shutting down some comments that were made along those lines during a discussion in a high school honors English class my junior year. At that time, I repeated what I had overheard my mother tell her friends. The time had come when she could no longer lift Nicole in and out of the bathtub. Nicole was outgrowing her diapers. How would she handle the onset of menstruation?

For most of my adult life, I failed to recognize that my parent's decision to place Nicole at Children's Rehab represented a loss for me as well as for them. Even once I realized what I had lost — the chance to continue to grow up with my sister — I never blamed them for their decision. I think, to some extent, that perhaps they did it in an attempt to be better parents to me. It didn't work, but it wasn't entirely their fault. Their responsibilities with me and with other things didn't end, or take a break to give them time to grieve. The world just kept on marching onward, and they had to go with the flow or drown.

I hadn't realized that acknowledging my loss didn't mean I had to be angry at them. I experienced a moment of freedom as I let that concept sink in.

I told Carol that I'd watched my mother decline, starting when she lost Nicole. Although we did visit my sister in the beginning, gradually those visits stopped. I imagine my mother reacting to her pain much as I did — by running. If she didn't visit Nicole, she wouldn't have to face her perceived failures as a mother. She wouldn't have to think about Nicole's future. If she were just getting by in survival mode — a term I use to describe those days when you have only enough energy to go through the motions of living — she would not have had the strength to deal with her feelings or be able to find answers to complex questions.

My mother also no doubt faced gender discrimination, which made it difficult for her to advance in her career and make ends meet. Moving to New Bethlehem seemed like a good idea at the time. But, then, she lost her job through no fault of her own. The company was sold and the new owners had different ideas for how they would do things. My mother suspected those who hired her knew this change was on the horizon and led her into a trap. I don't know if that's true, but even if it isn't, she found herself unemployed, isolated, and in debt for a house she purchased and remodeled. And she had no good local job prospects.

My empathy for her breaks down when I think about many of the things she did to me. I had done nothing to deserve to lose my cat. Friends of the family have said they believe my mother was trying to hurt my dad and my relationship with him when she took away my cat. Maybe, but it doesn't change the fact that she hurt me, and she never, ever took responsibility for that with an apology or even an explanation.

"You don't ever have to forgive her," Carol reassured me. "And even if you do, it doesn't mean what she did was ok."

I nodded.

"Forgiveness is for you, for you to find peace," she said. "It's not really about her. You will get there when you're ready."

A part of me was ready. I wanted peace. But, with so much of the story left to tell, I knew I had a lot of work to do. The worst parts of the story were yet to come.

- 11 -
HELL IS FOR CHILDREN

During my sophomore year, things were no better for me at Redbank Valley High School than they were at home. I was the target of a gang of bullies who, one day at lunch, began throwing tater tots at me and another girl. I tolerated it for a while and then fought back, throwing a carton of milk back at them. The teacher supervising the lunch period saw this, made me stay afterward to clean up, and made sure I got a detention. Because this teacher was a friend of my mother's, she wasn't interested in hearing what had precipitated my actions. The bullies went unpunished.

Another time, members of this same group decided to gang up on me in the school hallway. I responded to their pushes and shoves by pushing and shoving back. I wasn't hurt, but I didn't hurt any of them either, probably because they were all much bigger than I was. One girl in particular stood a full foot taller than me. She had broad shoulders and a broad waist, and when she pushed me, my body obeyed the laws of physics — I went flying. This angered me and I made sure to let her know it by pushing back. Although I didn't make her go flying, I did manage to trip her.

Later that afternoon came a ritual I knew well.

Every day, kids were called to the principal's office in groups. We would all leave our classes and congregate in the main office, waiting our turn for judgment. "What're you in for?" kids would ask each other and then laugh and point at whoever had the lamest excuse for being called.

Whenever the next name was called, the boys would look around to see who it was and razz each person, except for me. None of them knew me and probably wondered how a girl had managed to make it to the office at all.

The principal, known among students as "Myers" without the "Mister," was a thin man with dark hair graying at the sides and a mustache. By this time, he and I were quite familiar with one another.

"Sit down," Myers said quietly. I did as I was told, taking a seat directly across the gray metal desk from him, where I quietly remained with my hands folded in my lap.

He asked if I had pushed the largest of the bullies.

"No."

"Well, she says you did."

"She pushed me first," I said.

"So that means you have the right to push her?"

I took a deep breath and contemplated my answer to this trick question. If someone attacked me, I felt I had the right to use whatever force necessary to defend myself. But I knew the answer he wanted to hear was "no." So I said nothing.

Myers shifted slightly in his chair during the awkward silence. My hands fidgeted in my lap but I remained still otherwise.

"She says she never pushed you."

A shallow, sarcastic laugh escaped my body before I spoke. "Of course, she says she didn't." I was smiling but not feeling any joy.

"We can't keep having fights like this," Myers said, beginning his lecture. "You kids need to learn to get along with each other." He continued talking, but I didn't listen.

"Okay?" he said finally.

"Okay," I said.

Myers announced I would be assigned to detention.

I asked about the girl who pushed me.

"What about her?" Myers asked.

"Does she get detention, too, or just me?" I said, making sure to make a little bit of irritation, but not too much, audible in my voice.

"No," he said. "Why would she get detention? She didn't do anything."

I looked at him and shook my head as if to say, "You actually believe this shit?" I wanted to tell him both that he was utterly amazing and that if he had any sense of fair play, he would punish either everyone involved or no one. It was wrong to punish just one person when no school officials had seen the fight. The pattern was painfully obvious to me. I could get shoved, punched, kicked — or have food thrown at me — and the offenders would never be punished. If I fought back, I would be punished. I stifled my anger as much as I could, stood up, and left the room without another word.

―

In English class, we were assigned to write journals. We could write about whatever topic we chose, but we could not take the journals home. We wrote in them during class, and they stayed with the teacher, who read them and made notes in the margins about grammar, spelling, and content.

I was more comfortable with the impersonal piece of white lined paper before me than with any individual face-to-face. When I found myself unsure how to handle the sexual advances of an older boy, I wrote about it in my journal. Don liked to come on to me when Mark wasn't around, and I thought his attention had more to do with rivalry than any real interest in me. In any event, his advances were unwelcome. "I think Don is okay, but I don't want to have sex with him," I wrote. "Sometimes, he tries to push more than I like. How should I handle this?"

After handing in the journal that day, I felt relieved. I had addressed the teacher by name, so she knew this was a serious question. Soon, she would approach me, and we could talk about this problem. Maybe she could even help with other problems I was having.

The next day, at journal time, I eagerly opened mine, looking through the previous entry for comments written by my teacher. Surely, she would have something to say about what I'd written. But I found nothing. Not a single word. Though disappointed, I still held out hope that she would come to my aid. Day after day, I waited, but she said nothing to me. She must have read my journal since there were corrections to my grammar here and there. Why would she ignore my plea for help?

It was clear to me that my troubles were not her concern.

I was on my own, just a passenger riding along on the highway of hate.

—

One day that fall, Mark walked me home from school through the residential part of town. It was a beautiful day, with a bright blue sky sending rays of sunshine down through the trees along the sidewalk. When he and I reached the corner where we went our separate ways, we kissed.

At that moment, we both noticed a car going slowly by. A small face framed with graying curls that were dyed blonde stared silently out the window as an early 1970s sedan crept past at about five m.p.h. The sour older woman — our school librarian — didn't speak to us. She didn't have to — just the fact that she was there, creeping by and staring, was enough to make our blood run cold.

"We're in for it now," Mark said, his hands still on my shoulders as he stared back at the enemy until she finally drove off.

I didn't answer. I trusted this woman no more than I trusted any other school official. But I had no idea how vindictive she was, despite Mark's warning. How could she hurt us more than we already had been hurt, anyway?

The next day both of our names were among those called to the principal's office. Opening the windowed doors that led to the small office lobby, now crowded with other offenders, I noticed Mark coming towards me. His arms swung limply by his sides as he walked slowly down the dark hall. The light coming in a side window near the office brought his sandy blonde hair and sad face into focus.

"Wonder what this is about," I said, holding the door for him.

"Yesterday," he said. He closed the door and took me aside before we went in.

"Yesterday?"

"The librarian." His gaze was steady even though he couldn't hide the sadness in his eyes.

I looked at him for a moment but said nothing else. I had not yet developed Mark's cynical fatalism. Having attended Redbank Valley only a year, I still held a naive belief in the system, even though it had shortchanged me in the past. Mark, however, had attended school there all his life, and he knew what I was about to discover — that the system was more flawed than I could even imagine.

When it was our turn, we entered Myers's office and sat facing him.

Myers looked at us and sighed. "Kissing in the halls," he said. "This is not something we take lightly. You'll both receive a day out, and your parents will have to come in for a conference."

Mark and I looked at each other. "But we weren't kissing in the halls," I said. Myers looked up from his papers, so I continued. "Mark was walking me home yesterday. When we got to the corner where he goes the other way, he kissed me."

"So you weren't on school property?" Myers asked, his head tilted slightly to one side.

"No," Mark and I replied in synch.

"The librarian drove by and saw us. She's the one who turned us in, isn't she?" Mark said.

"Yes, she was the one," Myers admitted.

"So we aren't guilty," I said, expecting Myers to realize his mistake and let us go.

He sucked in a deep breath and let it out. He shifted in his seat and folded his hands on his desk. "Can you honestly tell me you two have never kissed in the halls?"

"No," we said together after looking at each other and back at the principal. By this time, we had both fidgeted to the edges of our seats.

"Well, then, I don't see that it matters," Myers said. "You admit you've kissed in the halls. It was just a matter of time before you got caught."

I stared at him, incredulous that he would still punish us, even if we weren't guilty as charged. Other couples practically made out in the halls and I hadn't seen any of them punished.

"But, Mr. Myers, please," I said, as my eyes filled with tears. "My mother gets so angry, and I'm afraid of what she'll do if she finds out." He listened, but his expression did not change. "Please, please," I begged.

"I can't," he said simply.

"Why not?" I asked.

"Because a member of the school faculty says she saw you two kissing."

"Yes, but not in the halls," Mark said.

"She lied," I added. Another tear made it out of my eye and down my cheek.

"I can't accuse her of lying," Myers said.

"Why not?"

"I just can't."

We went round and round like this for several minutes before I truly understood that I was unable to avoid being suspended for something I hadn't done — kissing on school property — by the principal of a high school that routinely used the afternoon announcements to congratulate teens on the births of their babies.

Yes, really. More than once, I heard girls as young as eighth grade congratulated on the school announcements for having babies.

Swallowing hard, my next tactic was to attempt to minimize the damage. "Can we at least not make my mother come in for a conference?" I pleaded in between sobs. "If she finds out about this, I don't know what she'll do."

"Please, you've got to help us with this. Her mother is going to flip," Mark begged. "You don't know this woman." He shook his head dubiously as he spoke and emphasized the word "know."

Myers listened without changing his expression. "All right. She won't have to come in for a conference," he said finally. "But she'll have to call in."

I breathed a sigh of relief and thanked the principal, realizing I had been shaking.

"Ok, you can go," he said simply. I stood to leave, my legs feeling like they were made of jelly and my chest numb from shock.

Outside the principal's office, Mark put his arms around me and tried to comfort me as I cried. He was genuinely afraid for me.

"You can just leave for school as usual," Mark said, adding we would try to find someone else to call in so my mother would not find out. "Then go home as usual. She won't have to know."

―

The next morning, I rose, dressed, and left the house as usual, my chest and throat tight from nervousness. Mark and I spent most of the morning trying to find someone in his family to call the school for me. No one would. They all said they understood our plight and felt bad for me, but calling and pretending to be my mother would be dishonest.

By midday, I accepted the fact that I would have to do the dirty deed myself. I called the school, asked for Myers, and said I was my mother. "She'll be dealt with," I said in my sternest voice.

Mark and I spent the rest of the day wandering around town, being careful to stay away from roads where my mother might see us. It was an overcast day, and the sky seemed to get even more gray as the hours passed. My body became increasingly tense as time to return home approached. Throughout the day, I checked my watch for reassurance that I had a little more safe time until there was no more safe time left.

I knew I couldn't hesitate or dally. It was important to walk through the door at the same time I always did. I said goodbye to Mark, and he told me he'd wait a block or so from the house for about a half hour to make sure everything was all right. As I left him, I tried my best to hide my nervousness well enough to keep my gait steady. If my mother saw me trembling, she'd know something was up.

I walked up the alley toward the brown wooden steps that led to the back door of our house. I didn't see my mother's car in the driveway and exhaled deeply to calm myself. She might not be home. That would be a blessing.

As I entered the kitchen, however, I saw my mother sitting in her usual spot on one of the bar stools with her feet up on the table. "Did you have a nice day?" she asked.

The question seemed a little strange. "Yeah, I guess," I replied, trying to act nonchalant. This was, after all, supposed to be just another day.

"Only 'I guess'?" my mother asked as I passed her to enter the powder room to the left of where she was sitting.

"Yes," I said, closing the door to use the toilet and trying to calm myself again. By then, I realized that she knew I hadn't been in school, but I hadn't figured out how. In any event, I knew coming out of the bathroom was not going to be a whole lot of fun.

Finally, I took a deep breath and opened the door. I felt something smash into my head, and for a moment, I thought I had run into the bathroom door or a wall. But it was my mother's open hand slapping me. She had aimed for my face but hit the side of my head when I instinctively turned away.

"You little bitch," she snarled with the fury of a rabid raccoon. I looked up to see her standing and another slap coming. "You lied! You lied!"

I could see my mother's narrowed eyes, full of rage. Her expression told me nothing I could say or do would save me now. I pushed past her and the empty barstool so that I could at least avoid being pushed into the walls or the pointed corners of the cabinets near the powder room door.

"What the track coach said was true," my mother said, shaking a fist in my face. "You are a little slut!"

My mouth opened slightly from the shock of her words and

I involuntarily began to make my way slowly back around to the other side of the bar toward the door.

"You and that boyfriend of yours, you … you ..!" She was so mad she could hardly speak. "I got this in the mail today. I know all about it." She drew out the word "all" as she held up a crumpled envelope and shook it in her fist.

I felt even more shock as I realized that the school had sent her a certified letter. If I had known that I would get beaten anyway, I would have let things play out differently.

"You were kissing in the halls, right in front of the whole goddamn world!" She paused but never took her eyes off me. "Could you possibly consider being honest about this?" She shook her head and shoulders mockingly. "No, of course not! You thought you could pretend to go to school and that I'd never find out!"

She had been walking slowly around the bar towards me as she yelled. I backed up involuntarily, and when I saw her raise her hand to hit me again, I turned and ran out the door, screaming for Mark or someone — anyone — to help me.

The next series of events happened so fast that I'm not sure which came first. A girl I knew from school had come outside and met me in the alley. Mark was there too, though I don't know who reached me first. "Call the police," I breathlessly begged the girl who was holding my arms at the elbows, much as I was holding hers. "My mother, my mother," I said, unable to complete the sentence.

Before I knew it, my mother's black Oldsmobile Cutlass appeared in my peripheral vision, and then she was dragging me away by the hair and pounding me with a fist made with her free hand. Everyone around me was screaming — me, Mark, my mother, the girl from school. Even other neighbors who had come outside to witness the raucous event were screaming. The voices ran together to form a terrifying, incomprehensible roar as I was dragged to the car for the ride home to the house and more beatings.

Later that evening, a local cop leaned against the kitchen counter, his dark uniform contrasting vividly against the pale yellow cabinets and off-white counters in the kitchen. My mother was sitting in the same barstool she had occupied when I got home. I sat opposite her.

"No matter what I do with this kid, she just doesn't appreciate it. I can't seem to make her understand that I love her and that I do these things for her own good." My mother's voice was calm and even. It was the most rational I had seen her in a long time. "This boy is too old for her, and she's too young to be having sex."

"We're not having sex," I protested.

"Then what about this?" My mother produced one of my journals, which she had apparently found while snooping in my room earlier that day. "Look, right here on this page, it says, 'It felt so good to be that close to someone.'" She looked up. "So, what's that supposed to mean if you're not having sex?"

"You can be close to someone without having sex," I said.

The cop listened but said nothing, turning his head back and forth from my mother to me like he was watching a tennis match from the sidelines.

"But you were 'that close' to someone?" she said, her eyes widening but not showing anger.

"You're taking that line out of context. If you read the whole thing, and I'm sure you did, you'd know we were just hugging."

"Shall I read the whole thing out loud now?"

"No."

"Why not? You said the whole thing would prove you weren't having sex."

"Yes, but it's private. It's none of his business," I said, referring to the cop.

"I think you need to go upstairs so he and I can talk," she said, tilting the top of her head toward the cop.

"Can I have my journal back?" I asked after I got down from my barstool.

"No."

"Why?"

"Because I might need it."

"For what?"

"Evidence."

"For what?"

"In case I decide to have Mark arrested."

I swallowed hard, turned, walked through the dining room to the foyer, and climbed the stairs. I had no idea what she could arrest Mark for since we had not had sex as she implied. But then again, he and I had been suspended from school for kissing in the halls when we hadn't. My heart was heavy as I plodded up the stairs and down the hall to my room, wondering what she and the cop were talking about.

I never got my journal back, and for a couple of weeks, I

didn't keep a journal at all, fearing it would not be safe. But then I realized I could use the drop ceiling in my bedroom to my advantage. Inside my bedroom closet were three shelves. If I climbed them, I could reach the ceiling tiles, lift one aside, and place my journal inside the ceiling. Then, I could replace the ceiling tile I had moved, closing the hole. So that's what I did.

—

My 15th birthday, less than a month after the suspension, came and went without a card, gift, or even an acknowledgment from my mother. My dad brought me two necklaces when he visited, but even those gifts, presented in my mother's presence, didn't prompt a reaction from her. I was certain this was just more proof of what I had believed for the past several months — my mother did not love me. All she wanted was a target for her anger — and someone to fetch her cigarettes and coffee.

—

Then, the lectures began.

Mark was crossing the street on his way to school one Friday morning as my mother drove past. When she got home from work, she ordered me to sit at the kitchen bar. Taking the seat opposite me and lighting a cigarette, she announced, "I saw Mark today."

I said nothing. I sat still in my seat, barely looking up.

"I know you and Mark are together in the mornings before school," she said. "From now on, you aren't allowed to leave for school until 8:30."

I remained still and said nothing.

"You know I could start taking you to Bellefonte every day. That would solve the problem."

About a month before this, she had begun an accounting job with a civil service agency in Bellefonte, a town located in the center of the state, a good two hours drive from the house. Since she had started the job, she made me go with her on occasion for no reason I could think of except to keep me from Mark.

"Of course, I could have Mark arrested," she continued. "That's another possible solution."

My mother half pursed her lips, giving me an ornery smile. Taking a drag from her cigarette, she looked quite pleased with herself.

I said nothing and remained still. She had been threatening to have Mark arrested since the day of my suspension two months before.

"I think I'll do that. In fact, I think I'll take Tuesday off. Yeah," she nodded her head in a show of satisfaction that complemented her mocking tone. "That would be a perfect time to do it."

I looked up slightly but did my best to hide the tremor her words sent through my body. It was already Friday. Because of the weekend, I was afraid I wouldn't be able to warn Mark until Monday for whatever good it would do.

"Don't you care?" my mother asked, leering at me like a schoolyard bully who had just stolen my lunch money.

"On what charge?" I finally asked.

"Interfering with the custody of a child."

I had never heard of the charge and did my best not to react in any way to her answer.

"This just doesn't faze you, does it?"

I said nothing.

"You stab me in the back. You don't miss an opportunity to show me what a spiteful little bitch you are. And nothing I do fazes you. You are truly amazing." Her voice was rising slightly, giving away her underlying anger, but she was still more in a mood to mock me than to berate me.

Lectures like these became a new daily ritual. Every evening after work, as well as on weekends, she'd make me sit down so she could spend two hours mocking me, shouting at me, calling me names and expounding on what a rotten person I was.

I learned how not to listen. Sometimes, I would concentrate on the pattern of tiny gold lines and dots against the white background on the table. Or I would study her face, thinking about the geometry of her inverted triangle lips. Other times, I'd use my eyes to trace the lines of my fingers in my lap, glancing now and then at my watch to guess how much longer I might have to sit there.

Every day, I would concentrate on how angry I was and draw strength from my silent rage. She still hurt me, but I could avoid letting her see it. I had to remain composed. It was my only defense.

"You say you love Mark." The words sounded more like a statement than a question, but then she demanded a response. "Right?"

"Yes."

"Well, if that's love, thank God I've been spared." She shook her head and took another drag from the ever-present cigarette, making sure to blow the smoke in my face. She knew I hated that.

I said nothing and held my breath till the smoke dissipated. Her comment didn't really make sense to me. Loving Mark meant taking great risks to be with him and treasuring that time. What was wrong with that?

"You're incapable of love." She reached toward the ever-present ashtray and flicked her cigarette with her index finger, sending a short cylinder of ashes downward to be with others of its kind.

I remained silent and still, wondering what she could think she knew about love. She told the cop she loved me, but here she sat calling me names like "spiteful bitch." Was I to believe that was love?

"God damn your rotten soul!"

I hadn't been listening, but the thunder of her voice crashing on the word "damn" made it through my auditory system and then to my brain.

"You are such a goddamn fucking bitch!" Her angry words tumbled from her mouth only to bounce off the mental walls I had built around me. "Hmmm," I thought from inside my emotional fortress. "We're getting creative with the cuss words now." But I said nothing.

"Do you really think you have the right to disobey me?" She got up to get herself another pack of cigarettes and then leaned against the kitchen counter as she opened it.

My head followed her, though I was careful not to really look at her. I said nothing, as usual, and silently contemplated the way she pronounced and emphasized the word "disobey." This, I believed, was at the root of everything that happened since she told Mark and me we had to break up. She couldn't control or manipulate me the way she seemed to be able to control and manipulate everyone else. It had nothing to do with Mark and nothing to do with my safety and well-being. It was simply a clash of wills. She hated the possibility that my will just might be stronger than hers.

"DO YOU?"

I hadn't been listening, and she was becoming angrier because I had missed a cue to respond. What was the question? Oh, yeah. Do I really think I have the right to disobey her? I knew the proper response and that giving it would allow her to verbally trap me with my own words. But I gave it anyway. There was no use trying to fight.

"No."

"Then why do you?"

"I don't know." But I did know. She was a tyrant hiding her anger, rage, and vengeance behind the title "mother." She had no concern whatsoever for me, my feelings, my safety, or my welfare. That, I felt, gave me the right to disobey.

It didn't matter what I thought, though, because she had her own theories, and she was going to expound on them again.

"Well, I know!" she bellowed, her eyes narrowing like the slitted pupils of a poisonous snake. She leaned forward and stepped slowly toward me.

Yup. I was right. She did know. She knew everything.

"Because you're a no-good filthy rotten bitch! You're a backstabber!" Her face was right in mine, but I had looked slightly away. As a result, her mouth was so close to my ear that I could feel her breath. She backed away after speaking and paused for what I saw as dramatic effect. "God damn your rotten soul!"

I said nothing and remained still except to occasionally adjust my position in my chair, only slightly, or to very slowly turn my wrist so that I could glance at my watch. An hour and 15 minutes had passed. I had about 45 minutes left to go.

My mother sat back down and put her feet up on the kitchen bar, as far across the top of it as she could, until her toe touched my arm. Then she pulled her knee up, bringing her foot back, and kicked me.

I shuddered and pulled back, hoping she had not been able to tell how much I both feared and loathed her touch.

She took a drag on her cigarette. "And that church." Mark and his family regularly made the journey to Pittsburgh to attend church. I had come to believe in God, too, seeing religious faith as a source of hope and comfort. My mother claimed the church was "wild and unstructured." Ironically, however, it wasn't much different from the Baptist church I had attended while living with her brother and his family — the very same church she had attended for a while.

As she exhaled blue smoke in my direction, she realized the ashtray was out of reach. She took her feet off the bar and sat up in her chair so she could reach it. Flick. The ashes fell. She took another drag almost immediately and leaned back. "How can you call yourself a Christian?" She tilted her head slightly, mockingly, as she spoke and then paused. "Well, how?"

I shrugged. No use in trying to explain things to someone who wasn't interested in listening.

"That church is wild and unstructured," she said again. "Any church that would encourage a little girl to defy her mother is doing the work of the devil."

Uh-huh. Yeah. That's what she would think. Of course, she was incapable of seeing the bigger picture — that the church was not encouraging me to disobey but merely to continue to believe in God. My mother tried to forbid me to believe in God. Since she couldn't, she didn't allow me to attend church, read the Bible, or show any outward signs of faith. But I also believed that many others before me had been persecuted for their beliefs, and I was willing to endure her persecution for the sake of God and my faith.

"You fucking little bitch. God damn your rotten soul!" She looked away and took a drag from her cigarette. She did not turn back to face me. "Get out of my sight."

I gladly did as I was told, glancing at my watch on the way up the stairs. The lecture, as usual, had lasted a little more than two hours.

—

During a subsequent lecture that weekend, my mother implied she might be taking me to Bellefonte instead of letting me go to school in town. After getting ready for bed — and thereby putting off talking to her for as long as possible — I crept down the stairs. She was sitting in an upholstered rocking chair in the dining room, reading by the bright light coming in from the kitchen. I asked her what I was to do in the morning.

"You'll go to Redbank tomorrow," she said in response to my question. "I'm taking off Tuesday to do some things." She paused. "You know what those things are, don't you."

"Arrest Mark," I said.

She nodded, held my gaze for a moment, and then turned back to her book. I hesitated for a moment, always vigilant to be sure I was allowed to leave before I actually did it, and then went back upstairs.

—

As soon as my mother walked in the door that Monday evening, she screamed, "Did Mark just leave here a minute ago?" She hadn't even made it into the kitchen, and I heard every bellowed word from upstairs in my room.

With a sigh, I went downstairs. One thing she couldn't stand was when I didn't immediately stop whatever I was doing, jump up, and go to wherever she was so that she could yell at me face to face.

"No," I answered as I entered the dining room on my way to the kitchen. Mark hadn't been at the house since the previous spring.

"Well, I just saw him a block away. How do you explain that?" She took off her coat as she spoke.

"I don't know. But he wasn't here."

"What kind of car does he drive? Does he have a dark green car?"

"No, he doesn't have any car," I said. It was true.

"Have you ever been in his car?"

"He doesn't have a car." I wanted to tell her that she was stupid for asking me if I'd been in a car that did not exist.

"I'm taking tomorrow off, and you know why, don't you?"

I didn't answer. I just stood still on the edge of the kitchen, about a foot from the edge of the dining room carpet.

"Sit down," she said as she made herself a pot of coffee and lit a cigarette. I walked over to my post, the barstool farthest from the dining room, and did my best not to even brush up against her back as I moved toward my seat.

"So what's my justification?" she asked as she moved toward her seat to sit down.

I was amazed that she apparently had nothing better to do than make me tell her why Mark deserved to be arrested. I said nothing.

She took a drag on her cigarette and said, "He's a sneak."

"Will you let me go to church if Mark doesn't go?" I asked meekly after a long pause in the conversation.

She snickered. "It's an unruly church. A church for imbeciles. They're nothing but holy sneaks. You don't need to go there," she said, and then took another drag, pausing her speech as she exhaled blue smoke.

"Can I go if Mark's family is not there?"

She didn't answer and shifted in her seat, staring at me all the while. She had emphatically told me before that I was not allowed to go to church, but I had to find out her real motivation. Was it that she didn't want me to see Mark there or that she didn't want me to go to church at all?

"You can even go with me to make sure I'm not with Mark," I offered.

For a moment, I thought a volcano had erupted as I finished my sentence. "I can't believe you'd even think I'd go to that goddamn place!" she screamed, her head actually shaking from the force of the words her lungs pushed out of her mouth. "You no good bitch!"

As she ranted on, pounding the bar with her fists to emphasize cuss words and the names she was calling me, I retreated into myself and was pleased to feel less uncomfortable with her ranting than I had in the past. I felt the truth was out. She wanted me to be miserable, and she would do everything in her power to see that I was. By refusing to allow me to attend church without any connection to Mark, she had, in my opinion, just admitted as much.

"I wish I had the old Johanna back," I heard her say. I came back to the real world for a moment so I could hear her analysis of my character flaws as they evolved through the years. "The lazy crybaby you used to be is so much better than this."

She spat more insults in between drags of her cigarettes, which she lit one after the other. "Whose fault do you think this is? Mine? These Christians help you sneak around, and you want me to join them? God damn your rotten soul!"

To my surprise, the lecture ended after only 45 minutes. Instead of ordering me out of her sight, my mother simply stopped talking, stood up, and turned to go upstairs, where she locked herself in the bathroom for the next 45 minutes. I heard bath water running and then the sounds of her splashing around. I stayed downstairs, eager to keep as much distance between us as possible.

While she was bathing, the phone rang.

"Hello?" I answered.

"Is your mother there?"

"She's in the bathroom. Can I say who's calling?"

"Mr. C."

"Who?"

"Mr. C."

"Ok, let me go get her." I set the phone down on the bar and told my mother that "Mr. C." was on the phone.

My mother said nothing and took the phone call in her bedroom, closing the door. When she emerged, dressed like she was going to work, she told me she was "going out to dinner for about an hour." It was 7:40 p.m. when she left. She returned sometime after midnight when I fell asleep.

—

"Today was supposedly the day she took off special to arrest Mark," I wrote in my journal the next day, Tuesday, Nov. 6, 1979. "I know something about her special day off. I listened to the radio this morning, and they mentioned it was election day and all state offices (one of which she works for) are closed."

When I arrived home from school that day, she was all dressed up. She didn't say anything about arresting Mark or even about not doing so. In fact, the only thing she said to me the whole night was, "You'll be going to Redbank for a while because I have to make some arrangements to transfer you to Bellefonte."

"She ignores me unless she has something mean to say," I wrote that night. "I feel like I'll be having a nervous breakdown."

—

Over the next two days, my mother virtually ignored me, except to point out that a canker sore I had in my mouth was just my "rottenness coming out."

Perhaps she was frustrated that all her attempts to break me had failed. After everything she had tried, it would be another event, outside both her control and mine, that would send me into a state of utter helplessness.

- 12 -
SECURITY

Growing up, I won a single battle, but it was a very important one.

I kept my Bankie.

The story of what Sean has playfully dubbed "the Acrylic Entity" began when I was two. My grandmother on my dad's side crocheted me a pink and red zig-zag afghan. I named it Betty and called it a "bankie" because I couldn't pronounce the letter L in the word "blanket."

I was obsessed with the name Betty and my parents did not understand this. Although I don't remember many of the details of the conversation, I know that my parents tried to convince me to choose another name for my new blanket. My dad suggested "Soft Joe" a couple of times, but I was insistent that it had to be Betty.

In fact, when I started kindergarten, I remember arriving at school and waiting in line to get into my classroom. One by one, the teacher greeted the children, asking their names. I so wanted to tell her my name was Betty but I chickened out at the last minute and told her the truth. She hung a name tag with my bus number around my neck, and I was known as Johanna from that day forward. I took comfort in knowing I had another chance to change my name. On the first day of school the following year, I vowed I would tell the teacher my name was Betty. But the following year, no one asked my name. Somehow, they all knew my real name. Damn!

I would wad up my new blanket in the basic shape of a doll and walk around with Betty and talk for her. The trouble was, I would not open my mouth when speaking as Betty. So no one understood her but me. And that was OK.

As I got older, Betty became an accessory to my pillow. I would put her on top of my pillow and lay my head on her to sleep. This continued for years without any significant changes. By the time I was in about third grade, my mother was concerned about the fact that I still had my blanket. And so she tried to convince me to get rid of it.

She failed. Time and time again, she failed.

Eventually, that summer, we held a series of intense negotiations that spanned several days. My mother wanted to throw Betty in the garbage, but I wouldn't have it. I finally agreed to give Betty to the cat in exchange for a bright orange afghan my mother was in the process of knitting. Just having come to an agreement was not enough in my mind. Betty would not leave my bed until the orange one was completed and in my possession.

My mother won the battle but lost the war.

My new, very orange Bankie — remember, this was the 1970s — simply took over where Betty left off. He was a pillow accessory. I remember being surprised because the new one was much larger than Betty had been, but after only one night, that was no longer an issue.

"What do you feel when you hold your Bankie?" Carol asked one day during a session.

I thought for a moment and probably smiled as I chose my words.

"Comfort," I said. "Safe. Loved." I paused again. "Joy."

"It's kind of what most people get from their mothers."

She was right.

"Why do you suppose she let you have him?" Carol asked.

Interesting question. My mother had taken away anything and everything of value to me but my Bankie. I don't think she realized when I was a teenager just how important he was to me, especially during the two years in New Bethlehem. I just slept on him. Once we moved back to Pittsburgh, I took Bankie along on vacations and even to sleepovers, but I always downplayed his role. I made sure she never saw me turn to him for comfort out of fear she'd take him away, too.

By that time, my mother was once again trying to get me to part with my Bankie. She tried to shame me, telling me it would be ridiculous to take him to college. She made sure to tell every guy I dated about my Bankie, making a point of saying, "She's going to take that blanket on her honeymoon."

Funny thing is I did.

Long before our marriage, Sean made an important declaration that neither of us has ever forgotten.

"Bankie is the source of all good."

He had been lying on the couch, resting his head on Bankie, much as I often did, when he said this about the afghan that would become our family icon.

It had been my college boyfriend, Ken, who first helped me bring my feelings to the surface where Bankie was concerned. He wanted to know about my past. "Tell me about your childhood," he'd say.

"Nothing to tell," I'd respond.

"What do you mean there's nothing to tell?" His tone was caring but playful, as if I was hiding a candy bar from him, and all he had to do was find it.

"I don't remember anything."

"How can you not remember anything?"

"I just don't."

Ken had asked me about high school, and I told him about North Allegheny, my classes, my teachers, and my friends' names. Clearly, he wanted to know more about the years prior to that. I had lived 18 years before meeting him, and only two of those years were at North Allegheny. There was a 16-year gap, and he was going to get to the bottom of it.

"Well, there's one thing I want to know," he said one day as I lay my head in his lap in a dorm sitting area. "Where'd you get that orange thing?"

I laughed. "You mean my Bankie?"

"Yeah. You sure do love that thing, don't you?" He was grinning like a mischievous kid who had discovered the combination of the lock on the candy jar.

"I just sleep on it like a pillow."

"You never sleep without it, do you?" he said, still grinning.

"No."

"Well, where'd you get it? I want to know."

Sighing playfully, I told him how the orange one was actually not the original and that the original one had come from my grandmother. I told him about my mother's crusade to get rid of it when I was in elementary school and how I'd ended up with the orange one.

"It's always been there, hasn't it?" Ken said. He was still smiling slightly, but his expression was definitely more serious.

Huh? I had never consciously thought about Bankie as anything but a comfortable pillow. After all, I could wad it up to whatever shape I wanted to get extra support for my neck, or to just feel the soft texture on my cheek. Having disconnected myself from most of my childhood memories, I was stunned by the suggestion that my blanket meant anything more.

Ken continued to insist that Bankie had greater meaning, and without ever consciously thinking about what I was doing, I began to allow my attachment to grow. By asking about something obvious like the blanket, Ken had made it inside the wall I had built around myself, even if he was allowed inside only for a fleeting moment. I don't know if Ken had any idea how important his questions would ultimately be.

"What was elementary school like?"

"Who was your best friend in first grade?"

"Who were your teachers?"

At first, I could answer only specific questions, like the names of my teachers. Facts such as these could be recited by rote without touching the dangerous emotions surrounding them. Of course, Ken was not satisfied with mere facts. They only made him want more. Sometimes, he would hand me my blanket, and I would hold it to my chest as I looked deep inside to find the painful memories buried beneath my protective shield and then begin to reveal them.

"You love that orange thing," he would say with a mischievous smile. Over the three years we dated, we would have many conversations about Bankie and what he represented.

"He's always been there," Ken would say when we would talk about my Bankie. "When everyone else disappeared, that orange thing was still there."

Continuity.

Bankie represented continuity in a world that changed by the day, by the hour, and even, sometimes, by the minute. He was security when the floor was likely to drop out from under me at any given time.

In fact, it once did. When I was about 12, we went to a carnival with members of my mother's family. My mother convinced me I needed to go on "The Rover," a ride that operated using inertia. It spun so fast that riders stuck to the wall while the floor was literally lowered. I had not wanted to go on it, and when I did go, I hated it, screaming in fear the whole time.

My mother thought this was hilariously funny, and she spent the rest of the evening telling and retelling the story of my screaming in fear to all her relatives.

—

Though it didn't last, my time with Ken was important in several ways. First, it helped me to unlock the fortress door to my memories and emotions. As these frightening scenes and emotions surfaced, I found myself taking comfort in my Bankie more and more often.

I always liked using my Bankie as a pillow at night. I remember my mother had convinced me not to take my Bankie on a trip to Acapulco. Sleeping was awkward. A pillow alone did not provide the cocooning I had come to enjoy. One of the great things about sleeping on Bankie is that he is flexible. I liked to wad him up and allow the folds of soft yarn to fill in the crevices around my neck and shoulders. I always felt supported. I vehemently disliked having to sleep without him and vowed that the trip would be the last time I would go anywhere overnight without Bankie. It was.

The connection with my past and the growing openness of my affection for Bankie called my attention to many other things I liked about the orange afghan. He is incredibly soft and I like to feel those worn, soft fibers on the tender skin on the inside of my arm. I also discovered I liked the feel of him on my cheeks and lips. Hugging him against my chest, the top of his wad touching the bottom of my face gives me a true sense of security. I found I enjoyed his familiar scent. All of these things worked together to provide me with a sense of comfort and security I had not found elsewhere.

Where Bankie was concerned, Sean never balked. He accepted the soft orange wad of yarn as an extension of me. He said Bankie wasn't an inanimate object. He was a living creature, an entity that just happened to be made of acrylic fibers.

As time wore on, I began taking Bankie with me on day trips as well as overnight trips. I found I could sling him up in the seatbelt on long car rides and sleep on him comfortably. The seat belt holds him in place against my shoulder and face, so I don't have to concern myself with keeping him in the right spot.

Though my friends are quite familiar with Bankie, most people never see him because he generally stays in the car when I go out. Their reactions when they see him for the first time are always fun. For instance, Sean and I became friendly with a couple of antique dealers who lived in Massachusetts. We were invited to stay over while on the road doing research for our first book on antique glassware. I don't remember exactly what it was, but someone made a confused comment about my Bankie.

"That is the softest blanket in the world!" Sean exclaimed without hesitation. Clearly, he had no problem with Bankie coming along on trips and he wasn't afraid to express his affection for the orange wad.

"He gets you," Carol would often say.

Yes. It is one of the beautiful things about our relationship that I have grown to appreciate more and more as I've healed in Maine. I always appreciated it. But that appreciation has grown considerably.

Sean likes to pretend Bankie really wants to sleep with him at night, and when I'm busy doing other things, he will ask if he can sit with Bankie.

I like to ask him why he loves Bankie so much.

"Because he's orange," Sean will say.

If I give him an odd look, he will follow up by asking why I love Bankie so much.

"Because he's mine," I'll say. The fact that he's always been there, even before I met Sean, need not be spoken.

Once, though, Sean shared the real reason he loves Bankie. "Because he's you."

—

Even now, or perhaps especially now, my Bankie is an important part of my life. I enjoy sitting with him while watching TV or riding in a car. And, when things get rough for whatever reason, I take a break and sit with him. If I'm really struggling, I might lie down with him in bed or on the couch. I do this often when fighting migraines. Instead of a flat wad under my head, I can craft Bankie into a longer wad, similar to a thick rope that feels like he's got his loving arms around me. Other times, that long wad feels just like a soft, acrylic lifeline — because this is what he is.

- 13 -
DEATH AND ITS AFTERMATH

Although I didn't show it outwardly, I needed my Bankie on Friday, Nov. 9, 1979. That day, I could not get my father out of my mind. I wrote him a letter during school, and at 3:45 p.m., I found myself standing in front of my locker, thinking about him with an odd nervous feeling in the pit of my stomach. I mailed his letter on the way home and then called as soon as I got in the door. No answer.

That night, my mother and I had canned tuna for supper, along with fresh-cut tomatoes. But neither of us wanted to eat. I washed the dishes and headed upstairs to my room as the phone rang. I answered the set on my mother's nightstand.

It was my dad's brother. He asked to talk to my mother. By this time, we rarely heard from my dad's side of the family. I would have barely recognized my uncle if I had seen him on the street, and that made his call all the more surprising. But it was obvious he didn't want to talk to me.

I told my mother who it was and waited for her to pick up the phone downstairs. When she did so, I hung up my end but promptly positioned myself along the open railing that surrounded the stairs so I could eavesdrop.

I heard my mother say something about "papers from Harrisburg" and then, "He always wanted to be cremated." I didn't know the details yet, but I knew my uncle had called to tell us my father was dead.

I sat there in silent disbelief as my mother continued her phone conversation. I heard my name and Nicole's and something about roses. I felt scared and refused to believe my dad was gone because he had been my only hope of escape.

I didn't want my mother to realize I had been listening. When she hung up the phone, I stood up, went into my room and sat in my rocker.

Moments later, my mother appeared in my bedroom doorway. "I have some bad news," she said. "Your father was killed in a car crash."

"No-o-o-o!" I screamed, jumping up and flinging myself into her arms. Although she confirmed what I already knew, hearing those words made me feel like I'd been the one hit by the car.

"I'm so sorry, Johanna," I heard her say through my sobs. As we pulled apart at the end of the embrace, she asked me what I liked to do to relax.

"Listen to music," I said, struggling to breathe.

"Then you stay up here and listen to some music," she said quietly. It was strange to see her showing so much compassion, but I was grateful. I chose an album for the stereo, located at the end of the hall just outside my bedroom door, and sat in my rocker. But I barely heard the music. It sounded as hollow and pointless as the motion of rocking back and forth in the chair.

The only semblance of comfort I felt was when I finally went to bed and held my Bankie.

The next several days are still a blurred memory of phone calls, radio news reports, and numbness that looked in my mind like colored streaks on an abstract watercolor painting. I listened to my radio that night after going to bed, as I always did, only this time I didn't switch stations when the news came on. I felt a strange compulsion to hear news reports of the accident as many times as possible as if hearing them would allow me to hold onto my dad just a little longer.

Apparently, my dad had left the restaurant where he'd had lunch and was on his way to work on Pittsburgh's Ohio River Boulevard when the crash took place. He was killed instantly at approximately 3:45 p.m. — when I had been standing in front of my locker thinking about him.

My mother was upset that we didn't find out about my dad's death until five hours later. Since the divorce had not been finalized, she was still legally his wife, and she felt that funeral arrangements should have been left up to her, not my dad's relatives. My mother and I had always known he wanted to be cremated after donating his organs, but his family chose a traditional Catholic burial.

Resentment began to build as I realized the only one to ask me what I wanted was my mother. How could my dad's relatives think that their feelings, beliefs, and opinions should matter more than mine? Did they honestly believe this tragedy hurt them as much as it hurt me? As his daughter, I was his next of kin. Was it too much to ask that my feelings at least be considered?

—

At the viewing, I reacted little to anyone except for my dad's girlfriend. When she entered the room, I ran and hugged her. When my dad's brother tried to hug me, however, I kept my body stiff and unyielding. He meant well, but he was almost a stranger to me.

In fact, the room seemed to be swimming with strangers. A few seemed to know who I was, but most ignored me. One stranger who did seek me out was my dad's brother's wife, my aunt. I remembered her vaguely from her family's visits to Middletown when I was a child and how my mother, always passionate and extravagant, seemed to clash with my aunt's reserved nature.

When my aunt finally managed to corner me, she seemed unsure of what to say and prattled on about a number of things. But at least she tried. I could see many others, including my cousins, eyeing me from a distance as if they were afraid to come too close for fear of catching whatever disease they thought I might have.

—

On the day of the funeral, all the strangers sat in chairs organized in rows facing the casket. I remember little about the actual service, except that I broke down crying — my only public show of emotion — when I tried to read a eulogy I'd written. I had every intention of continuing after getting myself together, but before I could do so, a stranger in a priest's robe pushed me gently aside and took the paper from my hands.

"In loving memory of my dad," began the droning monotonous voice as the robed stranger read the handwritten words from the paper in his hands. His voice rose and fell in a regular pattern, even when the rhythm didn't match the words and phrases on the page. I found myself unable to listen to this monotonous reading.

Instead, I bit my lip and fantasized about pushing him aside and taking the paper from his hands to show him how a reading was supposed to be done. I knew it would mean a fight, but I was used to that. I'd been in so many fights at school that they all blended in my memory, feeding my rage. My fear of letting anyone see my feelings worked against my anger, ultimately keeping me in my seat until the reading — if you could call it one — was completed.

When it was time to head to the cemetery, I stood looking toward the casket as the crowd dissolved around me. My stare remained fixed on the casket, and my mind raced as I tried to summon the courage to do one last thing in honor of my father. I had been cheated out of the right to present my eulogy, and I wanted more than anything to have another chance to be a part of the process despite all the adults' apparent determination to shut me out.

I wanted to remove my dad's tie.

My dad had passionately hated ties, and yet there he lay with one around his neck. "It's a barbaric custom," he would always say, comparing a tie to a noose. Why would anyone who knew him think he should spend eternity with a noose around his neck? Of course, I knew that the tie was attached only to what had once been his body and not his soul. Still, I thought it obvious that whoever had chosen his outfit either didn't know my dad or was a complete idiot.

Before I could gather the courage to act, one of the strangers had taken hold of my shoulders and was ushering me out of the room.

—

My mother asked my dad's girlfriend to ride in the first car with us. My mother had always liked her, even though she must have felt at least a little bit jealous of her. With everyone but me, my mother seemed to have a special sensitivity. My dad's girlfriend had not been accepted at this circus called a funeral any more than my mother or I had been, and this made them bond.

I remember little else about the actual funeral except that strangers were everywhere. Strangers carried the casket. Strangers stood and watched as the casket was lowered. The stranger in the priest's robe made more droning sounds. Strangers stood next to me and behind me. The only person I wanted there — Mark — was not there, thanks to my mother.

—

After the funeral, my mother went somewhere with one of her sisters, leaving me behind with other members of her family. I sat alone in the back room of an aunt's apartment staring at the books, stickers, and other items I'd brought along for entertainment. I could hear my mother's relatives out in the other room talking, laughing, and carrying on. Once in a while, someone would enter the room and ask me, only as an afterthought, if I was okay. "Yeah," I said each time, though my heart was screaming, "Okay? How could I possibly be okay? My dad just died!" But, as usual, I kept my emotions locked safely inside.

When my mother and her sister returned hours later, laughing hysterically, everyone sat for the table ritual, even though we were not at my grandmother's. My mother and her sister told everyone what a rip roaring good time they had. I felt left out and angry. How could they possibly laugh at a time like this?

—

The day after the funeral, we returned to New Bethlehem. One of my mother's sisters drove an ugly brown two-door that poorly imitated the shape of a Camaro. My mother rode in the front seat while two additional relatives rode in the back seat with me. All four of them were smoking, and I felt like I was choking, not just from the smoke but from the loathing that I always felt when among my mother's kin.

—

The following weekend, we went to my dad's apartment to begin cleaning out his things. The emptiness of the apartment engulfed me like someone throwing a burlap bag over my head. Dishes still sat in the sink, waiting to be washed. Dust covered the furniture, revealing no recent fingerprints. The bed was unmade, and a few articles of clothing were strewn about on the floor, evidence of my dad's activities as he got ready to leave the day he died.

Someone had brought in the mail, and when my mother

wasn't in the room, I quickly and quietly shuffled through the pile of envelopes until I found the letter I'd mailed the day he died. The letter had expressed hope that he could get custody of me and spilled my frustration, loneliness, and anger at my mother. I didn't want to give my mother ammunition to torment me once her sympathy began to wane.

—

The shock of my dad's death had barely begun to wear off when I had to return to the School From Hell. My mother wrote me the required excuse for my absence, and it said I had missed school "to attend [my] father's funeral."

Walking into the school building two days after the funeral, I quietly stepped up to the box office outside the school auditorium, and I handed my excuse to the woman on the other side of the glass. Without so much as a grunt, she opened the small piece of white paper with my mother's neat printing, read it, set it down, and picked up another piece of paper. On that, she signed her name and wrote the time before handing it out to me through the opening in the glass at the bottom of the window.

She shuffled papers as she continued to ignore me, and I stepped aside for the next person, disappointed that she did not attempt a few kind words.

—

For about three weeks after my dad's death, my mother backed off and gave me some slack. Then, the first week of December, she came upstairs and caught me listening to gospel music on a small black rectangular tape recorder.

"What the hell are you listening to?" she bellowed from my bedroom doorway.

"Music," I said meekly as I sat on the floor near the tape player, the only way I could really hear it. The tape recorder didn't have great sound, and I kept it low in an attempt to avoid getting into trouble.

"What kind of music?"

I said nothing. I didn't want to answer the question because I knew that no matter what I said, it would be the wrong thing.

"I said, 'What kind of music?'" my mother demanded as she came into the room towards me. Instinctively, I ducked as she picked up the tape player, ripped out the tape, and sent the player crashing to the floor with a metallic thud. "Stand up!" she shouted, bending slightly as she lifted me to my feet by the hair.

"It's only music!" I protested. "What's wrong with music?"

"It's music from that Satan-loving church!" she shouted. I could see the rage in her eyes as she shouted and waved her arms, her body leaning over towards me ever so slightly.

"No, it's not," I said. It was the truth. The songs had been taped from an album recorded by a singer who was not affiliated with the church. But by this time, my mother associated everything related to God or faith to be something evil from the church that she was certain was taking me away from her.

"Well, where'd it come from then?"

"An album."

"Where'd you get it?"

"I borrowed it."

"From whom?"

This was the kicker. She really didn't have to ask me where I got it. She knew. I hesitated, not certain what I should say, before finally opening my mouth to mumble, "Mark's sister."

"I knew Mark had to come into it somehow!" she shouted and slugged me across the face with her open hand. "God damn your rotten soul!" she shouted and hit me again.

At that moment, she caught sight of my Bible, which I had left out on the bed. She picked it up and then threw it down hard. "*You* are the devil!" she yelled.

Her irrational comment shocked me somewhat, but I kept my composure. She remained in my room for an hour and a half, screaming, calling me names, and trying to trap me with my own words.

It was back to business as usual.

- 14 -
THE RESPITE OF MAINE LIFE

Although I'd decided to become a photographer, life had other plans. I ended up becoming an antique dealer.

Sometime after I left the BDN, I wound up working for the *Ellsworth American*, a well-respected weekly that consistently has been named Maine's newspaper of the year. I enjoyed the job, my coworkers, and my beat as a reporter, which also offered plenty of opportunities for photography.

Then came Covid. The pandemic turned the news industry on its head, just as it did with virtually every other industry.

By March 2020, advertisers stopped advertising, thanks to the fact that pretty much every small, independent business was forced to shut down. Like most newspapers, the *American* was forced to cut staff to survive and they chose to lay off the last two hired in each department. I was among those let go from the newsroom. I wasn't angry. My husband was able to keep his job as an engineer, and I knew we'd be fine. I did look for another job, but I also sensed my newspaper career was done.

After Covid lockdowns ended, we left our place on the Maine coast and moved to a small town near Moosehead Lake in central Maine. After the move, We kept driving past this shuttered antique shop not far from where we live. Once, we parked the car, got out and looked in the windows, wondering what was to become of all the inventory. Finally one day in October 2020, as we drove past the shop, we noticed a real estate agent's "for sale" sign in front of it.

"So, you want to run an antique shop?" Sean asked.

I thought he was kidding.

He wasn't. Two months later, we owned the place.

We learned the shop had been closed for most of the previous 10 years. During that time, another person bought it but was unable to be open consistently due to health and family issues. We didn't actually buy the business, just the building. And the contents. Lots and lots of contents.

During the winter of 2021, I learned the secret to weight loss. Spend a Maine winter in an unheated building doing manual labor. I dropped two sizes, and because this is such physically demanding work, I've kept it off.

But let me back up a bit. The building had been stuffed to the point that we weren't actually sure what was in it. It had a furnace in the basement, but a sticker on it noted that the last time it had been inspected was in 1989. Nope, we weren't going to try to fire that thing up. Instead, I bundled up in layers. I even bought boots in a size too big so that I could wear three pairs of socks at a time. I often warmed up at a combination deli and gift shop within walking distance up the road. I took lunch and bathroom breaks there, too, and started to get to know the employees. Each day's work was a treasure hunt. I never knew what I would find as I worked to uncover and organize what was there.

We honored one of our cats by naming the shop The Lily Cat: North Woods Antiques and Buttons. We added the term North Woods because we are not far from the real North Woods, a huge swath of northern Maine that has no paved roads or amenities. In fact, the shop itself is not far from where the 100-mile wilderness begins on the Appalachian Trail. I added the term "buttons" to the name because I'm an avid button collector and planned to offer the largest selection of antique and collectible buttons in Maine. It also made sense to add those words to differentiate the shop's social media page from existing pages featuring cats with the same name as our Lily.

I launched our social media page the day we closed on the real estate and shared the process of cleaning out the building and setting up shop. I started making what I called "departments" by grouping like items together. And I had fun with it. I created "Miss Johanna's Home for Wayward Hardware" for both hardware and the assorted and sometimes unidentifiable metal objects I found. I also had two tubs that I dubbed "Parents Without Partners" and stuffed them with lids that had no bases and bases that had no lids. I hoped to eventually reunite these singles with their mates. It never seemed to work out, however.

We threw away tons of trash, including most of the stuff in the Parents Without Partners bins. As I went through what had been stuffed into the building, I began to wholesale off the salvageable items. We even gave a few things away, like an air hockey table and an interior door.

The building needed a lot of work, including a new roof,

a new garage door, new lighting, and a stair railing. We hired contractors to do the roof and install the garage door. Sean did the work inside with my unskilled assistance.

When the clean-out began, Sean and I weren't sure we would be able to open by the time summer began. But we did! We brought in some of our own stuff and began buying additional merchandise.

We like to say that Lily is our company CEO. Our other cars also have titles. Macy, who died in the summer of 2024, was our office supervisor. Abbot, aka Little Guy, is the document shredder, and Pash is our food reduction expert. Her role has nothing really to do with the shop, but she does it well. The cat loves food more than any cat I've ever known.

Not long after we began cleaning out the place, a woman stopped in to see if I would save her anything broken, even if I thought it was trash. It took me awhile to figure out just what she was looking for — it wasn't what I would call real "trash," but then again, others might. Eventually, I figured it out, and this person has since become one of my best friends.

I got to know several other people similarly. They came to the store while I was cleaning it out and bought a lot of, well, odd things that some might just toss. One woman bought a single table leg. Another bought random metal things like a single andiron. It turned out they were multimedia artists, and they all know each other. Through them, I've gotten to know others who have also become my friends. We have since dubbed ourselves the Junk Angels. We find and trade things we think the others in the group might want or use. I'm no multimedia artist, but I'm good at finding things. And I love looking through things. It's the thrill of the hunt.

I had friends in Pennsylvania, even some good ones, who still keep in touch. But the process of making friends was easier for me in Maine. In Pennsylvania, everyone always seemed to be so busy. It wasn't easy to set up a lunch date. I always felt like I was trying to break into an already well-established group. In contrast, I made friends quickly and easily in Maine.

—

Today, the antique shop is a source of great joy. Most customers are wonderful, and I like to joke that the ones that aren't at least make fodder for good stories. Because we are located in an area known for tourism, many visitors come back year after year. I've also gained a following from the locals who like to buy things they can recycle into something else. Running the shop makes life very busy, especially since Sean still works a full-time job. I consider the shop to be my job. I work at the store during our regular business hours, waiting on customers and writing up sales. I also keep the books and find inventory, which I then clean and price. Sean helps with building maintenance, and he mans the shop on Saturdays so I can do other things.

We both love buying the best. We buy at auctions and estate sales and sometimes from people who come to us with estates to settle or who just want to downsize. Often, we find things we want to keep for ourselves. If we grow tired of them later, they can be sold at the shop.

The best part is I never had to completely give up photography. I use words and pictures to tell our story on social media and to generate marketing materials. Most of the pictures I take are snapshots done with my phone but I do take the real camera out on occasion to shoot the beauty of the Maine landscape.

—

Our current home had been just a summer camp for the former owner. We converted it into a full-time residence. It's not uncommon for Maine people to have camps in addition to their homes, and many out-of-staters own camps up here, too. Although some camps are just regular houses, many are simple living spaces that are frequently not suitable for year-round use. Some are even off the grid, so there's no power or indoor plumbing. Ours had plumbing and a propane heater. We put in flooring, finished a couple of walls, and added a heat pump.

We've got a garage that research indicates used to be a bunk house. It's insulated, with indoor-outdoor carpeting and a regular ceiling. It had an electric meter but no proper indoor wiring. Sean rectified that. We also added an actual garage door since there had been only a man door. We have a John Deere tractor that Sean uses for plowing and occasional earthwork that now lives in the garage.

Our town has a year-round population of around 1,500 people, but, thanks to all those camps, the summer population swells to around 6,000. We really have almost everything we need right here in town — a grocery store, an independent pharmacy, auto mechanics, schools, shopping, a doctors' office, and a hospital. The only thing we don't have nearby is a veterinarian, but we found a good one within a reasonable driving distance.

If you want to shop at chain stores, you need to drive about an hour and a half to Bangor. Most people don't do it often. If you have to go to Bangor for a single purpose, you try to schedule other stops and make a day of it.

Generally, though, people here plan so they don't run out of something essential after hours. Life here isn't for those who want the convenience of 24-hour shopping. I like that about Maine.

The slower place of life has affected me emotionally, too. I find myself happier with less. For example, in 2014, not long before we moved to Maine, we bought a new Chevy Sonic hatchback with a 6-speed manual transmission and turbocharged engine. But its main appeal was the color — a metallic specialty color Chevy called dragon green. It has been the best car we've ever owned. In 2024, it turned over 200,000 miles. Except for a new throttle assembly at 150,000 miles, it has needed no significant repairs.

It's a great car for the store, too. It gets an average of 37 mpg, and with the two back seats down, we can stuff an unimaginable amount of cargo into it. The funny thing is that with every other car I've owned, I've gotten new car fever not long after 100,000 miles. At that point, I began to fear breakdowns and the accompanying repair bills. Not this time. I'm totally content with this car and I don't fear breakdowns. If it happens, I will deal with it. I think the healing process has allayed my fears and given me more confidence to handle whatever comes. It has also allowed me to just be content with what I have, whether it's a 10-year-old car with high mileage or a flatware box I can reuse for something else.

Another thing I love about Maine is the people. Sean and I started going for breakfast regularly at a restaurant in town not long after we moved up here. When the waitress learned we were new in town and that Sean regularly had to travel out of state for work, she gave me her phone number in case I ever needed it when I was home alone. I treasure that sheet of paper with her name and number and, even more, I treasure the fact that a stranger cared enough to make herself available. This kind of friendliness and concern creates a real sense of community that goes beyond anything I'd ever known before.

- 15 -
THE SETUP

During my sophomore year of high school, I passed the time during Christmas break home alone. My mother might be a bear when she got home in the evening, but in the meantime I had a few hours of peaceful solitude. I was used to being alone and even enjoyed it. My mother often assigned me errands to run in town, which was within walking distance of the house. For the most part, however, I could spend the time doing whatever I wanted, free from her unpredictable moods and unburdened by the fear that she would find fault with me or what I was doing, at least for the moment.

My reprieve was short-lived. It was interrupted the day after Christmas by the ring of the doorbell. I went to the back door to see Danny, the husband of one of my mother's co-worker friends from the garment factory. I opened the door, intending to ask him what he wanted, but before I could get a word out, he stepped through the sliding glass door and into the laundry room.

My mother had maintained her friendship with his wife, Joy,

and we had visited their house on a number of occasions. They had also visited us at our house.

The previous summer, Danny had stopped by the house without Joy. He had been standing in the kitchen talking to my mother when I entered the room. "Why don't you go get your bikini on and show Danny?" my mother said.

I groaned and made a face. Ever since the sixth grade, when I was already well-developed physically, my mother had been after me to show off my thin but muscular and curvy body at every opportunity. "I never had a body like yours," she'd say. "You don't know how lucky you are. If you got it, flaunt it."

When she didn't respond to my groan, I gave her a pleading glance. I always felt uncomfortable showing off my body just for the sake of doing it.

"Oh, come on," she said. "What's so bad about looking good?"

Realizing that arguing was no use — it never worked before — I turned around and trudged up the stairs to change.

When I came back down, I stood there like a convicted man waiting for his execution.

"Turn around," my mother said.

I obeyed.

Danny was smiling but said nothing.

My mother continued to make me pose so Danny could see my body from other angles before allowing me to slip away.

"Danny says you can model a bikini for him any time," my mother told me later. When I didn't answer, she shook her head in disgust.

I regarded Danny and Joy in much the same way I did my mother's relatives — strangers who'd no doubt heard what a rotten little brat I was. This couple had no kids, so I spent most of my time during our visits listening to the three of them talk. I learned that Danny was a cop and a black belt in karate and that he was under investigation for an alleged sexual assault on a Clarion College girl. Joy loved to make fun of those involved in the investigation, including the college girl. My mother joined in these jokes, and the three of them seemed certain that all that happened was nothing more than a ploy to keep a good cop down.

"My mother's not here," I told Danny, closing the sliding glass door after he passed me and entered the kitchen.

"That's okay," he said, turning to face me once he was inside the kitchen. "I came to see you."

Saying he knew I was having problems at home, he announced he'd stopped by to see if he could help. We talked for a moment, but I was careful not to say much. I didn't want anything getting back to my mother, especially since I wasn't sure what this man could do to help anyway.

What I said didn't matter. He had no genuine interest in talking or helping me. He was there to take the bait my mother had all but offered him over the summer. I remember very few details about his sexual assaults. What I do remember, I don't particularly care to describe.

The assault took place only six weeks after my dad died. Yet another adult was proving that I did not matter, that I was nothing but a tool or an object to be used and then discarded.

When it was all over, he acted as if we had done nothing more than play a game of cards and that we were now the best of friends. After he left, I cried.

―

A couple of days later, Danny called and said he was on his way down and would stop at a fast food joint on the way.

"What do you want to eat?" he asked.

"Nothing," I said. "You don't have to come."

"Oh, that's okay. I don't mind," he said as if he were doing me a favor. He continued to press the issue, insisting that he visit with a bag of fast food.

Finally, I gave in, though I don't remember what I told him to order. It didn't matter. I didn't intend to be there. As soon as I hung up the phone, I got my coat and left the house. I planned to spend the afternoon wandering around town, hoping not to run into him and wondering how I would answer my mother's questions about what I had done all day.

He actually waited! He was out of sight when I returned to the house six hours later. Shortly after I got there, however, he emerged from his hiding place and pulled into the driveway. I hadn't thought to lock the door. Another assault followed.

―

Danny returned a third time, unannounced. I was in the kitchen when I heard the sound of the car. I peeked out the window above the sink and saw his blue sedan turning into the driveway, located near the back door.

Sucking in my breath with a start, I turned instinctively to run. My entire body was shaking; it was all I could do to grab a coat and figure out how to get myself to the front door and out. I plunged through the door with no thought of locking it or even checking to see if it was closed. I sprinted across the street and through the weeds that led to the home of Mrs. Krepp, my Spanish teacher and the only adult I believed had any genuine interest in my welfare, even if she did think my mother was the saint she pretended to be.

I don't remember much of anything that happened once I got there, only the fact that I had to listen to her grown daughter go on and on about how it was my duty to report this in order to protect other women. I spent the day shivering under a blanket even though the temperature in the house was around 70 degrees. No one else was cold, but I simply could not warm up.

Mrs. Krepp called the police, and the cop who answered the call was the same one who had been there the day of my suspension from school. I found myself with no choice but to trust him if I was ever going to get Danny to leave me alone.

I would also have to tell my mother. I dreaded that but I had no choice. I stayed at Mrs. Krepp's place until dark, when I anticipated my mother's return, and then went back to the house.

My mother was taking off her coat and preparing to hang it in the hall closet under the staircase when I walked in the front door. The only lights on in the house were in the kitchen, making the hallway dark and full of shadows.

"Did you go to the hardware store like I asked?" Her tone was unusually pleasant, without any anger or mockery. It made me feel a little more confident than I would have ordinarily.

"No," I answered.

"Why not?" Thankfully, she still didn't seem angry.

"Mom?" I hesitated as she looked up at me. Her coat was in the closet now, and she was walking back towards the dining room. "I have something to tell you."

"What?" she asked, still walking. I followed.

"Danny has been coming over," I said and then searched for the words to explain what had happened. I was still young enough not to fully understand it. I don't remember much of what I said. I probably blocked out the words as soon as I spoke them, much as I blocked out the actual events. Somehow, though, I managed to relate to her what happened when Danny showed up, and that this time I had run for safety at the home of my teacher, who called the police.

I was a little afraid of how she would react, especially since Joy was her friend, one of the few friends she had.

She didn't yell or get mad, however, and maintained the even, approachable tone that she'd had since I first got home. "Are you sure?" she asked a couple times, her tone indicating that she did not believe I was lying. "Joy is going to hate us. I want to be sure I understand you correctly before we do anything," she said.

The cop came over to the house shortly after our initial conversation, and we sat in the living room. It was the centerpiece of the house, though we seldom used it. When it came to decorating this room, my mother had pulled out all the stops, covering the back wall entirely with smokey mirrors to give the room the illusion of size and adding expensive linen wallpaper and an off-white carpeting that was more plush than anywhere else in the house.

The cop sat in one of two light blue upholstered chairs with cane backings. My mother was seated catty-corner to him on one of her blue-striped loveseats. I sat next to her in another chair. The only light in the room came from a single lamp positioned on an end table.

The cop had a long, thin notebook open, and he made notes in it as he asked me to tell my story from the first time Danny arrived at the house until I ended up at my teacher's house. He was patient and kind, speaking softly and explaining why he needed the intimate details.

He asked me if I had been a virgin. I said yes, and it was the truth.

My mother listened without a word but I heard her shift in her seat after I answered that last question. The interview continued.

"Did you fight back? Did you scream, kick or punch Danny, for instance?" the cop asked.

"No, I don't think so," I said. I was too naive to have had any warning of what was coming, and when I did realize what was happening, I was frozen. I pointed out my assailant was a cop who knew karate. What could I have done?

"He's not a cop," said the real cop, addressing both my mother and me. "He told you he was a cop, but he's not. He's a security guard at Clarion College." Court documents confirm what I'd overheard during visits. Danny was dismissed from that job in May 1979 after soliciting a college student for sex and threatening her after she turned him down. The dismissal was upheld on appeal in 1981. My mother made me model the bikini in the summer of 1979, and he assaulted me in December of that year.

My mother knew what he'd been accused of doing when she set me up. Next, she went in for the kill.

"She led him on."

I looked up with a start upon hearing my mother's voice,

as did the cop, who was done speaking and was about to ask me more questions.

"She led him on," my mother said again. "He figured you were having sex with Mark, and he was entitled to a piece for himself."

I couldn't figure out how Danny's erroneous assumptions could make me guilty, but I didn't allow myself to believe this example of her twisted logic.

"A 15-year-old girl doesn't lead on a 30-year-old married man," the cop said.

At last, a voice of reason.

"Well, she admitted she didn't fight him."

"What was she going to do? He told her he was a cop and a black belt in karate." The cop's voice was still quiet as he questioned my mother's reasoning and said my reaction was not unusual.

My mother's words didn't surprise me in the least. She was nothing more than a vindictive woman who opened her mouth whenever she had an opportunity to create shock value.

But this cop? This man who had sided with her less than four months before was actually defending me to her now. That was a real surprise. Did he manage to figure out that this woman might not be the perfect mother that she seemed?

—

"I've been thinking about this," my mother said a day or two later after hanging up her coat upon her return from work. Again, the only light came from the kitchen, and her silhouette looked like a shadow. "And I guess I can understand how you felt. I don't think you led him on anymore."

"How big of you." The words popped into my head but never

came out of my mouth. I felt I deserved her admission, but more than that, I felt she was totally unjustified for accusing me in the first place. Admitting her error did not undo the damage, and nothing she could have said would have made me forgive her.

Perhaps my mother realized this because once she changed sides, she did so with a vengeance. She supported and even encouraged me as I continually refused to let Danny plea bargain out of the charges. She repeatedly said she wanted "to see him rot in hell" and even went out and bought a shotgun in case he ever came around again.

—

The state filed charges against Danny. Because I was under the age of 16, my name would be kept confidential unless the case went to trial. Then, I would have to testify. So, I could either let him plea bargain or risk becoming a public spectacle.

For reasons I don't fully understand, I chose the riskier path. Maybe it was because I knew in my heart that I had done nothing wrong. Maybe it was because I didn't want to regret it later. Maybe it was to prove something to my mother. Whatever the reason, I'm amazed I was so strong and determined.

In the weeks that followed, the cop told us each time Danny tried to make a deal. First, he tried to plea to the least of the three charges if I would drop the other two. I wouldn't. Then, one by one, he tried to get me to drop the other charges. I wouldn't. Finally, he pled guilty to all three charges. I no longer remember the sentence, though it wasn't harsh. Whatever it was, it spared me the agony of testifying in court and having lawyers attempt to break me by accusing me of lying, much as my mother had.

At this point, I was in what I now refer to as "survival mode." You go through the motions of life, get through each day, and move on to the next, but you don't really live. You survive.

—

The assaults were one of the first things Carol and I discussed. I still don't remember many details about the assaults. I remember Danny coming to do the door and coming inside, and then I remember being on my back in the dining room. What happened between his arrival and the beginning of the attack, I don't know. I don't remember how I ended up on my back or what was said.

Still, Carol persisted, asking for the details. I was uncomfortable. I didn't see the point in recalling any of these things.

But Carol had a plan. She aimed to prove that I could remember the details of what happened and still be all right.

Really? The idea seemed preposterous. But I needed to know how to handle my emotions, especially during physical intimacy when I would withdraw suddenly and say to Sean, "No! No! Stop! Don't touch me!" It would then take me 20 minutes to a half hour before I would calm down enough to even talk about it with Sean.

Something would trigger those withdrawals, Carol said. It may have been a sound, the shape of a shadow, the feeling of being touched in a certain way. In order to get past this, I would need to believe I could remember and still be safe.

I told her all I could remember, and I reread diaries I had kept at the time, hoping they might trigger memories. But the entries only described my shock that Danny would see me "that way." I wrote about my anger at my mother's finger-pointing and blame, and I wrote a few basic details about the case as it wound its way through the court system. But I included no details about the attacks themselves.

Carol asked how I felt about the attacks. I didn't know what to say. I reacted in the usual way — intellectualizing rather than allowing myself to feel. The only real emotion I could connect with was my anger at my mother. After all, she set me up. Carol and I talked about how I could not comprehend a mother wanting to show off her teenage daughter's sexuality, especially to a known sex offender.

This brought up other strange aspects of my mother's behavior while I was growing up. I remember shopping for a swimsuit when I was in kindergarten or first grade. She wanted me to choose a two-piece, but I insisted it was "itchy" and, so she allowed me to get a one-piece. Even when I was very young, she had wanted me in a more revealing swimsuit.

I began to develop physically at age 8, and my mother made a big deal of this. She was always pointing out to me the increasing size of my breasts and other features of my changing body, and she indiscreetly told all the other neighborhood adults. I could hear every word of what she told them, even though I was not a part of the conversation and, instead, was playing with other kids a short distance away. They probably heard, too.

After my parents split up, my mother would talk about my body with her siblings and other relatives. While trying on clothes in anticipation of starting seventh grade, my mother and one of her sisters discussed my body in detail without including me in the conversation or even acknowledging that I was present. It was as if I were a doll or a mannequin.

During the last year or so that we lived in Middletown — when I was about 10 — halter tops came into fashion. When other neighborhood girls began wearing them, I wasn't allowed. But then, suddenly, my mother realized how grown up I looked in halter tops and began showering them on me like a snow squall. By the time we moved, when I was 11, my mother routinely encouraged me to wear halter tops and to encourage the inevitable catcalls from men working outside. Sometimes, she would even tell me to walk past them and look sexy. At the time, I had no idea how abnormal this was. I thought I was supposed to show off my body, and I did so when she asked, even though it made me uncomfortable.

By the time we moved to New Bethlehem and met Danny, I had become involved in church — against my mother's wishes — and my faith came with a new sense of humility that my mother just couldn't seem to tolerate. I had bucked her by refusing to wear halter tops and other sexy clothing on a routine basis, and it would seem that she decided that if I weren't willing to be provocative on my own, she would force me to be.

After we left New Bethlehem and I started school at North Allegheny, my mother and I had a reconciliation of sorts. I had given up the boyfriend, given up church, and was doing my best to become the daughter she wanted. This meant getting back into being sexy. Though I couldn't wear halter tops and other revealing clothing to school, my mother made sure I dressed provocatively elsewhere. I remember a senior class social event to which I wore a rather revealing dress. I had the attention of all the boys, whether they would admit it or not, but I was very uncomfortable. I kept looking down at my dress to make sure it wasn't revealing anything more than it had to. My mother was in her glory, both sending me off to the event and hearing stories about how I caught so many boys looking at me.

Although I went away to college, my mother did her best to continue to encourage me to show off my body. Desperate for details, she would carry on an ordinary conversation with me and then suddenly ask something like, "So, have you ever seen a penis?"

I never knew what to say. Even after I had, in fact, seen a penis, I told her I hadn't.

When that didn't work, she tried again a few weeks later, telling me that doctors recommend having a pelvic exam starting at age 21 or whenever you become sexually active.

At that time, I was 19.

She asked if she should make an appointment for me.

Again, I disappointed her, telling her it wasn't necessary.

"So, how do you feel about all this?" Carol asked.

I still didn't know what to say. I didn't know how I felt besides being confused. I was slowly able to begin discussing how appalled I was that my mother would treat me like a sexual object and that she wanted to control my sexuality as if I were a whore and she was my pimp. I realized being appalled meant I was angry.

Carol pushed harder. What was behind the anger?

It was a mixture of both fear and sadness. I was angry that my mother thought my sexuality was more important than my safety or well-being, and that she would even blame me for being raped. But behind all that, I was sad and hurt about being mistreated by the very person who was supposed to love and protect me. If I wasn't worth the love and protection of my own mother, then what worth did I have?

Sean traveled for work and Carol would ask me my worst fears about being home alone. I would say it was that someone could break in and rape me.

My worst fear has not come true, thankfully, but I did experience a situation that was a lot closer than a mere discussion of what could happen. I had a boss sexually harass me, giving me a written reprimand for "fraternization" with him — claiming verbally that I had a crush on him.

Whoa! I didn't have any kind of crush on this man. It seemed to me he was quite possibly setting me up for sexual assault. If an assault did take place and I reported it, he had the perfect cover, putting in writing his notion that I had a crush on him.

I walked out the same day. I didn't even let him finish the conversation.

I called Carol that day from the company parking lot, even before leaving to meet Sean and several coworkers at a nearby restaurant.

We discussed the situation in our sessions, which all came back to my worst fears and the possibility they might come true.

"And then what?" she'd say. "What if it did happen?"

I thought it was a strange question. If I were raped, my worst fear would have come true. "Then what?" was a ridiculous thing to ask because it couldn't get any worse from there.

But that wasn't her point, though she didn't initially tell me this. She simply persisted, right down to the details — the assailant is gone. What do I do next?

I would call the police, I said.

"Then what?"

Huh? Another "then what?" In describing my worst fear,

I never considered what would happen next. I would simply picture myself sometime in the future, broken, as a result of what happened.

Carol led me through the process of actually thinking about how I would handle my worst fear. She pointed out that the answer to one of the "then whats" could be that I would call her.

"We'd work on getting through it together."

I was stunned. The possibility of getting through it and coming out OK despite it had never before occurred to me. But it made sense when we talked about the fact that I would have not only her but also Sean and my friends to help me through it.

The cup of heartache did not have to overflow.

—

My work with Carol definitely helped me to realize I could be OK despite having been sexually assaulted. At age 15, however, with the wounds still fresh, I did not think that was possible.

By mid-January of my sophomore year in high school, I began having crying fits that came on for no apparent reason. On some level, I suppose the reasons should have been obvious. The sexual assaults had taken place just three weeks earlier. And my dad had died just two months ago. However, I was unable to make the connection between the crying and those recent devastating events.

The school nurse called child welfare after I flipped out. I spoke briefly with a child welfare investigator, and the school nurse and guidance counselor suggested I ask my mother if she would speak with him, too.

I was surprised when my mother agreed to meet this man

the following Friday evening. I was shocked that she didn't ask questions or insult me. It was as if I had merely scheduled an evening to play board games.

The day he was to visit, things were different.

"Who the hell is this man?" my mother demanded. She had wanted to go out to eat, but I reminded her about our appointment. "Where did you meet him?" She fired off the questions faster than I could answer.

I told her I thought he was with the school somehow. At that time, I honestly didn't know where he had come from or how he was supposed to help. I knew only that the nurse and guidance counselor were nice to me, and they recommended the meeting. I was willing to try anything to get my mother to lay off.

She glared at me, and after holding my gaze for a frightening few seconds, she turned and went upstairs to change clothes.

—

The social worker's name was Charles. He was rather pudgy with dark brown hair that was slightly wavy. He dressed casually in a striped polo shirt, knit slacks, and these awful brown leather loafers that reminded me of the wooden shoes they were supposed to have in Holland. We sat in the living room. My mother had her usual cigarette and I could see our reflections in the room's mirrored wall.

Charles said little. He didn't have to say much because my mother's mouth never seemed to stop moving, except to occasionally wait for a response from me to echo what a good parent she was.

"She just doesn't understand that I love her and that I do these things for her own good." I had heard that line before.

"This church is like some kind of cult. They sneak kids around and encourage them to disobey their parents." I'd heard that line before, too.

Charles nodded, and I felt any hope sink into my stomach.

"I'm not trying to hurt her by keeping her from this boy and that church. I'm trying to protect her." By that moment, my mother had extinguished her cigarette, and it made her look strange.

"But—" I protested.

"But what?" she asked, turning towards me. She was dressed in one of her business suits, her legs crossed so that one black high-heeled pump dangled above the other. Her tone was neutral, her expression almost soft, as she offered me the opportunity to speak up.

Charles turned to look at me.

"But what about how I feel?" I finally managed to ask and then swallowed.

"What do you mean?" my mother asked, still calm.

"How do I feel at church? I know how I feel at church, and it's not something bad."

"I don't deny that you had an emotional experience at church," my mother said, much to my surprise. But that statement merely led to her negativity. "But what you felt wasn't God. You were elated with your defiance."

I glanced at Charles.

"Things would be golden if she would just obey," my mother said, turning her head to face him.

"Most people agree that parents have the right to say who their kids can see, fair or not," Charles said.

The hope that had sunk into my stomach leaked out my toes onto the carpet, where it quickly evaporated.

I was too young and inarticulate to realize I should have told Charles about my mother's fits of rage, the beatings, the taunts about Mark, and the name-calling. I didn't even think to tell him about how she set me up for sexual assault and then accused me of leading on the assailant. As it was, Charles seemed to approve of every word my mother said. And he never asked me a single question.

I didn't see Charles again until the following Friday, when the guidance counselor pulled me from class. I really didn't want to talk to him. But I tried to put a friendly smile on my face and went to see him anyway, more out of curiosity than out of any real hope.

The guidance counselor led me back through the administrative offices to an empty table and chairs, where I sat down. Charles entered through a side door and sat down next to me, leaning his arm on the edge of the round table. "You have to make a decision," he began. "I think you're being unreasonable about the church."

I tried to protest, but not too much, because the office secretarial staff were all within earshot. Although Charles and I were sitting by ourselves, the shelving and filing cabinets that separated us from the secretaries were only about shoulder height. Otherwise, the office was open. I could see the tops of the secretaries' heads, so I knew they could hear.

"Well, who am I to judge?" he said, a comment which thoroughly confused me. I thought his job was to judge.

"You know, I changed my mind about thinking you were capable of making intelligent decisions," he continued.

My jaw dropped open slightly. I had expected him to be unwilling to help — my mother was good at conning her friends into believing her self-righteous nonsense about how this was all for my own good. But I had not expected Charles to treat me with such disdain when everyone in the office could hear. I was sure they were listening, too.

"You need to grow up and appreciate what you have!" he barked. His hair was silhouetted against the light coming in from the window behind his pudgy body. I could barely see his rather nondescript face as he spoke. But I heard the words. "You don't have anything to complain about whatsoever. I am amazed that you would even have the gumption to say you are being abused. You're just a spoiled brat looking for attention, and you've wasted my time!"

His words sent a wave of despair over my body. I fell limp against the desk as I began to sob. I had clearly run out of options. Not only did this man refuse to help me, he thought ill of me. I pushed down the feelings of worthlessness that tried to surface and tried to regain my composure. I knew I would soon be sent back to class, ready or not.

The school nurse, whose office was next door to the room where this happened, was not pleased with how Charles criticized and humiliated me. She suggested I ask for another caseworker. At first I considered it, but then changed my mind. I continued to refuse when she suggested it again several times over the coming weeks. Would another caseworker really be able to see past my mother's smoke and mirrors?

Fat chance.

—

By this time, Mark and I seemed to always be fighting. I had endured all I could from my mother, both emotionally and physically, and the heat of my anger seeped through the cracks in my armor to burn him. He frequently commented on how I'd changed since he met me. I tried to explain the pressure I was under, but he didn't seem to understand.

The relationship had really been floundering by late winter, but I clung to him because he was truly all I had. Even my dad's fiancée, who had kept in touch for a while, stopped writing, becoming one more in a long list of adults to abandon me. I was afraid to lose Mark because losing him symbolized the end of all hope that I wasn't the monster my mother claimed I was.

Circumstances had forced me to consider the possibility that she was right. Otherwise, why would God have taken my only hope of escape and continually allow adults to abuse me? It must be, I reasoned, because I deserved no better. My failing relationship with Mark seemed to be another sign that the core of the evil I'd experienced over the past year came from inside of me.

Whether I believed that 100 percent or not, the undeniable fact was that I was stuck with my mother unless I wanted to become a street bum. As appealing as that sounded at times, I knew that, in the long run, it was not the answer. Somehow, I needed to find a way to make living with my mother tolerable until I turned 18, about 2 1/2 years later. And that would never be possible as long as Mark and I were together. Plus, my mother had left her position in Bellefonte and found another job in Pittsburgh. We would be moving back there over the summer before the beginning of my junior year.

All those things combined had me convinced I had to end it with Mark. Each time I tried — about once a week from March to June — he would become upset, crying and pleading with me to change my mind. Most of the time, I took him back, telling my mother I did so just to stop the emotional outbursts. The truth was I didn't really want to break it off. By the time school was out for the year and I knew for certain that I would be gone before summer's end, I broke up with him again, this time for good. I felt I had no choice. It would be impossible to continue our relationship with two hours of backwoods highway between us in addition to my mother's objections.

The last time I saw him was shortly after he graduated. I was hitting a tennis ball against the wall of the elementary school behind my mother's house when he pulled into the parking lot in a yellow two-door car he'd just bought. He had a pair of black sunglasses perched on the top of his head, and the way the blonde highlights in his hair matched the car made him look like Malibu Ken posed in a Barbie sales brochure.

He wanted me to take him back but gave up after only a few moments and turned his car around to leave. As I watched him go, I felt a strange mixture of relief and sadness. Relief because I had finally severed the last of my ties to the two most horrible years of my life. Sadness because I hated to see him in such pain. Despite our inability to stay together, this good looking kid from the outskirts of this tiny town had saved my life more times than he would ever know. He had been the only drop of sanity in an insane world, the only dependable element in my life, a person I still trusted even if I couldn't stand to be around him anymore.

It would be years before I could let anyone get that close to me again. In the meantime, I vowed to try to become the daughter my mother wanted — someone worthy of love or at least a little kindness.

- 16 -

LESSONS FROM CATS

Kira Kat was born in my house on April 30, 1999.

She was part of a litter of five kittens whose mother was feral. I'd been volunteering with a cat rescue group in Pennsylvania that had trapped a feral cat, intending to spay and release her. However, when they caught her, they discovered she was about to give birth and asked if I would provide foster care. I took her in, and on April 30, 1999, she gave birth to Kira and her siblings.

The mother was feral but did not lash out at me. She just didn't have any reason to trust or want to share space with humans. Her kittens picked up on her state of mind and were entertaining me with tiny little hisses within a week. By the time the kittens were nine days old, the mother allowed me to handle them, albeit begrudgingly. As they grew, I formed a deeper bond with them and socialized them so they could eventually be adopted out.

The mother cat had other plans. When the litter was about five weeks old, she managed to chew a hole in a window screen and escape. Before she could come back and get her offspring, we caught her in another trap, let her milk dry up, had her spayed, and then released her.

By that time, the kittens were eating solid food and using the box. They adapted easily to the new situation, seeing me as the mother. After a meal, they'd all climb up on me and sleep.

Kira, a gray longhair with a white spot on her chest, was the boss. When I put two trays of food down, she ate with her front feet in one of the trays so no one else could eat from that dish. The other four had to share the other tray of food. She also seemed to be the ring leader. If Kira climbed to the top of the cat condo, the others followed. If she climbed up to sleep on the top step of the staircase, everyone else climbed up to sleep on the top step with her. I wound up keeping her. She was what cat rescuers call my foster fail.

We had an older cat, Big Zepp, who had been the boss. When she met Kira, they touched noses and then Big Zepp hissed. Instead of backing away and showing deference to the resident cat, as most kittens do, Kira hissed back.

Big Zepp was old and when she died about a year later, Kira slept in all her spots to let the other cats know she was the new leader.

We'd brought Kira Kat with us to Maine on a couple of occasions. She traveled reasonably well and didn't require much time to become comfortable in the new surroundings. But, her health had started to decline about a year earlier when the Great Bipolar Incident began. We brought her to Maine in mid-January 2015, knowing it would be her last trip.

She was senile, ridiculously skinny, and struggled with constipation. It was agonizing trying to determine when suffering outweighed quality of life. As a snowstorm moved across southeastern Pennsylvania, we called a vet who made house calls to help Kira Kat cross the Rainbow Bridge. She died in January 2015, just a couple of weeks before I moved to Maine permanently.

It was a devastating loss, and although I know on an intellectual level that it was the right thing to do, I still feel like I betrayed her by ending her life.

I remember describing my wonderful relationship with Kira Kat during a session with Carol. I said Kira never knew hunger. She never knew thirst. She never knew it to be too hot or too cold. She never knew inconvenience, for that matter.

"Kira Kat was really special, wasn't she?" Carol asked.

"Yes," I said. I love them all but I loved her like no other.

"What do you think was so special about her?"

I could do anything I wanted with her, I said. I could pick her up and cradle her like a baby. I could throw her over my shoulder like a sack of potatoes. I could wrap her around my neck like a scarf. I even had a photo of her draped over a family member's shoulder, in which she's not even trying to hold on.

"So what does that demonstrate?"

For a moment, I was stuck.

Carol paused, giving me a moment to try to figure it out, before she revealed what she was getting at.

"Trust," she said. "Kira Kat taught you trust."

Wow, I thought. That had never occurred to me, but it was so true.

She loved me and she trusted me unconditionally. At the time, what Carol said was a revelation. I remember thinking that

Kira Kat was the first one to ever trust me, the first one I trusted to love me unconditionally.

But, as I would eventually discover, Sean also loved me unconditionally. Talking about Kira Kat allowed me to see love and trust in their most simplistic form, without all that other stuff that human society uses to complicate things.

When she was still healthy, I took a photo of Kira with the zoom lens from another room. She's looking right at the camera with this almost haughty expression. Her facial features and the gray fur surrounding them filled the entire frame, her green eyes jumping out at the viewer as if to say, "I Said … My dish. Is. Empty."

I have that photo in a frame on my desk, a reminder of the special family member who first made me aware of what it was like not only to love, but also to trust.

Over the years, many wonderful cats have shared my life, taught me important lessons, and helped me heal. Here are a few of their stories.

—

It was a writing mentor who helped me see myself in my cats. At that time, I had two — Big Zepp and Wee-Cat.

Zepp was a longhaired tortie who showed up as a stray in 1985 after I dropped out of college. I found her outside my apartment, eating scraps. I put out small pieces of cheese to lure her closer, each time placing the cheese closer to my door. Before the end of that day, she was inside my apartment eating a can of tuna.

Next I found myself headed to the store for cat food and a litter box. Despite the no-pets rule in my apartment, I couldn't put her back outside. I ended up moving to a place where I could keep her.

I never thought she was all that big. But people used to tell me she was, so "Big" became a part of her name. I used to describe her as moody and matriarchal. Perhaps she wasn't all that matriarchal, but she was the boss of the other cats, and she most certainly was moody.

When I found her, I was still dating my college boyfriend, Ken, and working in an automotive garage. I kept my hair short but decided to put a couple of curls in my bangs for a night out. Ken had been holding Zepp, and when she saw the curling iron, she literally freaked. Her claws came out, and she growled and struggled to get away. When she made it free of his grasp, she ran away and hid.

She'd obviously been abused and beaten, just like me.

I used to occasionally give her scraps from the table. I remember one time, giving her a piece of meat and then deciding I was finished with my meal, I approached her with a second piece. She saw me coming, growled and spun away, protecting the meat she was eating.

Wow.

Of course, Zepp could also be silly. She enjoyed chasing long strands of spaghetti, which she would eat, and she would often spontaneously start to spin in a circle, chasing her tail.

One afternoon, I fell asleep on the bed instead of accomplishing whatever it was I'd set out to do. I awoke to find Zepp curled up in my armpit, purring.

Yes, she was both fearful and happy, angry and silly, distant and loving. And she eventually overcame her emotional baggage and began to trust, much like me.

A couple of years later, I adopted a white longhaired kitten I named Kayleigh. She was tiny, only about 6 inches long, and I used to say she was a tiny little wee cat. Her name evolved from Kayleigh to Kay-Wee and, finally, to Wee-Cat.

She was an impulse purchase. When I saw her in a pet store, she reminded me of Puff, my first cat in Middletown, a furry companion who loved me unconditionally and loved me best.

I wanted to take her home that day but was told she needed to have vaccinations and be wormed. I could get her in a couple of days. In the interim, I returned to visit. As I left one day, she climbed up on the cage bars and hollered. I was buying something else and remarked to the clerk that the kitten wasn't happy. The clerk made a face and said something derogatory about my kitten.

I didn't think anything of it until I brought her home and noticed that she backpedaled whenever I reached for her. If I wanted to pet her, I could, but I had to do it on the sly, bringing my hand toward her from behind where it wouldn't frighten her. Eventually, she would let me reach for her but continued to backpedal from strangers.

I wonder if that clerk or one of her colleagues did something not so nice to her before I could bring her home. It would make sense. Something caused her to be frightened whenever a human reached for her. Eventually, however, her confidence grew to the point where she was no longer fearful.

Like Big Zepp — and me — Wee-Cat started out with emotional baggage but became more secure over time, learning how to trust and overcome fear.

—

Macy actually showed up in about 2014, a few months before Kira died. I'd been outside, and our garage door had been open. When I walked toward the garage, I heard a meow followed by some rustling as Macy emerged from a hiding place among the boxes and crates we had in storage in the garage.

She walked towards me and let me pick her up. She was beautiful, about half white with patches of mixed gray and cream-colored fur. She was also really skinny.

I went inside to get her some food and water. She ate hungrily and purred in thanks. I didn't bring her inside because Kira was ailing, and I didn't want to stress her out with a new cat. My plan was to get Macy spayed and provide shelter, as I was doing for several other outdoor cats. Before I could bring her in, however, one of the outdoor cats ran her off.

At that time, I was working as a weekly newspaper editor and I wrote a column about losing Kira. A neighbor about a half mile away responded, and we chatted via email. After a few exchanges, the neighbor emailed, saying she didn't want to rush any decisions, but she had found a cat. She sent a pic, and I knew before I even looked at the photo, that it was Macy. I compared the photo the neighbor sent with photos I had taken of her. The markings were identical. It was the same cat.

"I'll take her," I said without hesitation. The neighbor had named her Macy after a character in a soap opera that I had actually watched, and I kept the name.

I moved to Maine not long after adopting Macy, and she came with me before Sean moved with us full-time. We had hired a contractor, who worked with his wife, to finish the house in

Maine and get it ready to move in. His wife had said her goal throughout the project was to touch the cat. I'm not sure if she ever did. Over the years, though, Macy became much more confident and relaxed. She was my faithful companion, sleeping with me at night and snuggling with me every time I sat on the couch until cancer took her life in the summer of 2024.

Macy had obviously been someone's cat before I found her. Otherwise, she wouldn't have known to come out of hiding in the garage to get help. She had been thrown away, just like I was. I'm glad I was able to share 10 years of my life with her and to teach her that she could trust and that she would never have to go without food again.

—

Lily came to us around 2009 with the help of two teenage boys, who found her as a kitten in a local park. She was obviously sick. Her nose and eyes were runny, and, although she was black and white, she looked dull gray. The black areas looked dull and faded and the white was dirty and gray.

"We knew you'd know what to do, Mrs. Billings," one of the boys said. Yep. I did, and a $150 vet bill later, I had a new cat.

Lily took her meds until she started to feel better, and then she gave us a fight. She's stubborn and will refuse to move from a spot on the couch just because we want to sit there. Although she loves me, she has bonded with Sean. He is her preferred human, and, when Lily decides to sit on my lap instead of his, he jokingly calls her a "cheater." We've enjoyed quite a few laughs over this.

She's not afraid of the vacuum cleaner and refuses to move when we're vacuuming even if the vacuum touches her.

Most cats will jump up off your lap and leave if you move. Not Lily. She just repositions herself. She sleeps on Sean and, after he gets up, she sleeps on me. If we want to roll over, she's like a dead weight. As far as she's concerned, we belong to her and she's not going anywhere just because we flop around.

From Lily, I learned confidence. Why should she see herself as less than her human companions? Being bigger doesn't give us more rights. While I find that amusing, I can't help but see the logic in it.

—

I met Pash in 2016 in Maine while Sean was traveling for work. I had gone to a local animal shelter to do a story for the newspaper where I worked. I couldn't resist looking around at all the cats and noticed Pash and another one in a cage together. As soon as I reached out, Pash stood up on her hind legs to head-butt my hand, even before it even came down to her level. When I tried to pet the other cat, Pash interfered. She wanted all the attention.

At that time, we already had Macy and Lily and I wasn't sure it was a good idea to bring another cat into our small house. But I could not get Pash off my mind. I texted her picture to Sean who showed it to his colleagues. "Looks like you're getting another cat," one of them said.

He agreed to the adoption and we brought Pash home. She settled in quickly and introductions to the other cats were easy. She didn't challenge anyone for the top cat position. But she was adamant about getting attention and love from her new people.

Pash is an all-black longhair and we call her our dust bunny with eyes. When she curls up on a chair or the couch when the lights are off, we don't see her unless she opens her golden eyes.

She still likes to stand up for love, which is what I call it when she stands on her hind legs to reach a hand for pets.

Pash loves to eat. We keep dry food available at all times but feed everyone canned twice a day. Pash believes the frequency for canned food should be double. She will follow us into the kitchen whenever we go that way. She will sit by her bowl and look up at us, then down at her bowl and then back up at us.

She loves to hunt and "kill" her toys. Whenever she kills a toy, she will holler until one of us stops what we're doing and acknowledges her prowess.

While she's not obese, she's definitely not lacking in girth and her fur makes her look even bigger. She has 24 toes — normally a cat has 18 — and her big feet and girth combine to create an adorable waddle when she walks.

What I learned from Pash is to freely express joy and appreciation for the little things, like a good meal, a hug, or playtime.

—

Sharpie didn't exactly teach me anything but he did save my life.

Sharpie was an all-black feral cat, who showed up one day in about 2006 at our house in Pennsylvania, meowing loudly enough that I thought he was a female in heat. I trapped him and had him neutered — at which time I learned he was male — and released him.

Although he spent most of his time in the fields across the road, Sharpie ate his meals at our house and started hanging around, becoming friendly with the other outdoor cats. He was always careful to keep his distance from us while happily kneading the air with his paws.

One summer, Sean and I found ticks on the tame outdoor cats and decided to treat them all for fleas and ticks. This meant luring Sharpie and another semi-feral cat, Dexter, into the sunroom with food, and then closing the door behind them. Dexter hid. Sharpie, however, literally climbed the sliding glass doors, overturned furniture and broke a few things. After we got the treatment on the back of his neck, we opened the door, expecting never to see him again. Instead, Sharpie must have realized what we did was good for him. He not only came back but also decided he would allow himself to be touched and even picked up for 10 to 20 seconds at a time.

Over the years, and especially after the deaths of the other outdoor cats, Sharpie became more comfortable around us. He would greet us at the front door, walk around our legs, rub against us, and even allow an occasional pet. He enjoyed being nearby when we worked in the yard or sat outside to enjoy nice weather.

In 2015, when we had plans to move to Maine, we knew we could not abandon Sharpie. So, after packing up the moving van with the last of our belongings, we greeted him out on the front porch as usual, hoping we could figure out a way to get him into a carrier. We succeeded after several tries and some scratches from the terrified cat. And then the yowling began. Sharpie yowled for 12 hours, for 600 miles across five states.

Although it's not uncommon for relocated outdoor cats to attempt to return to the place of their origin, Sharpie adapted quickly to life in Maine. He would spend the day outside and then return in the evening for a meal before sleeping in the garage on the seat of a one-horse open sleigh. Though he was never our pet, he continued to enjoy being around us. Whenever we would return home after a day out, Sharpie insisted on walking us to the door of the house before he would go into the garage for the night.

Then, one winter day while my husband was away on business, Sharpie didn't come home. I checked for him several times, calling his name to no avail. I finally found him the following afternoon and used his favorite food to lure him into the garage. He walked very slowly, as if he were in pain. The next morning, he didn't fight my putting him in a carrier for a trip to the vet. I learned Sharpie had a fever and an infection, which could be easily remedied. The problem was he also had diabetes. Treating it would mean twice-daily injections, among other things, that would not have made him happy. He loved life and he loved us but he always did so on his own terms.

If I had my way, he would have gotten to enjoy one more perfect Maine summer. But it was not to be. And so, as dusk fell, ending a cloudy day, I held him in my arms as he crossed the Rainbow Bridge.

I couldn't shake a strong sense of his presence as I left the vet's office. It continued after I arrived home and a nor'easter began delivering blowing snow. The feeling was especially strong when I went into the sunroom near the front door, no doubt because this is where I had interacted with him. I assumed it was just grief for this cat I loved but never owned, and I went to bed.

I awoke a couple hours later, Sharpie on my mind. I lay there for a couple minutes before I decided that using the bathroom might help me get back to sleep. As I walked across the floor toward the stairs, I could see a positive reading on our carbon monoxide monitor. As I descended the steps, I smelled something burning and saw that the downstairs was filling with a hazy smoke. I opened the hopper of our pellet stove to see a billow of smoke rise up through the fuel. I turned the stove off and opened the windows, despite the storm.

Our smoke alarm did go off but, by that time, I was already up and remedying the situation. The CO levels had been rising quickly and I'm certain that my being awakened before the smoke alarm went off mitigated a situation that could have been much worse. Even if the CO didn't kill me — and our three indoor cats — we might have been overcome by smoke.

The next morning I still felt a profound sense of loss but I no longer sensed Sharpie's presence. He found a way to thank me for all the love and care he had received during the 12 years had been with us. His work here done, I imagined him greeting his old friends on the other side of the Rainbow Bridge. Reunited, he and Dexter walk together down a sunlit path, their tails entwined, just like old times.

- 17 -

THE GOOD DAUGHTER

Crazy Sam was a hitchhiker.

My mother gave him rides to and from Pittsburgh starting sometime during the summer between my sophomore and junior year of high school when she was in the process of moving us back to Pittsburgh. At that time, I had broken up with Mark, and I was determined to be a good kid to earn my mother's love.

My mother had found a job as the head of the payroll department in a downtown Pittsburgh department store and had begun commuting from New Bethlehem.

I asked if she thought picking up hitchhikers was safe.

"Oh, he's harmless," she responded with a dismissive wave of her hand. But she did say he had been discharged from the military for mental reasons, which is why she called him Crazy. Sam was his actual name.

I raised my eyebrows and shrugged. She seemed to be in better spirits since taking this job, and she was actually moving forward with plans to relocate.

I met Crazy Sam once after he had been riding with my mother for about a month. I was going to work with her that day so that we could look at real estate together that evening. After leaving the house at 6 a.m. through early morning fog, we came to a tree-lined stretch of highway that was empty except for a greasy spoon diner. My mother slowed and pulled over.

"Get in the back," my mother ordered as a thin blonde man with blue eyes approached the car holding two Styrofoam cups. He was wearing blue jeans, sneakers, and a lightweight jacket to fend off the morning chill. I got out of the car and climbed into the back behind the front passenger seat as Crazy Sam said "hello" and slid into the front.

Neither greetings nor introductions were formal. Crazy Sam handed one of the cups — which no doubt held coffee — to my mother as she looked at him and gestured with her head toward the back seat. "That's my daughter, Johanna."

"Hello," he said, looking back over his shoulder. His face was friendly, with a warm and genuine smile that put me at ease. He certainly hadn't seemed surprised to see me that morning, so he must have known I'd be coming.

Crazy Sam took my mother's coffee cup as soon as she finished taking a sip. He seemed to instinctively know when she wanted another sip and also when he should take the cup from her. He performed his job flawlessly, somehow managing to drink his coffee during the breaks in his duties. Free of the pressure to provide coffee services myself, I realized for the first time that there was safety in numbers. Whenever someone else was around, my mother was less likely to berate, criticize, or slug me.

Sunlight began to grow brighter as it filtered down through

the trees, lighting the pavement enough to change its appearance from black to gray.

"So, where are you looking to buy?" Crazy Sam asked.

My mother rattled off the names of several locations, but none of them meant anything to me. Obviously, the two of them had discussed her plans in enough detail so that something general like "north of the city" was already understood.

"So, which school district is that one in?" asked Crazy Sam, referring to one of the properties my mother had described.

"I think North Hills."

"Mmmmm. Yeah, that's an okay school," he said, nodding his head just a little.

I felt the car swerve as my mother crossed the double yellow line and punched the pedal to the floor. The car downshifted, and we flew past the two cars we had been following. Sam never flinched.

"I love it when I can pick 'em off like that," my mother said, satisfaction dripping from her lips. She continued as if the previous conversation had not been interrupted. "The last one we're seeing today is in North Allegheny."

He perked up. "Aaahhh, yeah, I went to North Allegheny. Good track team."

Crazy Sam had my attention.

"So be honest," I said, leaning up toward the console between their seats. "Who has the better track team? North Hills or North Allegheny?"

"Oh, North Allegheny, for sure. Though North Hills was always a pretty good competitor."

"Johanna wants to go to North Allegheny," my mother offered.

"Not necessarily," I said, leaning back into my seat. I didn't know where my mother wanted to live, and that made it dangerous to get my hopes up or even voice a strong opinion one way or the other. "But I've heard they have the best track team in the area."

"They're pretty good in all the sports," Crazy Sam said.

My mother listened, her bottom lip jutting out farther than the top one, and her cheeks filled with air in an "I don't care one way or the other" expression. Soon, Crazy Sam and I were doing most of the talking, evaluating the merits of all the school districts in the area, with an emphasis on their sports records. I tried hard not to sound too passionate or to let on that I had great plans for the spring track season. This move was a new start for me, and finally, I would have my chance to be somebody. I was afraid that if I seemed too interested, my mother would change her mind like she had when she was going to send me to live with my dad. Or she might make good on her threats to send me to a juvenile detention center where she thought I really belonged.

—

My mother finally settled on a townhouse in the North Allegheny School District. She and I were on an emotional high as the movers came to pack our belongings for the trip from New Bethlehem to our new home. A move would give me my much anticipated fresh start, much as it would give my mother new territory in which to feign sanity. Once the movers left, we followed in the car for a while, stopping to eat at a restaurant that had the air conditioner turned up too high. Sitting there shivering,

I suggested I go out to the car and get my Bankie so we could cover up with it.

With a big grin, she said, "Go ahead."

I went out to the car and retrieved my special blanket and my mother and I sat on the same side of the booth so that we could wrap it around both our shoulders. Sitting together under it, we laughed and carried on like a couple of pre-teens. I don't remember what we said to each other or what was so funny aside from sitting under the blanket, but it remains one of my best memories of my mother.

Sadly, neither the high nor our connection lasted. We spent the night in our new townhouse on the floor in the dining room because our furniture would not be delivered for another day or two. When my mother left for work, she left me alone all day in the unfurnished home without a morsel of food or even enough toilet paper. I was instructed to wait for the phone company, the cable company and the delivery of a new sleeper couch.

I was pleased when representatives of both utility companies showed up before 11 a.m. I began to eagerly await the arrival of the sleeper couch so I could walk to a shopping plaza about a mile away and get something to eat. But 11 a.m. became noon, and then it was 1 p.m., then 2, then 2:30. I kept opening the refrigerator and freezer doors, hoping that maybe food would appear. I knew from opening them earlier that nothing was there — and nothing was in the cabinets either — but I could not stifle the compulsion to keep looking.

As 3 p.m. rolled around, I finally called my mother. She

asked if the cable and phone guys had been there, and I said yes. Then she asked about the sleeper couch. I said it hadn't arrived.

"Can I please go get something to eat?" I asked.

"What if the guys with the sleeper couch come when you're out?"

"I don't know. Can't we call them and find out when they're going to be here? I'm hungry."

"No," she said. "You need to wait."

I sighed. "I'm so hungry. I don't know if I can wait."

"Well, you're going to have to." My mother's voice had become stern. Not quite angry, but stern enough that I knew she was dead serious. She probably had to curb her anger because of coworkers being within earshot.

"Okay," I said with a sigh and hung up, stifling my anger. On some level, I knew what my mother was asking of me wasn't fair, but dwelling on it wasn't very comforting. I wanted to mold myself into the perfect child so that she wouldn't hate me and try to make my life with her work, no matter what the costs to myself. What other alternative did I have? My dad was gone, and there was no way I could go back to the hell of the previous year.

The sleeper couch was finally delivered at 4:30 and my mother was home by 5. We went out to eat, and I eagerly devoured the first food I'd had in nearly 24 hours.

—

"Now, don't be a smart ass," my mother told me before we left to enroll me at North Allegheny Senior High School.

Eager to get a new start, I assured her that I wouldn't.

I was a little nervous during the 2-mile car trip to the school, which many in the area said looked more like a shopping mall. Made of white brick three stories tall, it is situated on a busy section of highway. Because it sits slightly downhill from the road, you don't immediately see the glass doors and windows on the first floor that make it look like a school. All you see are the second and third stories, rising toward the sky with only a few vertical rows of thin windows. Having been built not long before I enrolled, the school was air-conditioned, making the traditional large rectangular panels of classroom windows unnecessary.

We parked in front and walked in through one of several sets of double glass doors trimmed in black metal. Inside was a spacious open area with a section blocked off for cafeteria seating. A small glass-front office was located to the right of the cafeteria area and this is where we had our meeting.

A man with a vague resemblance to Myers took us into his office. He had a rather square face with a serious expression that made it clear that he was none too impressed with the tiny girl in front of him. He had my birthdate, so he knew I would not turn 16 until well into the school year, making me younger than most of my 11th-grade peers. And he was even less impressed with the district from where I had come.

"Redbank Valley..." he mused, nodding his head ever so slowly.

Oh, God! I wanted to throw my head back, spread my arms wide, and shout, "I am not *from* Redbank Valley!" I had gone to school there, yes, but I was not from there. I felt like the name was tattooed on my arm, and I would have to cut out a section of my biceps to get rid of it.

I didn't have to shout. My mother intervened. "It was not a

good school district," she offered. "She got straight As and never had to take a book home, even though she lost her father only nine months ago. She needs a challenge. That's why we're here."

Not a bad argument, I thought.

The guy, whose name I don't remember, eyed my mother curiously before proceeding. "We have a number of academic programs. I'm not sure which level would be appropriate."

"The top," my mother answered without hesitation.

Mr. Forgotten Name shifted in his seat. "We have academic programs here that go beyond the typical academic courses you might find at a school like Redbank Valley."

I cursed my invisible tattoo but said nothing, leaving the verbal warfare to my mother.

"My daughter went to Norwin before Redbank Valley," my mother began. I saw Mr. Forgotten Name's eyes dart to her face when she said Norwin. "She was in the top academic grouping there and Middletown before that. And Middletown is a very good school."

I suppressed the urge to smile. My mother seemed to know what she was talking about and even Mr. Forgotten Name seemed impressed.

"She deserves a chance with the best," my mother added.

Hmmm. I didn't think my mother believed I deserved much of anything except a good smack across the face or a yank to my feet by the hair, but here she was making an argument that I did, and I couldn't help but get sucked in by her enthusiasm.

"Well," began Mr. Forgotten Name. "Our best program is Advanced Placement."

"That sounds like a good place to start," my mother said. I

watched the exchange, enjoying my mother's ability to elicit the responses she wanted from this man, who probably thought that he would scare us off with his subsequent description of the AP program. AP was like taking college courses in high school. At the end of the year, students who did well enough on a special exam could earn college credits before ever setting foot on a college campus.

My mother listened and nodded, glancing at me now and then as she listened. I could see she wanted me in the AP program.

"Kids who take AP classes have to qualify," he said, "and frankly, I'm a little hesitant to put her in an AP class without any of the testing that the other students went through. I don't want to set her up for failure." He spoke about me as if I weren't there.

"I'm sure she can handle it," my mother said.

Mr. Forgotten Name gave me a questioning look. I held his gaze for a moment and then began asking questions of my own. How many AP courses were there? And what subjects did they cover?

High school juniors could try one AP course, he said, and then take several the following year. The senior AP courses covered various topics, including math, science, and English. The AP course for juniors was American history.

I wanted to pantomime, tying a noose around my neck and hanging myself as I dropped my head to the side and stuck out my tongue. I had promised not to be a smart ass, and I would keep that promise, but I did not relish the idea of another year of American history.

"Isn't there another subject?" I asked, explaining that I'd had American history in eighth grade at Norwin and then again in ninth and 10th grades at Redbank, where the subject had been divided into two year-long courses. If I took this AP class, it would be my fourth year in a row of American history.

Mr. Forgotten Name assured me that American history was my only choice if I wanted to be in the AP program.

"Okay," I said with a shrug and a little giggle. "I guess since I've had it three years in a row, I have a bit of an advantage over everyone else."

Mr. Forgotten Name was still not convinced, and he spent the next several minutes trying to make sure I understood that I would need to spend a minimum of two hours a night doing homework for this one AP class alone.

But I was undeterred. I was eager to be challenged at school for something other than a fistfight. Besides, I knew I had the brains to succeed, even at this elite level.

Of course, my real goal was to run track in the spring. My mother wanted to see me in the AP program, and I figured the more able I was to please her, the more likely I would be able to run track without her interference.

—

Though I wasn't all that nervous, I found the first day at North Allegheny to be a bit overwhelming. The basement and first floor of the building held the cafeteria, locker rooms, pool, and gym. Most classes were held on the second and third floors, which were set up like figure eights. The joke was that the room numbers had been thrown up at random and then attached to the door nearest where each one landed. This explains why I found myself wandering the halls long after the bell, looking for the right room and wondering if Crazy Sam was good at walking in circles.

Time would certainly prove, however, that even if Sam had been crazy, the school district was not. Teachers cared more about teaching than spreading rumors and putting kids in detention. Even the size of the district was the antithesis of Redbank Valley. My graduating class alone numbered more than 650, almost half the entire student population of Redbank Valley, from kindergarten through 12th grade.

I didn't know the numbers then, but I knew North Allegheny was big enough to give me the anonymity I craved. There were so many other kids — and all the juniors were new to this building along with me — that I could stay locked safely inside myself while contemplating how to find my place in the new environment.

I never did emerge from my shell. On the surface, I seemed to grow into the perfect kid, just as I'd planned. I made friends and went to the movies, parties, ice skating, and swimming. I got excellent grades and held a part-time job while running both track and cross country. But the reality was that the wounds of the previous two years had taken so much out of me that I was unable to form meaningful relationships. It would be years before I'd realize that I had kept everyone at arms' length and that my apparent success at North Allegheny was nothing but a ruse. Still, the school environment gave me hope without inflicting further damage, and that would be enough to guide me to eventual success, both vocationally and emotionally.

On the first day of AP history, the teacher seemed surprised to see my name on his roster. "Where did you move from?" asked Dr. Sheffer, looking at me through intense eyes underneath a patch of short-cropped brown hair that was combed to the side, ending in a curly cue.

The words "Redbank Valley" fell from my lips, poisoning the air, and I hoped I wouldn't choke.

"Redbank Valley?" he said, his voice rising almost shrilly. "Where on earth is that?"

"I'm not *from* there," I said, silently cursing the invisible tattoo that everyone seemed to see. Of course, that wasn't the answer to the question he asked. It was just an aside, a piece of information I was compelled to share in my attempt to dissociate myself from that place before answering the question.

While the rest of the class concerned themselves with the syllabus and several textbooks required for the class, Dr. Sheffer called me aside.

Uh oh, I thought. My records have arrived from Redbank, blowing my cover, and this teacher knows what a loser I am. Surely, he was calling me aside to tell me that I didn't belong.

But he said nothing about my past. He merely gave me the same warnings I had received from Mr. Forgotten Name, adding that there would be no shame in opting out of the class later.

I told him I was sure I could handle the work and then returned to my seat.

Dr. Sheffer announced that for each class, someone would be assigned to lead the discussion on the readings, an activity that required more preparation than usual. No doubt, thinking it would be a great way to test my preparedness, Dr. Sheffer assigned this job to me for the next class.

That day, I sat in front of a classroom full of North Allegheny's elite achievers, none of whom I had known more than a day, in a test to see if I would sink or swim. I got off to a slow start, asking a general question, which left my classmates clowning around and not taking me seriously. Next, I asked a more pointed question about how the readings might have been different if the writers had been other people. My peers quickly settled down and got into the business at hand. I had won their respect, at least for the moment.

I got a B on the first test. I was strongest on the essay questions, and this helped to counterbalance any weaknesses elsewhere. As we were looking through the exam booklets after the first test, I noticed that Dr. Sheffer had written "you belong" on the last page. It was his way of saying that I had proven myself capable of keeping pace with my peers despite having come from Redbank Valley.

—

During the first few weeks of school, I went to the guidance office to find out if my records had been transferred from Redbank Valley. I wondered what would happen when the people at the new school found out that I had been suspended and had spent as much time in detention as in class. I wasn't sure what they could do, but I was nervous about it nevertheless.

"Your grades are here," said the guidance counselor, a friendly, dark-haired woman.

"What about my behavior records?" I asked.

"We got those too, but we purged them."

Wow! I was not to be automatically branded as a "bad" kid! If I could stay out of the principal's office, I might actually have a chance!

—

I still got in fights, but not always at school.

I had begun babysitting an 8-year-old girl, Stephanie, and when I found out a neighborhood bully was frequently throwing snowballs with rocks in them at her, I took it personally.

John was in eighth grade, but he was huge. I had to look up about a foot to see his short, cropped, straight blonde hair. He was stocky, too, built like a football player. In contrast, Stephanie was a tiny third-grader with a wonderful imagination and a head of curly brown hair.

Stephanie acted as if the assaults from John and his friends were no big deal. Perhaps she said this only because she felt powerless to stop them, a feeling I knew well. In any event, I felt that a huge eighth grader had no business picking on a third grader, and I put myself in charge of stopping it.

I was outside one snowy January afternoon when Stephanie got off the bus. Thud. I saw a snowball crash to the ground as she and a handful of other elementary school kids began walking up the hill toward home. Thud, another one hit, and then another. Finally, I was able to locate the source of the snowballs, and it was John, standing in the bushes part way up the hill that led from the bus stop to the condos and townhouses where we all lived.

"Hey, knock it off!" I yelled. I could see John turn to look in my direction, and then he promptly threw another snowball. I began walking toward Stephanie, who had gotten hit despite her best efforts to dodge the snowballs.

John saw my arrival as another easy target presenting itself. As I put my arm around Stephanie and began to lead her out of range, John came out from his hiding place in the bushes, ran right up behind me, and rammed a snowball into the back of my head.

I whirled around and began pounding him with a vengeance. I was small but fueled by the rage I kept hidden so well. His open-mouthed expression showed both fear and surprise. He had not expected to be knocked to the ground and then repeatedly punched in the face, especially by a girl half his size. As his friends stood by, their jaws hanging loosely from the bottoms of their faces, I pounded this kid repeatedly, all the while lecturing him about his sins.

"You are sure some big hot shot," I said through clenched teeth as I let another punch land, "picking on a third grader. See how impressed I am?" I punched him again. His arms were swinging wildly as he lay on his back, trying to fend off his tiny attacker, who now had her knees buried in his chest to keep him on the ground. "You had better leave her alone!" I warned, hitting him at just the right time to punctuate the words "better" and "alone."

"Hey! Leave him alone!" I turned to see his mother standing on the porch of his townhouse, which was not far from where I had leveled him. "How dare you pick on a younger kid!"

"Pick on a younger kid?" I said as I removed my knees from his chest and stood. John scurried away on his back, using his hands and feet like a crab soccer player.

"I may be older," I yelled, moving slowly in her direction. "But in case you haven't noticed, he's twice my size!"

"I don't care! I don't want you picking on him!"

"Listen, Lady. He was picking on *me*. He rammed a snowball into the back of my head, and he did that because I tried to stop him from picking on a third grader."

She continued yelling, though I didn't listen. I continued my argument as well.

"A third grader. Did you hear me? This rotten kid, who you claim to be defenseless because he's younger than me, was picking on a third grader!"

"You just stay away from my son!" she bellowed finally.

"Then you keep him away from me and Stephanie!" I shot back.

"I will!"

"Well, good!"

John never bothered Stephanie again, to my knowledge. He never made the mistake of getting too close to me again, either. Making sure to keep a safe distance away, he would yell, "Hey, Psycho!" whenever he saw me. At first, I ignored it. Then, I was out running one day when he was with a friend, and he yelled it. I changed my course so that I'd run right by them. When I got to where they were sitting, I stopped and calmly asked him what he had said.

"Oh, nothing," he insisted, raising his hands slightly and shaking them as he leaned slightly backward.

Once his defensiveness and fear showed, I knew I had him. I pushed a little harder. "Hmmm. I swear I heard you yell, 'psycho,'" I said. "I'd hate to think you were calling me names when we all know what happened the last time you pissed me off."

Knowing full well that humility was only a punch away, he continued to stammer as he denied saying anything. I admit, I enjoyed watching him squirm. "Okay," I said, looking straight at him as he dodged my gaze. "I'm going to finish my run. But I better not hear any more yelling from you."

He assured me I wouldn't and kept his promise. He never bothered me again.

Living my mother's lie was difficult. I could not tell my friends or even one of a few trusted teachers what was really happening, at least not in any real detail. Some things spilled out inadvertently from time to time, but never any real details about how I lived in constant fear. Keeping people around me allowed me to fool myself into thinking I was not alone. But because I had to keep these people at arm's length, I lived in emotional isolation. Although I appeared to have more friends at North Allegheny than at Redbank, I was unable to allow anyone to get close to me as Mark had, and this compounded the loneliness.

In the fall of my senior year, one person almost made it past the armor, but I panicked and sent him away. Part of the problem for me was that this relationship was beginning to look too much like my relationship with Mark. And although that relationship meant good things, like camaraderie, laughter, and even trust, I associated these good things with my mother's rage. After all that's what they led to in the past, so I reasoned that it would be the same the second time around.

My mother contributed to my paranoia by nagging. "I think

you're getting too involved," she casually commented one afternoon. "Too involved." That's what she had said about Mark. The parallels were frightening.

My mother criticized everyone else as well. Whenever one of my friends would leave the house after a visit, my mother would strike up a conversation with me that included an analysis of all my friends' faults, in both appearance and character. These statements all run together, being said about virtually anyone I associated with, regardless of gender.

"He's chubby."

"She's jealous of you."

"He's not as smart as you."

"She's using you."

"He's a loser."

"She's not really interested in your friendship."

"He's too uptight."

"She's overweight."

"He's dumb."

"She's too religious."

"He's a liar."

The only people my mother seemed to approve of were boys I admired from a distance, those who had not gotten close enough to threaten her position as the only person with any influence or control. Of course, I didn't realize this pattern yet. I merely saw my mother's analysis as a sign that I had better end things with anyone significant before she interfered and made my life miserable.

Somehow, though, I would manage to climb out of the pits of hell without being shackled by such pessimistic beliefs. Before leaving North Allegheny, I would experience true joy, even if only for fleeting moments, and this would propel me beyond my mother's cynicism to a world where possibilities exist, even after a life of tragedy and heartache.

- 18 -

SPEED

Where I got the idea that I needed to run is a mystery. Almost as far back as I can remember, though, running competitively was chief among my goals. I wanted to go out for track in seventh grade, but Norwin didn't have any kind of organized running program in junior high. I waited until ninth grade, but by then, I was at Redbank Valley, where the opportunity I had longed for was yanked out from under my feet. Finally, I made it to North Allegheny, certain my talent and eagerness to work hard would earn me a place on the team. I was right.

In January of my junior year, the track program's unofficial "winter workouts" began. Three days a week, athletes went down to the school stadium and independently followed instructions for workouts posted for their events. Intending to be a sprinter, I practiced with a senior named Heather, a quarter-miler who taught me the meaning of humility.

We were to run a series of quarter-mile sprints. Standing at the edge of the parking lot — the track was covered with snow — we took off at what seemed like a break-neck pace. I lasted all of 100 yards, only a fourth of the total distance. Out of breath with my chest heaving, I slowed for the second 100 yards and watched my teammate's form grow smaller ahead of me in the distance. At about the halfway point, I could take it no more. I had to stop and walk. Catching my breath, I began jogging the last 100 yards to where my teammate stood waiting for me.

Shocked though I was with my inability to keep pace, I refused to accept defeat. I would not believe I lacked talent but rather that I would have to work harder than I'd anticipated.

Admitting to Heather that I was now in awe of her, I simply started at a slower pace for the next one, my goal to finish at this same speed. Heather took my admiration in stride, encouraging me to keep at it because that was the only way to improve. Her easy-going and supportive attitude amazed me since I had seldom encountered such encouragement before.

Although I had worked hard for two months until official practices began, I was surprised to find a number of sprinters faster than I was. Several days before the first away meet, I asked the assistant coach, Mr. Sabados, if I would be going. He said he wasn't sure. I wasn't surprised, yet I was. Two years before, I had beaten a girl who went to the state competition in the 100-yard dash. I knew Redbank had been in an easier, less competitive division in track than North Allegheny, but I found it hard to believe this state-caliber sprinter would not have even made the North Allegheny team. It looked like that was the case.

I did end up going to the first away meet, though not in the event I had chosen. Coach Sabados said he wanted me to run the quarter mile. "But I want to be a sprinter," I protested as I looked up a good foot and a half to his face.

"Well, let's just try this and see what happens," he said.

"Okay," I sighed, certain that things weren't lining up in the universe the way they should. I would have to believe that they'd work themselves out later.

Although I thought he had me pegged wrong, Mr. Sabados was onto something that even the negative name-caller at Redbank had noticed. I had speed, yes, but I also had considerable endurance. I had forgotten until years later that the Redbank coach had thrown me into a couple of quarter-mile time trials before my mother made me quit. I had easily kept pace even though I thought I didn't belong in their events.

I did go to the first meet, placing second in the quarter behind Heather. I ran the quarter in a number of meets afterward, always placing second. I remained determined to outrun Heather and came to practice faithfully in an attempt to do so.

I never did, though. By the third or fourth meet, I found myself running the half mile instead of the quarter. We had several good half-milers, though, and I struggled to place in each race. Finally, with a special regional relay event coming up, the coaches had me join a time trial for a three-quarter mile run, the same distance as one leg of a medley relay. When I easily beat all the distance people on the team, I earned the right to run that leg of the relay.

What the coaches saw in me had gone over my head as the success I wanted continued to elude me. I could run any number of events and do okay. But I didn't seem to be outstanding at any of them.

Discovering the events that most suited me happened nearly by accident. Our team had made it to the district team championships, and the head coach, Mr. Cerny, offered me a choice. I could run the half-mile, which I had done before, or I could run the mile, a distance I had never run, even in practice.

For me, the choice was easy. I could run the half and have the same old mediocre race, or I could try my hand at something new and see what happened.

"I'll try the mile," I said.

Mr. Cerny grinned, and I grinned back. He was quickly becoming a father figure to me since I had lost my dad only a year before. I'm certain he had no idea how much he resembled my dad. Mr. Cerny had dark hair, combed to the side where it lay flat. In contrast, my dad had a full head of chestnut brown hair along with a beard and mustache. But their facial structures were similar, and Mr. Cerny's build was similar to that of my father. Most striking to me was the resemblance in their stances and mannerisms. Both men carried themselves with their backs slightly arched so that their bellies jutted forward. They held their shoulders back so that their arms stuck out slightly at their elbows.

If Mr. Cerny had wanted me to run a marathon that day, I'm sure I would have at least tried.

As it was, the mile was the right choice. I kept pace with the pack without any trouble despite my lack of training and experience. I placed second with a respectable time of 5:41 and a feeling that I had found my niche. The quarter and the half were almost sprints, and I always liked having already run them better than actually running them. But the mile was fun. I had tasted a moment of joy, and I was hungry for more.

Fate would help feed my hunger. One of my teammates had dropped out of the mile race due to a twisted ankle, and she felt she wouldn't be able to run the two-mile. I could hear Mr. Cerny's sigh as he stood facing her, contemplating what to do. I listened to the banter with interest and couldn't avoid feeling a little smile creep up from my belly to my face. I had an idea.

Mr. Cerny had the same idea. He turned to me with an exasperated look, as if this were the craziest thing he would ever consider, and said, "Well, you want to run the two-mile?"

Like Forrest Gump being offered a selection from a box of chocolates, I said simply, "Okay."

I went into the race with a mixture of nervousness and elation. I was high from what felt like a victory in the mile, even though I had placed second. I felt like I could do virtually anything, even run a two-mile. At the same time, I felt a bit of apprehension because I'd never run more than half this far, except for once in seventh grade. Yet here I was, crazy enough to step onto the track with a bunch of experienced distance runners. It was just as conceivable that I could be left in the dust as keep pace with them. I wouldn't let myself dwell on that possibility, though, and set off at the gun, determined as always.

I ran most of the race at an easy lope in about sixth place. I wasn't satisfied with this placing, but I was afraid to run harder for fear of losing steam later. A girl from one of the other teams surely never knew that she was the reason for my eventual success. At the beginning of the backstretch for each lap, she'd pass me, and then I'd get annoyed enough to pass her right back by the end of the backstretch. And so it went, lap after lap.

Finally, as the end of the race approached, I passed her at the end of the backstretch and kept going toward the finish line just a few yards away. I flew past every other runner that stood between me and the end of the race until I saw Mr. Cerny's bugged-out eyes and wildly waving arms off to the side of the track. "Whoa! You've got one more lap!"

I don't know what my face looked like, but it felt like my jaw dropped so low I could trip over it. I slowed, gathered my composure, and ran the last lap. I didn't have quite enough left to sprint past everyone in the last 100 yards, but I managed to come in third with a time of 12:40.

Everyone wondered what would have happened if I had not miscounted the laps and sprinted before I was supposed to. But I wasn't the least bit embarrassed. I had done well — really well — and had recovered enough from my goof to still place and earn points for the team.

"You're going out for cross country, aren't you?" Mr. Cerny asked, more than once, in fact.

"Yes," I said each time, glad to have someone actually wanting me around.

The joy of running had me flying so high that not even my mother could bring me down.

—

Eager to reach out and grab success by the neck and yank it to my breast — and thereby control one tiny aspect of my out-of-control life — I sought the opportunity to run more distance races. But my next two-mile run in a district invitational didn't end on a high note. I imagine my less-than-stellar performance was due to a combination of inexperience and pain from a chronic cough. Whatever the reason, I didn't feel as high as I had before.

"Don't worry about it," Mr. Cerny said. "You're going out for cross country, aren't you?"

I grinned. "Yeah, I am," I said, realizing that the fall cross-country season would give me ample opportunity to train for distance races the following spring.

Our next meet was the district qualifier. Runners from various teams competed for a chance to try for medals in the district meet. I qualified, even taking a few seconds off my previous time. But in the district meet itself, I choked, coming in last of the 12 who had earned the right to run this race.

I was devastated. At last I had found my race, but I still couldn't capture the success I wanted so desperately. Making matters worse was the fact that everyone else on the team who had qualified for districts had earned a medal. I fought the tears as we got on the bus to return to our school, and when we stopped at a fast food place to eat, I got off to join my teammates only because Mr. Cerny had come back onto the bus looking for me.

No one had any idea what the race had meant to me or why my poor performance hurt so badly. For the rest of the team, it was just another track meet. But for me, the race represented so much more. Running had brought me the only joy I had ever known, except for time spent with my dad and with Mark, both of which were still too painful to remember. I saw winning as the only way to give my empty life meaning. I had not won therefore my life remained meaningless.

I had started in January, unable to make it around the track once, and less than four months later, I qualified to run a mile and two-mile against the best runners in Western Pennsylvania. Too engulfed by my pain to see the bigger picture, I would have to wait almost 20 years to comprehend that this was a victory in itself.

—

Speed was intoxicating. The faster I ran, the faster I wanted to go. Speed was freeing, redeeming, and oddly calming.

My mother felt it, too, though she rarely walked anywhere, let alone ran. She drove like a madman on the two-lane roads between New Bethlehem and Pittsburgh, thinking nothing of passing in a no-passing zone, passing more than one car at a time, or passing on a curve. In fact, she was downright proud when she managed to do all three of these at once. She sought the freedom of speed just as I did but in a different medium.

"I want a Corvette," she announced toward the end of my junior year as we were driving past a Chevrolet dealership near the high school.

I turned and looked at her with a grimace as if she had suggested we rent a spaceship and visit the moon. "Ok, whatever," I finally said with a laugh, unaware that my mother was not discussing a fantasy but rather stating her intention.

"Would you like having a Corvette?" she asked a minute or so later. Her face glowed with mischief against the blurred background of businesses and restaurants along the highway.

"Well, sure!" I said. What 16-year-old would say anything different?

Her interest in the Corvette was another one of her bouts with extravagance. Her darling little brother, who lived in the Norwin School District, owned a 1977 model that he took to shows. Candy apple red, it had a turbo hood and a custom paint job showing a wildcat with his mouth open. Inside its mouth was a scene of a dove flying over the Pittsburgh skyline with a full moon behind it. My mother and uncle made a deal that kept the car in the family, a situation that also offered my mother the chance to get everyone in the neighborhood talking.

Although I would be 17 in less than three months from the date she bought the Corvette, I had not even attempted to get a driver's license. I had little extra time, and I knew my mother did not have the patience to teach me to drive. Because she had difficulty not being in control, any time she attempted to teach me ended with her screaming before we were even out of the driveway. I decided not to bother learning. But the Corvette provided an incentive like no other. When she said the car was mine if I learned to drive, I paid for private driving lessons.

It was clear she was delighted with the car's shock value. On the one hand, I wondered if it also represented all the things she wanted to tell me but couldn't — that she was sorry for her fits of rage, for hitting me, for accusing me of leading on the man who sexually assaulted me, for my dad's death, for failing my sister, for uprooting me four times in six years, and for the loss of my dog and my cats.

On the other hand, I'm sure it gave her one more thing to lord over my head, to push my buttons and keep me under her control. More than once, when in one of her "get out of my sight" moods, she'd tell me to leave and take the car with me. She knew I wouldn't, but she also knew she could make me feel bad by suggesting it. And she succeeded.

My mother had fun with the car, experiencing the thrill of both its speed and ability to attract attention. But then she seemed to lose interest in it, much as she had lost interest in everything else.

But I was living the 17-year-old's dream. And once I learned to drive, the car provided an infinite source of the speed I craved.

That summer, I got a part-time job at a local fast-food restaurant. When Dave, the assistant manager, came to work in his vintage Camaro, I joined everyone in admiring the car. He took me for a short ride, and then I reciprocated with a ride in the Corvette. But I didn't stick to the short stretch of road in front of the plaza where the restaurant was located.

"Where are we going?" he asked as I went through the traffic light at the end of the plaza rather than turning back in.

"Somewhere where we can go *fast*," I said, turning to face him briefly with a wide grin. The car accelerated smoothly, almost imperceptibly, reaching 100 miles per hour without even a moment's hesitation. I checked my mirrors and, seeing no one behind us in any of the three lanes, I cut over from the far left to the far right, avoiding a slower vehicle that had been in front of me.

"How fast are we going?" Dave asked, grinning with the excitement of a little boy with his first toy car.

"A hundred and ten," I said calmly as if I were quoting the price for a pack of gum.

"A hundred and ten!" he said, laughing. "My god, you just crossed three lanes of traffic at 110!"

"You ain't seen nothing yet," I bragged. "I've had this baby up to 140."

We were on the clock at work, so I didn't have time to take it up to that speed, but Dave didn't seem to mind. He'd already been thrilled by the speed of my car.

When we returned to the restaurant, he took great delight in telling everyone about our adventure. It was a moment of glory for me, my recklessness earning me a few moments of honor among my peers.

—

I trained hard over the summer, running four or five miles a day so that I'd be competitive by the start of the cross-country season.

It was a completely different kind of running than I was used to. The changing terrain made it interesting, and I discovered I was good at running uphill, though not terribly so at running downhill. Downhill running was supposed to be easier, but my strength and unusually small size made it easier for me to climb hills than for my larger, taller peers. They had the advantage of going down, however, where they could utilize their longer strides.

In the first meet of the season, I placed third. I wanted to win but I was pleased with third, considering that only two people from two entire teams had managed to run faster. But in the next meet, I placed a disappointing 10th. I did well in the next race, but the one after that was mediocre. Although I didn't expect to immediately be a cross-country standout, I was frightened by my inconsistent performances. I felt that if I could do well in one meet, I should be able to do about the same in the next one. It never occurred to me that this kind of inconsistency was normal for a beginner.

My mother's attitude certainly didn't help. The following week, when I placed second, running my best time on our home course, her reaction was, "Well, why didn't you win?"

She had been sitting in the green velvet rocking chair in the corner of our living room which was furnished in much the same way as our living room in New Bethlehem had been, complete with a smoky mirrored wall. She had a romance book open in her lap and barely looked up to speak.

A puff of air escaped my throat in a reserved show of dissatisfaction — too great a show of such emotion might have dire consequences — turned and went upstairs without another word.

I was steamed, not just about the comment, but about her lack of support. She had only once come to a track meet, early in the season, presumably to watch me run, but she could not lower herself to sit on a bleacher. I was embarrassed that she actually drove down into the stadium to a no-parking zone, where she sat in her car to watch from inside it. It was hard to see the other kids' parents so interested in their events while my mother couldn't even rearrange her schedule for the district meet because she had to get her hair done that day.

Despite the fact that she would not support me, she sat there dismissing my good news as inconsequential. As angry as I was about her lack of support and lack of interest in me, I took her comment as another sign that I would never make the grade.

—

Frustration continued to mount during cross-country season. Although I began to build a more consistent performance record following those two bad races, I could never quite reach the lofty goals I set for myself.

When we went to invitational meets, I wanted a trophy so bad I could taste it. Yet each time, I missed one by only a few places. In the first invitational, I placed 13th, but trophies were given only to the top 10. At the next invitational, where trophies were given to the top 20, I was 21st.

In the district qualifier, our team easily earned the right to compete in districts. I managed to place 20th, which would have earned me a spot at districts even if the team hadn't made it. Although I placed a very respectable 30th in the district meet, I went away disappointed, aware only of the fact that I had not done as well as I had hoped.

—

In the Corvette's mechanical speed, I found a source of comfort. When the tension got so high that I needed release, I would take off down McKnight Road — a three-lane open highway that wound its way into a suburban Pittsburgh shopping district — hitting speeds of 110 to 140. The Corvette's speedometer didn't peg until 160, but instinct would take over, keeping me from getting it there. I reasoned the stretch of road from where I lived wasn't long enough for that kind of speed. Of course, none of those stretches of road are suited for that kind of speed. But I didn't care. I would try to beat the traffic lights, which usually managed to slow me down, but not appreciably.

Sometimes, I filled my appetite for speed by drag racing. Driving any Corvette, especially a flashy one, meant getting the attention of every muscle car driver in the area. When another muscle car and mine were first in line at a traffic light, a race was inevitable.

I raced many cars, from Mustangs to Trans Ams to vintage muscle cars with custom paint jobs. I even raced an older man in Buick. One day, around dusk, I was headed north toward home, sprinting from the traffic light at the end of the McKnight business district, when I let the engine's power explode out into the open road. As I picked up speed, I noticed in my rearview mirror an approaching vintage red Chevelle SS with two white stripes running from the hood to the trunk. I had to maneuver around one or two cars to catch up with me as I slowed for the light ahead.

As I saw him pull up next to me, I suppressed an overpowering urge to grin as I pretended not to notice, my eyes glued to the light governing the cross traffic. When it turned yellow, I held my breath and watched the red light in front of me and waited for the color to change, my hands tight on the steering wheel, left foot on the brake, right foot poised to jump on the gas even before completely releasing the brake.

The light turned, and I punched the accelerator, sending the car surging forward. The pitch of the engine rose as the speedometer climbed. Out of the corner of my eye, I could see a brief hesitation as the Chevelle shifted manually. The Corvette's automatic had a quicker, cleaner shift, helping me to gain the lead. My lack of fear furthered my lead as I continued to hold my foot down on the accelerator until I was flying at well over 100 m.p.h.

I inched ahead for two miles until the next traffic light began to grow larger as we neared it. Waiting to hit my brakes until the last possible moment, I held my lead till the very end.

The Chevelle reached the light a moment after I had stopped, and, glancing out the passenger side window, I saw it back up about a foot so that its nose was even with mine. It was a clear challenge. I looked over and grinned at my competition, a young kid with straight blonde hair who grinned back. I could see he had a passenger but could not see the other person's face.

Winning strategy meant I had no time to study the other driver or his passenger. I turned to face forward, my eyes turned to the lights governing cross traffic and then switched my attention to the light in front of me as it was about to turn green. I had won the last race, but clearly, my competition considered the finish to be unofficial. This was for real.

As the light turned green, I punched the accelerator and held on to the steering wheel as the Corvette picked up speed like an Olympic sprinter coming out of the starting blocks. The Chevelle shot forward with me, the tires screaming as they raced in useless circles on the pavement. I could make the tires on the Corvette squeal if I wanted, but I saw no point in wasting energy on what amounted to little more than a sound spectacle. My car's engine and mechanical parts had more important things to do, like getting to the finish line first.

The Chevelle pushed harder, and as I saw its nose approaching my passenger-side window, I pushed down on the accelerator a little more. The tip of the orange speedometer needle continued to move towards 110. As the other driver met the challenge, the Chevelle picked up speed, matching my increase in speed until we were doing 120. With about a mile of open road ahead of us, I pressed the accelerator just a little bit harder, and the speedometer needle eased towards 130, more than three-quarters of the way around.

The Chevelle apparently had nothing left, its nose dropping out of my peripheral vision as the Corvette, which still had plenty of power to spare, raced ahead unchallenged.

With a triumphant smile, I let off the gas and hit the brake for the approach to the next regulated intersection. Coming to a stop, I looked for the Chevelle but didn't see it for a moment until it came to a stop next to me, steam pouring out from under its hood.

"Is that me or you?" asked the blonde driver as he looked out his window first toward the front of his car and then to mine.

"I think it's you," I said, feeling triumphant that I had won so decisively but respecting the other driver for having the guts to push it to the limit.

Unfortunately, I couldn't see that I deserved the same respect for pushing my racing body to the limit every time I ran a race, even when I failed to win.

—

Despite the frustrations, running still brought me moments of unparalleled joy. Whether I won or not, my workouts released endorphins into my brain, elevating my moods and giving me a fleeting sense of purpose and self-worth.

On some level, I realized that perhaps bringing home trophies or medals in my first year of competition was expecting too much of myself. However, I was also driven by the belief that expecting success would result in better performances than if I went easy on myself. Analyzing the situation, I considered the possibility that cross country really wasn't my best sport. My favorite race was still the mile, and another complete track season lay ahead of me, full of inviting possibilities.

I could not allow myself to lower my expectations, however. I was a senior; it was my last chance. Sure, I was a rookie and a talented one who achieved all the more through dedication and hard work. But that didn't change the fact that I had only one more season to prove myself before graduation and that I was competing against kids who had four years, sometimes more, to train. The conflict between realistic expectations and my lack of training time worked together to put me under enormous pressure — in addition to the stress my mother constantly put on me.

As graduation approached, the burden my mother laid on me grew exponentially. She knew I was smart, and I was. After all, I'd earned the respect of the not-too-easily-impressed Dr. Sheffer. Therefore, my mother reasoned that I should be able to get a free ride to college on an academic scholarship.

But such plans for me would not pan out. I was no prodigy. Every one of my honors and AP classmates was at least equally capable. No matter how hard I tried, I could not make her understand that the only way for me to go to college — since she said she could not pay my tuition from her pocket — was to go through the financial aid process. It was a reasonable conclusion drawn from sound evidence, but that never was good enough for my mother.

What I didn't realize at the time was this expectation was not motivated by her belief in me but rather by her greed.

The problem appears to have been that she had already spent most of the more than $65,000 she received from my dad's death. In fact, at $10,000, the Corvette represented two years of college tuition, room and board.

She'd also bought a mink coat, diamonds, and other jewelry, a new luxury Oldsmobile for herself, and trips to Hawaii and Acapulco, yet her spending never slowed. No doubt she still had cash on hand, and she couldn't let the financial aid people know about this. No wonder she didn't want to apply for financial aid.

I understood that she was being unfair, and I began to reject the notion that I had somehow brought it on myself. I actually believed I could solve the problem by becoming independent. When I would reach the point where I needed nothing from her, I could refuse to tolerate the behavior. College was the most logical first step in my plans to get out of the house and reach this goal.

To placate her in the meantime, I applied to a couple of Ivy League schools, but I had every intention of choosing a college based on my criteria, not hers. First and foremost, any college I considered would have to have a track program. My mother would simply shake her head in dismay as I threw bucket loads of college brochures in the trash with no other explanation than "no track team."

When she tried to get me to enroll in college early so she could continue receiving Social Security death benefits, I found the courage to buck her, mostly because I couldn't bear the thought of giving up my dream. After all, I lost the opportunity to run track in ninth and tenth grade because we moved to Redbank

Valley. Had we stayed put, I could have joined the Norwin track team in ninth grade, which would have put me on equal footing with my now more experienced peers. After being cheated out of two years, I was indignant that she would force me down a road that would mean losing a third. I would enroll early in college if I absolutely had to, but I would not do so willingly.

Running was, indeed, a powerful motivator.

—

Running was also my escape, keeping me away from home for a couple more hours each day. The less I was home, the less ridicule and fewer temper tantrums I had to endure.

January's start of winter workouts was a relief after several long months of being home almost every day after school. This year was a bit different in that I knew to follow the workouts for the distance runners rather than sprinters. I quickly made my mark as the best miler and two-miler on our team.

In the second meet of the season, I found myself up against the district champion in the two-mile. I suppose I could have let myself get psyched out, believing I didn't have a chance, but I never allowed myself to consider the possibility. When the race began, the district champ started slowly, and everyone on both teams held back to keep pace with her. Even though we all knew she was playing with us, no one wanted to dart ahead, knowing that would be utter foolishness. If she was saving her energy for later so, then, must we.

Suddenly, as we began the second lap, she darted ahead like a bird of prey headed for dinner. I immediately took off after her as if I had to get the prey first in order to survive.

My coaches were ecstatic. "That's the way, Jo! Go after her!" Mr. Cerny shouted, practically dancing across the outside lane with the vigor of a kid who just landed a date with the homecoming queen.

Despite my best effort, the district champ won the race, and I placed second, probably a good 15 seconds, or 100 yards, behind. As she crossed the finish line, she turned to look behind her to see what my coaches had been yelling about. Her expression seemed to say, "Who *is* this girl, and where did she come from?"

Later that season, I felt a peculiar mixture of anxiety and excitement to see that a trio of distance runners from the team we were about to run against had hit mile times 10 to 15 seconds faster than mine. The anxiety was natural since they were good, and a good race against them could not be a matter of chance. The excitement came from knowing that victory was possible if I ran well.

At a moment when the anxiety was peaking, I mentioned to Coach Cerny that I'd seen my opponents' times in the newspaper.

"You have nothing to worry about," he said casually. "You can run with them."

His answer took me by surprise, yet it didn't. He always said it was easy to run against "the fish," meaning the runner who is not in shape or not competitive. But the real victory was achieved when you rose to a real challenge. "There's no such thing as luck," he would say, usually to the collective groan of the rest of the team. "You've got to make your own breaks."

I disagree with the part about luck. Luck is circumstance. It was luck that my sister was profoundly disabled, my father was dead, and my mother teetered on the brink of total insanity. But making one's own breaks was something I could believe in. I had made my own breaks by convincing my mother I needed to stay in high school instead of going to college early. I would go on to make my own breaks by becoming a nationally award-winning journalist. And I would make my own breaks by giving these three opponents a hard race.

Because I was a virtual unknown, these three girls didn't take me seriously. They figured they had first, second, and third place in the bag with nary a heavy breath. But by the first half of the first lap, they began to realize they had underestimated the competition. I stayed with them. No matter how hard they ran or how hard they tried to unnerve me, running in a pack around me, they couldn't shake me. I was determined to keep pace.

As we raced toward the finish line, I opened up with a sudden burst of speed, and each of them attempted to match me. We crossed the line in a cluster, and I was judged to be third by about a 10th of a second. Although disappointed that I hadn't won, I was pleased with my performance and my time, more than 10 seconds faster than my previous best. It represented big possibilities for the future.

As it turned out, a college recruiter had come to watch someone else — the three girls I ran against, perhaps — and was impressed with my race. We talked several times, but I put him off, mostly because I knew my mother would never accept my taking an athletic scholarship. Though I never understood why, she had repeatedly told me that an athletic scholarship simply "wasn't good enough." Since my survival meant keeping peace in the house, I let this opportunity slip by and lived to regret it.

That spring, I once again qualified for districts, this time in both the mile and two-mile. Although I failed to place, I ran much better races than the previous year. I had accomplished a lot in a short time, but I remained disappointed that the level of success I truly desired still eluded me.

—

As graduation neared, my mother's sullen moods increased. She had begun to resent any time I spent with friends and tried to discourage me without ever saying I couldn't go out.

"So I suppose I'm stuck here all night alone," she'd say, and when I didn't answer, she'd continue. "Well, go ahead. Have a good time, and by all means, don't worry about me."

When that failed to stop me, she began insisting I make her dinner, but most of the time, she wouldn't eat. I would be left to clean up everything while she sat silent and still in the kitchen, her lips pursed in a frown, making me work around her as if she were a statue.

Guilt was indeed a powerful deterrent, but not quite as powerful as my desire to escape, even if only for a few hours.

—

By July, I began counting the days till summer's end, eagerly looking forward to a long-awaited escape to life in a college dorm. I started my freshman year at Penn State with my tuition unpaid, and my mother continuing to fight the system. She continually refused to provide the required documentation or to clarify information when asked. I would eventually have my aid revoked because of it.

The worst part of all this was that she was telling her family, coworkers and her few remaining friends that she was paying for my college education. When I would drop out three years later — burdened with nearly $10,000 in debts from loans taken out to cover the shortfall created when my college aid was revoked — I would face the scorn of these people, all of whom mistakenly believed I was unmotivated and ungrateful.

I had no idea that financial aid snafus would be the least of my problems.

- 19 -
EXIT STRATEGY

My mother was hours late picking me up on the last day of my freshman year at Penn State. What had been my home only the day before was now an empty cell made of painted cinderblock walls rising from a gray floor. All my belongings were packed neatly in boxes and stacked on the bare mattress that had been my bed for the previous nine months.

My roommate, along with everyone else in the building, was already gone. I paced the floors, periodically glancing at my watch, wishing I had some other way to pass the time. I knew that if I left to take a walk or get a meal, I risked upsetting my mother by being gone when she arrived. I hoped that by staying put and having everything ready, she would have no reason to be angry or to criticize me.

But, as usual, she found something. I don't remember what it was, only that she screamed and ranted the entire time we loaded the car. I'd forgotten just how bad it could get and realized that I had accomplished nothing over the previous nine months. I had gotten out of the house, yes, but what good was that when I had to return to the same miserable environment for the summer?

My mother calmed down by the time we arrived home and got the car unpacked. We got along relatively well at first, but over the summer, our relationship gradually deteriorated.

"I'm hungry," she announced one day as she sat in her favorite chair. "How 'bout going and getting me a Wendy's hamburger?"

"Ok, what do you want on it?" I asked since this was back in 1983 when you had to list exactly what you wanted on every sandwich.

"Nothing. Just a hamburger."

"You want a plain hamburger?" I asked, wanting to make sure I understood precisely what she was asking.

"Yeah, a plain hamburger," she said, nodding her head as if to say I was stupid to ask for clarification.

I headed to the fast food place about two miles away and ordered exactly what she'd told me she wanted. When I returned, I gave her the bag and her change and then turned to go upstairs.

Part way up the steps, I was summoned back downstairs with an angry scream. "Johanna!"

"What?" I sighed as I spoke the word, drawing it out.

"What is this?" she asked when I reached the doorway. I could see her holding up a half-wrapped sandwich.

"It's your hamburger," I said, trying not to sound too angry, though my blood pressure was rising.

"You know I would never want a plain hamburger!" she shouted, her forehead wrinkling over narrowed eyes. "I can't eat this!" She tossed it down on the bag with a snap of her wrist as if it were poison.

"But that's what you told me to get," I protested, trying to stand as still as possible to avoid aggravating her further, even though my chest felt like it would explode.

She turned her head to the side and then faced forward again as if she had started to shake it and changed her mind half way through. "What do I always get on my hamburgers?"

I shrugged and told her the truth. "I don't know."

She exhaled as she lifted both her arms and set them down again with a soft thud. "You ought to know I always get five slices of tomato." Her chin jutted forward as she spoke, punctuating her statement.

"I'm sorry, I honestly didn't remember that." I lowered my head slightly and shrugged.

"Well, if you loved me, you'd know that." She turned her head to look away.

"What?" I asked, incredulous and unsure if I possibly could have heard that correctly. "You're telling me that if you love someone, you automatically know what they want on their hamburger?" I was certain my eyes were as wide as my open mouth.

"Yes," she snarled without turning to look back at me.

"Do you want me to go get you another hamburger?"

"No."

"How about I slice a tomato for you to put on it?"

"No." She hadn't stuck out her lower lip, but she was pouting just the same, much like a 5-year-old would when told he can't have ice cream.

"Okay," I said, throwing my arms in the air as I turned to leave. As I climbed the stairs to my room, still amazed that she would say such a thing, I vowed I would not return home the following summer.

Of course, I still had the rest of this summer to contend with, and it was fraught with the same kinds of pitfalls. I was expected to fall back into my old routine of servitude, which now included grocery shopping. Standing in the kitchen, I questioned my mother on what we needed so that I could make a list.

"Get some ice cream," she said as she glanced into the freezer to see what it did and did not contain.

"What kind?"

"Get something I don't like."

"You want ice cream, but not anything you like?"

"Yeah, get it for yourself. I don't need to eat it." Her tone was pleasant enough, and, knowing how the strength of her sweet tooth always seemed to be at war with her desire to be thin, her comment actually made sense. I felt a twinge of sadness for her. At 5 feet 4 inches and about 140 pounds, she was not fat by any means. She had a bit of a belly, but her arms and legs were muscular, and she could dress to hide what little extra weight she had. Yet I was always aware that she wanted a body more like mine — I stood just under 5 feet tall and maintained 92 pounds. She wanted to look like a distance runner but without actually doing any distance running.

When I returned from the store, my mother helped me unpack and put away the groceries. Working together peacefully, I was feeling safe until she suddenly bellowed, "You got chocolate ice cream?"

"Yeah," I said, my voice rising toward the end of the word

to express that I was really asking why she had questioned me about it.

"I hate chocolate ice cream!" she shouted, tossing aside the half-gallon cardboard container. "Why couldn't you think of someone else besides yourself and get something I like too?" She turned to look at me and her eyes really did seem to be questioning me.

"You told me to get something you didn't like," I said flatly.

"I can't believe you'd be that insensitive," she said, looking at the ice cream and then back at me.

"You told me to get something you didn't like," I repeated, busying my nervous fingers by slowly putting the other groceries away.

"Now, why would I say that?"

Didn't this woman's brain have memory cells? No more than an hour and a half before, she had told me to get ice cream, but not a flavor she liked, because she didn't want to be tempted to eat it. Now, she was claiming she never said that. No matter what I said, she would make me feel stupid.

She snorted, shook her head, and turned to leave the kitchen.

I put the rest of the food away and prayed for fall to come quickly.

—

That summer, between my first and second years in college, my mother decided to sell the Corvette. "You understand, right?" she said after offering some sort of justification for her decision. I told her I did, and even believed it. I had never really allowed myself to think of the car as mine anyway. It was just another tool for her to use to manipulate me. Selling it left one less weapon in her arsenal.

In addition to selling the Corvette, she traded in her Oldsmobile and used the two to buy herself a Mercedes. She also bought me a used 1980 Fiat Strada, a light blue four-cylinder compact car. I named it "Pokey" in an ironic honor of the Corvette. It was a car I could take to school, providing me the independence necessary to avoid another end-of-the-year moving disaster. That car would set off an important chain of events.

When Ken saw the car at the beginning of my sophomore year, he playfully warned me that "Fiat" stood for "Fix It Again Tony," and this car proved that saying true. Things always seemed to be going wrong, whether it was something important like the fuel pump or something seemingly minor like a broken window crank.

Meanwhile, my mother got me a job as an "extra" at the department store where she worked. As an extra, I would not be assigned to any one department, but rather, I would work wherever they needed me during school breaks or over the summer.

One morning, when the Fiat was in the garage for repairs, I needed a ride to work. My mother said she would take me, but she was running late, as usual. As she was getting ready, she lost one of her contact lenses and called me to help her find it. Her customary screaming and ranting accompanied our attempts to locate the contact. Since I was already supposed to be at work by that time, I told her I wanted to call my boss to let her know I'd be late.

"NOOOOO!" she screamed, "Get your ass back in here and help me find my contact!" I knew this was a bad call and one that would have consequences for me and not for her. But I obeyed out of habit.

When I got to work, I ran into my boss, who demanded to know why I was late and didn't even have the courtesy to call. I found myself shamed into silence. What explanation could I possibly offer? That my crazy mother — who this woman regarded as a sane colleague — had forbidden me to call? I simply nodded my head in agreement as my boss angrily told me what I had done was irresponsible and that it better not happen again.

I was becoming painfully aware that appeasing my mother was no longer an option. This had to stop.

I took a big step just a few days later when I put a stop to my mother's physical abuse. That was when I walked away from her screaming and calling me names over her difficulties assembling a shelving unit and then blocked her punches when she tried to hit me.

Her next tactic was withdrawal. If ranting, screaming, and throwing punches couldn't control me, then she would punish me by shutting me out. She didn't speak to me until the day I left for my summer job as a counselor at a Girl Scout camp. I had sought the opportunity more because I would live at the camp — and away from my mother — than because of what I would be doing.

—

When I arrived back at Penn State in late August, I was grateful for the escape. But I knew it was only temporary. With no relatives I could depend on, I feared that come early May, I would find myself with nowhere to go but back to my mother.

Adding to the knots in my stomach was anxiety over my

tuition, which remained unpaid for my freshman year. My mother had finally filled out all the financial aid forms, but she refused to claim Social Security death benefits as part of her income for my senior year in high school. Her rationale was she had lost that income so she should not have to claim it. Whatever her reasons, the computer into which aid applications were fed repeatedly rejected her answer — it would not accept that she received no death benefits when my father was listed on the application as "deceased."

I met with several university aid representatives, who explained to me what was happening. It seemed so simple, I couldn't wait to tell my mother that all she had to do in order to end this ordeal was to include death benefits on the correction forms she had repeatedly received. Those administering aid realized these benefits had been cut, but they still had to be recorded for the application process to continue.

"I know that's what they say!" she shouted into the phone. "But they're going to factor that income into your aid eligibility!"

"But—" She cut me off.

"Tell those assholes I have not received that money since you've been in college, and I refuse to claim it."

There was no use arguing, even though I knew she had received benefits through my 18th birthday, which took place in October of my freshman year at Penn State. I hung up, glad she was 150 miles away. Returning to the aid office, I explained between sobs that I had no idea how to get my mother to understand what needed to be done and that I feared I would not be able to attend classes this year. Although it required extra paperwork — which I had to run from office to office on my own — the university allowed me to stay in school, and aid office employees continued trying to get my mother to cooperate.

My mother was an intelligent woman, and now I realize she knew exactly what she was doing. She wasn't confused by the aid process at all. She was punishing me for not dropping out of high school to enroll in college early so she could keep receiving Social Security benefits. And she was hiding the fact that, because of my father's death, she'd received more than enough cash to pay my tuition had she wanted to.

—

My grades during my sophomore year were proof that something was most definitely wrong. My semester GPA for the fall was 1.5, and for the spring, it was 1.88.

Penn State's business program didn't allow freshmen to take any business courses, so I didn't get even a taste of what I was getting myself into until my sophomore year — when my world began to self-destruct. I did okay in accounting, but I didn't like quantitative business analysis and actively despised economics.

Penn State's class structure further discouraged me. Classes like these were held in auditoriums filled with hundreds of people. The instructor, looking as small as a piece of lint, stood in the front of the huge room with a microphone and an overhead projector. You could not ask questions because no one could hear you. My accounting classes were smaller, but the instructor didn't show up half the time, instead leaving us to play a videotape of her lectures. If you had a question, you had to try to track her down outside of class.

I responded to the academic environment by having what

I considered a "perfect week." That meant I didn't go to a single class from Monday morning to Friday afternoon. In my mind, classes were a waste of time anyway, so why bother?

It was clear that what my mother wanted for me was not going to work. Knowing she'd have a fit if she found out about my grades, I said nothing. But I knew I couldn't continue this way. Changing my major only brought scorn from my mother. After she berated me, I silently stewed. Over the years, this tactic had proven to be the safest course of action. I stewed not only because of her disapproval but also because of the financial crisis she created for me. As the counselor said, my mother had no right to dictate my choices, especially while only pretending to be my benefactor.

—

The stress I endured took its toll on my entire being, starting with my running during my second collegiate cross-country season. We typically did our most difficult workouts on Mondays and Wednesdays, leaving Tuesdays, Thursdays, and Fridays open for team members to run 5 to 7 miles on their own. Just as my world was starting to close in on me, the coach decided to tighten the reins by having us do controlled pace distance runs on Tuesdays and Thursdays.

For me, running alone had always served as meditation time and a chance to get away from everything and everyone, especially the problems my mother was always creating for me. Running in a big group while the coach drove by in a van, shouting times at mile intervals, took away my precious solitude.

At Penn State's main campus, time alone is scarce at best. I had a roommate, and although I could predict her comings and goings to a point, most times, I didn't know when or if I could have the room to myself. No other place on campus offers the least bit of solitude. People are everywhere, hallways, parking lots, stairwells. Virtually every nook and cranny of the campus is inhabited 24 hours a day, seven days a week, when school is in session. Even classrooms are inhabited during off hours. If you're lucky enough to find a solitary spot, your solitude will be repeatedly interrupted by people passing through. To lose the ability to be effectively alone overwhelmed my already overloaded psyche.

It wasn't long before I dreaded going to practices, and that scared me even more. Running was the only thing I cared about and yet I didn't want to do it.

I looked into transferring to other colleges but never contacted the coaches who had tried to recruit me, fearing the possibility they would no longer want me. I was beginning to wonder if I had lost whatever it was that had made me a good runner. Plus, the financial problems my mother was creating would have made transfer difficult, if not impossible.

As my world came crashing down around me, I made the painful decision to leave the team. Foolishly, I thought walking away from my athletic problems was the answer to what was bothering me.

—

It was amid the turmoil that I found an ally — Ken.

Like many college girls, I went to frat parties. Although beer was freely available, I seldom drank because drinking came with its own set of problems. I'd already found that beer and my temper didn't mix. Still, I enjoyed the music and dancing.

A friend who was also on the track team accompanied me to a party in April of our freshman year. Before long we were dancing mostly with Ken and his friend Jim. They were both tall and skinny, but Jim looked a bit more proper than Ken with wavy brown hair, glasses, and a pouty expression that you could picture at a prep school. Ken had what I call a hopeful mustache — there was just a little bit of hair on either side of his lips but not much in the middle. He was much quieter than Jim, letting his friend do most of the talking.

"Where you from?" Jim asked above the noise of the banging dance music.

"Pittsburgh," we both said. Rhonda was actually from Canonsburg, located a half hour or so south of the city. But Pittsburgh was a simpler answer.

"And you?" I asked.

"Oh, we're from a tiny little town I bet you've never heard of," said Jim.

"Try me," I said. After all, I had heard of New Bethlehem.

"Tunkhannock," Jim said.

Thinking he had said Duncannon, which is located near Harrisburg, I said I'd heard of it.

"You have?" He perked up, lifting his head a little higher, and smiling with real pleasure. "Wow!"

I realized my mistake as the boys walked us home but said nothing. I didn't want to disappoint Jim since my comment seemed to have made his whole day.

But it was Ken with whom I had bonded. He and I wrote letters over the summer and were pleased to be able to continue the relationship in person at the start of my sophomore year. When my world began crashing down on me, Ken was there for me, offering a patient listening ear and encouragement to follow whatever path I believed was best.

—

If my childhood were a watercolor painting, the time in Middletown with my family intact would begin on the left side of the canvas with mottled shades of pastel yellow and peach interspersed with white. Norwin brings in shades of blue and yellow, a little bit darker than the Middletown colors, but still bright. On the far right of the canvas, the colors for North Allegheny would mirror those of Middletown, except they'd be darker as if they were made up of both Middletown's and Norwin's colors.

In between Norwin and North Allegheny would be a black stripe done with heavy oil paints that refuse to dry. The thick muck of tacky blackness would spill from the borders of that stripe, covering up small sections of my time at both schools.

This stripe represents my time at Redbank Valley.

Like a swamp too mucky and dangerous to cross, the black band from Redbank Valley kept me on the right-hand side of the canvas, from where I could access only memories of North Allegheny. Ken helped me to build a bridge over the tacky, wet oil paint on my canvas to reach the other side. There I stood on the left side of the canvas, looking at images from my past that I had kept so deeply locked away that I barely remembered them. The longer I stood over there, the more familiar these images began to seem. I recognized a little girl who liked caterpillars and red bugs and who played wagon train with her disabled sister.

It would be almost a full 20 years until I could uncover the muck of the black stripe and begin to remember my life in New Bethlehem. But by first looking at Middletown and Norwin, I began to emerge from the coma in which I'd existed. As I came out of survival mode, I could finally begin living.

This process was not without its price, however. As I began to recall these things, even seemingly happy things, I began to remember the pain. To my horror, the emptiness I felt was not just because I needed to escape my mother's clutches but also because I had lost my father, my sister, my dog, my cats, my friends, and even my home several times over.

—

Although I couldn't actively remember what had happened during those two years in New Bethlehem, I began to experience some of the pain from that time. And with that came the rage.

When Ken and I went to see the Clint Eastwood movie *Sudden Impact* on campus, a guy sitting behind us thought the rape scenes were fodder for jokes. As the screen showed a flashback to a brutal gang rape, he made remarks like, "Hey look, he's having fun with his girlfriend!"

The movie scenes, combined with his rude comments and my stifled memories of sexual assault, were just too much. As he made another rude remark, I rose from my seat, whirled around, and, in one fluid motion, plunged my fist into his face. Since he was in the very back row of the theater, I had no concern about blocking the view of others. I let my fists work freely like a cartoon character's running legs while I berated him for his rude and unappreciated remarks. His friends sat there in stunned silence until long after I turned and sat down again.

Watching the rest of the movie, I felt tense as I battled with the barrage of frightening feelings creeping up on me. But at least the jerk was silent.

When the movie ended and the lights came on, we stood to leave. I kept my back to the macho idiot so he could see the red lettering on the back of my white Converse t-shirt. "USA/TAC Women's 20K Championships." Although I don't really know why, I wanted him to know I was an athlete. Perhaps I felt some fear that he might retaliate, and I wanted him to know that I was strong enough to make retaliation difficult.

Whether it was my shirt or his conscience, he made no move to further aggravate me. To my surprise, he caught Ken's eye and said, "Sorry, man." Ken simply nodded and frowned. I thought it strange that this guy would apologize to Ken and not me, but since I didn't look at him, I wouldn't have known if he tried to get my attention.

I'm sure Ken never expected to see such fury come from me. But he didn't judge. I told him that I'd been assaulted when I was 15 and that this person's comments upset me.

"Mmmmhmmm, yeah," he said, and then a grin began to creep up to his face. "That and he deserved it."

—

By the fall of my junior year, things had begun to make some sense. I had chosen my own major rather than the one my mother had chosen for me, and I returned to school eager to work hard at it.

I also began to run seriously again. I had never actually stopped my daily distance runs but I had not thought about competition for much of the previous year. As things had begun to fall into place in my personal life, I began to think I could make my mark even without running for the university team.

The second week of school, Ken and I entered a 10K race about 45 minutes from campus. At the end of the race, a man approached me and identified himself as the coach of a cross country team at a small college somewhere nearby, the name of which I no longer remember.

"You beat all of my runners," he said.

I grinned.

"Do you go to school?"

"Yes, at Penn State."

"Are you on their team?"

I hesitated a moment before saying no.

"Would you want to transfer?"

I could kick myself now for saying that I didn't. I suppose it was because Ken, the only person I trusted at that time, was at Penn State, and I was frightened of being alone again.

—

At the end of September, Ken and I ran the Pittsburgh Great Race. Streets were closed to allow the runners to make their way through the city to finish at the Point, the city's famous park situated at the meeting of the three rivers that flow through the city.

Starting in a mob, it took us 30 seconds to make it to the actual starting line. But the course was relatively easy, and I flew along like the Corvette racing the Chevelle. In the fifth mile, I passed a dark-haired girl who looked surprisingly like the unbeatable high school district champ in the two-mile. Could it really be?

When I got to the finish line a few seconds behind Ken, I breathlessly refused to get water or refreshments until I saw this person finish. As she came into the chute a couple of minutes later, my eyes darted to her name, printed on the detachable lower portion of her race number. Yes, it was who I thought it was.

My time was just under 40 minutes, which wasn't incredibly fast, but it was still good enough to put me 27th out of 2250 female competitors and 870th against the entire field, estimated to number about 13,000. But I had beaten our high school district champ! Yes, it was actually possible I could achieve great things on my own.

—

That fall had brought some other unexpected good news. The track and cross country teams had a new coach. A different coaching philosophy might be just what I needed! I trained hard and ran road races almost every weekend as I contemplated the potential of returning to the team. I knew cross country wasn't my sport, so I waited until the season was over before approaching her.

I was scared. Surely, a nobody who had quit once would not be the coach's idea of the perfect recruit. But to my surprise, she was receptive. My universe was, indeed, returning to order.

—

At an away meet during the indoor track season. I ran the two-mile in 11:35, considerably faster than I had ever run it before. When I came across the finish line, my coach was unimpressed.

"You didn't compete," she said.

"What?" I had just run my best race ever in the two-mile, and she didn't think I had competed.

"You may have run your best time, but you didn't compete," she said, looking directly into my eyes. She was tiny like me, with bobbed dirty blonde hair and small features. And, like me, she was not someone who let others get away with anything. "When someone passed you, you didn't try to go after them. You just let them go."

She was right. Instead of taking off like a spooked horse, the way I had when running against our district champ back in high school, I just ran as fast as I thought I could without any real concern for where I finished in comparison to others. I had lost my belief that anything was possible, and it had actually worked against me.

I resolved to do whatever I could to get my edge back.

—

By outdoor season, the coach was training me for the 10K, which is 6.2 miles or 10 kilometers. The distance, which translates to 25 laps around the track, was perfect for both my speed and endurance; plus, I had run road races this distance almost every weekend.

The challenge of the distance was boredom, something that could send the ill-prepared runner into lala land. When I raced the 10K on the track, I tried to envision myself at Pittsburgh's North Park, where I had run many 10K races. I knew the loop around the lake there well enough to know what the scenery would look like at various points, and I used this to distract myself from the boredom.

Two days before a big invitational meet, I joined two other runners and the coach for a car trip to Virginia for my shot at representing Penn State in the 10K. Because this race took so long, we would run it in the evening, the day before the rest of the meet.

A teammate began running on pace to qualify for the national competition but missed it, having slowed by the end when the competition was too spread out for runners to effectively use each other. I had been on pace to qualify for the eastern regional competition, but I also slowed enough to miss qualifying by about a minute.

Still, I placed sixth and earned a medal. I was ecstatic.

Later that evening, we walked into the hotel room where the rest of our teammates were waiting. The coach announced that two of us — one of whom was me — had medalled. Everyone applauded. They were applauding for my teammate, but they were also applauding for *me*. For a brief moment, and for the first time in my life, I felt like I truly belonged. It was the highlight of my running career.

—

By all accounts, things were beginning to happen for me. I ran faster times in practice than I had run in races in high school. I was going to away meets, and though I wasn't the star, I was scoring points for the team. And I had two more years of NCAA eligibility yet.

But those two years would never come.

I did fairly well academically during my junior year, either making the dean's list or coming close. But I was feeling burnt out. When I calculated that I'd need two or maybe even three years to finish my new major, I felt hopelessness wash over me. And Ken was nearly finished with college, which meant I would be alone on campus.

I despised school and I wanted out. Fortunately, I had Ken on my side. He probably didn't realize the importance of his genuine interest in my past, but he suspected I needed an escape. My track coach was supportive, though she warned me that it might not be as easy as I expected. I knew that, but I also knew it was impossible to convey to someone else that I truly had not other choice. No longer doomed, I set out to make a life for myself.

- 20 -

GAINING INDEPENDENCE

The first time I saw a manure spreader in action, I thought I would split a rib laughing.

As an adult living in a rural town not far from Allentown, I've seen a wide variety of manure spreaders, but none of them touch my funny bone quite the same way as the one Ken's family used. Pulled behind a tractor, the long rectangular wagon had a number of mechanical arms that would fling the manure — which I'd always known by another name — up into the air. Not only was the sight of it hilarious, but also a joyous metaphor for purging myself of the manure in my life.

Living on a farm certainly was an adventure. The summer I spent with Ken's family opened my mind to possibilities and new ways of thinking that I'd never considered before. These things stuck, not unlike the way the manure sticks to the ground, ultimately improving it. Although I was 20 years old, emotionally, I was a young child and, like a growing tot out on her first adventure, I saw this lifestyle as a reflection of what life could be, and the possibilities were exciting.

As a result of my experiences in New Bethlehem, I was apprehensive when Ken told me he was from "a small town." But Tunkhannock, which has a population about double that of New Bethlehem, is no more than 45 minutes from downtown Wilkes-Barre and Scranton. Not nearly so backwoods, Tunkhannock welcomed me, coddling me safely in her breast in a way that New Bethlehem never would. A loyal core of residents live in Tunkhannock and will probably die there, but strangers are not usually considered undesirable. The only time I was aware of town gossip was when a person interviewing me for a job asked, "So, are you still living with Kenny?"

Life in Tunkhannock would form a new basis of trust in my world, thereby paving the way for me to create a satisfying adult life in other towns I'd come to call my own.

———

By sharing Ken's rural lifestyle, I learned to appreciate chickens.

It was during my sophomore year at college that Ken first took me home to meet his family — parents, two brothers, a dozen or so Holstein cows, and about two dozen chickens.

"What are those?" I said shortly after stepping inside the barn and looking toward the corner coop containing the cluckers. They walked about, their heads darting forward and back as they pranced and pecked at the ground.

"They're chickens," Ken said, barely able to suppress a laugh.

"I know the white ones are chickens," I said, shaking my

head and half-grinning to indicate that I wasn't as stupid as he thought. "I mean the brown ones."

"They're chickens," he said, giggling like a school boy.

"But they're brown!" I protested, aware that I was actually more ignorant about such things than I had realized.

"They're brown chickens." Ken emphasized the word "brown," his body still shaking gently from the giggles. "Haven't you ever seen a brown chicken?"

"No," I admitted. "I thought all chickens were white."

"These are Rhode Island Reds."

"You mean there's more than one kind of chicken?"

"You got a lot to learn there, city girl."

My introduction to chickens was but one source of laughter for Ken.

"Oh, my god!" I said the first time we rode up the dirt road that led to his house. "A street sign! I can't believe there's a street sign at the intersection of two dirt roads!" I was laughing out loud like a person listening to good stand-up comedy.

Ken glanced at me with his mischievous, half-grinning expression. "Mmmm-hmmmm. Yeah, that's real funny," he said, nodding his head and trying not to laugh as I sat in his car, giggling in the seat beside him.

I'd never seen a real dirt road before, let alone one with a street sign. I'd always assumed dirt roads were located in obscure places and were either abandoned or seldom used. A dirt road intersection with a street sign seemed absurd, but I came to accept the concept as one more surprising possibility among many more to be discovered.

—

Faced with the proposition of integrating myself into Ken's family, I hoped to create the least possible disturbance. I felt my presence was an imposition, even though no one made me feel it was, and I didn't want to take advantage. I planned to get a job, pay rent, and move out on my own as soon as possible. Independence was my eventual goal, after all.

In the meantime, I would experience farm life, and that meant hauling hay, among other things.

Baling was the biggest part of the haying process. One of the tractors would be hitched to the baler, a green machine that sucked up the hay and formed it into heavy rectangles, and tied each bale with twine to hold it together.

Ken's youngest brother, who was still in elementary school, didn't have to help, but I joined Ken and the middle brother, who'd just graduated high school, on the hay wagon for the slow, bumpy ride through the fields, the baler making its chunk-chunk, chunk-chunk sound ahead of us. I liked to sit on the bales piled at the back of the wagon while Ken and his brothers imitated pro wrestlers and otherwise acted like typical boys. I wasn't quite tall enough to reach the bales coming off the baler, so one of the boys would have to grab them, and I'd help stack them.

One or two people would unload the wagon while the rest of us went up into the loft to drag the bales from the pile where the conveyor had dropped them to the back of the loft for stacking.

It was hot work, always done when the weather was expected to be dry — rain would ruin mown hay — so rain would be unwelcome even if it would cool us. Like Ken and his family, I wore jeans to avoid getting my legs scratched up by the sharp pieces of dried hay that invariably stuck out from the bales. The loft of the barn was huge — probably the same square footage as a small ranch house — and the second floor of the loft was hot even with the ventilation provided by the large square opening where the conveyor entered to drop its cargo.

By the time the hay made it from the fields to a neat stack in the loft, we were all exhausted. But it was good, honest work, and with it came a feeling of accomplishment. As an athlete, I was never afraid of hard physical work, and hauling hay — even when I really didn't want to do it — always left me feeling that I'd done something worthwhile for my body as well as my mind.

Ken's family also grew field corn, sweet corn, and other vegetables, and I spent the summer in awe, watching the veggies develop from seedlings in the early summer to full-grown ripened food by the time they were sold in late summer or early fall.

We'd had a small strawberry patch in Middletown, but never had a vegetable garden that I remember. It's possible my parents intended to have one, or even that they did until Nicole's handicaps became apparent. In any event, the many facets of farm life filled me with awe.

—

"When are you coming home?" My mother had called my dorm at Penn State in early May — before I'd left to live with Ken's family — and asked that very question. I'd mailed her a letter explaining my decision, but I wasn't sure if she had received it.

"I'm not," I said, my heart pounding inside my chest, which was beginning to feel tight like someone had cut off my oxygen supply.

"What do you mean you're not?" she asked, her voice rising with the anger I always expected.

I took a deep breath and released it slowly to calm myself, glad she was 150 miles away. "I'm moving to Tunkhannock," I finally said.

"What?"

I breathed in and out again as quickly and quietly as I could. "I'm moving to Tunkhannock."

"What do you mean you're moving to Tunkhannock?" Her tone was belligerent.

"I'm going to go up there and look for a job," I said.

"Fine, good-bye." I heard the click of the receiver as she suddenly hung up. I stood there in my tiny dorm room next to the phone for several minutes, trying to regain my composure.

Not long after I moved in at Ken's, my mother called again to tell me she wanted my car back.

I discussed the situation with Ken and his parents, who were clearly perplexed, sitting in the living room quietly looking at me with open mouthed faces. Would a mother actually behave this way toward her child? Was this young woman in their home delusional? Neither answer seemed logical, I'm sure. They had only their son's faith in me to assure them they had supported the right side in this war they could barely comprehend.

Next came the hate mail.

"You've enrolled in the school of hard knocks," my mother wrote. "Don't expect me to pick you up when you fall." The rest of the letter chided me for making the "selfish" decision not to return to Pittsburgh.

"You can always come home," began the last paragraph. "If you don't know that, you are truly beyond hope. As far as I am concerned, you, Ken, and his family no longer exist."

Despite her statement that I could always come home, I knew I wasn't really welcome unless I was willing to become an indentured servant. Besides, how could I be welcome if I didn't exist?

I had nothing. No money. No decent job. Everything I owned fit into a tiny car that barely ran. But I had a dream of a safe, happy, and fulfilling life. I could not give up my dream for material comforts that came with impossible conditions. For the time being, my dream of what could be would have to be enough.

—

That summer, Ken continued to gently push me to reveal my past, as well as the feelings that went along with it.

I'd always wanted to play soccer, and in the fall of my sophomore year, I bought a plush, stuffed soccer ball and named it "Tribble" after the creatures on Star Trek. Everyone called it "Treble," so I bought another one and named it "Bass." I actually intended for Bass to be a gift for Ken who had played soccer for Penn State's Wilkes-Barre campus. But I enjoyed having Bass and Tribble together so much that Ken allowed me to adopt Bass.

Eventually, Bass and Tribble had two kids, Midrange and Volume. Bass was slightly larger than Tribble and both were close to the size of real soccer balls. Made of cloth, the two kids were about the size of baseballs. Being without the fur that their plush parents had, they actually did look like babies.

"These guys are your family, aren't they?" Ken asked late one night when we were hanging out together in his family's finished basement.

"Yeah, right," I said with a laugh. I was lying on my back on the couch, and he was beside me as we both played around with the soccer balls.

"I'm serious," he said. He was half smiling, as he usually was.

I gave him a playful frown.

"It's the family you lost." He picked up Bass. "This guy's your dad. That's why you like to carry him around so much. To keep him close."

I stared at Ken with my mouth open in surprise as I took Bass from him and held him. It made perfect sense. There were four soccer balls, two parents, and two kids. The argument that they represented my parents, my sister, and me was startling in the symbolic truth it held.

A wave of emotion washed over me, and I wasn't sure what to make of it. Before I knew it, I was crying. I tossed Tribble aside and refused to hold her. I held on to Bass and began to sob louder.

Ken held me and tried to calm me, worrying that the sound of my cries would wake the rest of the house.

I was in so much pain I didn't care. Tears running wild on my face, I cried, loud wailing sobs. "I want my dad," I said over and over, barely able to get the words out. I could hardly breathe. "It's not fair. Why couldn't she die instead of him?" No longer concerned about my waking the rest of the house, Ken just held me until I fell asleep, exhausted.

—

To support myself and pay rent, I got a job as a waitress at a local diner. During my first week there, the owner came in and started chit-chatting. Since he had not personally hired me, we had to be introduced.

"What did you do before you worked here?" he asked.

With a shy smile, I told him I'd been a college student.

"A college student?" He shifted in his seat so that he was no longer leaning casually backward. "So you didn't work before?"

"I had a work-study job."

"Do you think you earned more than $3,000 last year?"

"Probably not," I said. I had worked part-time for $3.70 an hour at one of the Penn State dining halls.

"Well, you know what?" His short, cropped, graying brown hair blended in with the dark brown paneling behind his nondescript face. "You might qualify for a special program."

"I might?"

"Yeah. It's for people like you who haven't held a full-time job before so you can get extra training. You have to go and fill out an application, and then we can say, train you as a cook in addition to your work as a waitress. That'll make you more valuable to us and give you further opportunity here."

"Ok." It sounded good to me. "Does everybody who works here do this?"

"Oh, no," he said, shaking his head and eyeing me with an expression similar to that of the traveling vacuum cleaner salesman who'd once sold my mother an overpriced Kirby. "Only people we think have potential, and then only if they qualify."

I listened as he gave me directions on where to put in my application and even gave me the afternoon off to do it. "Just don't tell them you already started work here. You have to fill out your application before you start working, or you can't get the extra training."

Although I thought his explanation of this special program was a bit odd, I didn't want to jeopardize my job and, therefore, my ability to earn my keep. So I did as he asked and then waited for someone at the restaurant to mention the extra training. When nothing was said, I asked and got the brush off.

"Huh? He doesn't train waitresses as cooks. You're either one or the other," said a fellow waitress whose shift overlapped mine. She continued to go about her work as if I were a pesky kid trying to get a free soda.

I never saw the diner owner again, and I didn't know his name. Other employees gave me basically the same answer as my fellow waitress. So, when another job offer presented itself, I took it. Within a couple of weeks, I left that job to take another one. Although I never missed a rent payment, I realized I was no better at being a waitress than I was at being a college student. I found I could handle the customers just fine, but I disliked the fact that my hours changed from day to day, week to week. Plus, my anxieties made me feel I didn't fit in with other employees.

As I grew increasingly aware that I was not meant to be a waitress, I began searching for other options. I discovered a technical school nearby and decided to enroll in an auto mechanics course. I'd always been fascinated with cars and wanted to know more about them. It seemed like a good way to explore what I wanted to do with my life.

By the time I contacted the school, the auto mechanics course had already begun and enrollment was closed. So, I enrolled in a diesel class. It wasn't my first choice, but it had to be better than waitressing. I wouldn't learn about carburetors since diesel engines don't have any, but I figured many other elements of diesel and gasoline vehicles would be basically the same.

I qualified for financial aid through the Job Training Partnership Act, or JTPA, a now-defunct Pennsylvania state program designed to provide training for low income people. During the application process, I got an earful from the woman who reviewed my file. "You don't have a very good track record," she told me to my surprise. "We went through this process before, and you didn't stick with it."

I was confused. "What do you mean I didn't stick with it?" I asked, thinking I'd never gone through the program before.

She explained I had — only a couple of months before — when I applied before starting work at the diner.

"But I never got any additional training at the diner," I protested as I realized this was the diner owner's special program.

"Your training started the day you started work!" she snapped.

Aghast, I realized I'd been had. The diner owner never intended to train me or help me in any way. He wanted only to get the state to subsidize my salary, and he could get my labor for less. And I had lied to help him do it.

But what could I do? Tell this woman the diner owner told me to lie? I felt I couldn't risk coming clean and exposing his fraud for fear of incriminating myself. Worse yet, if this woman believed the diner owner over me, which in my experience was the most likely scenario, I wouldn't get the money I needed to pay tuition for mechanics school.

So I did the only thing I felt I could do and accepted responsibility for someone else's misdeed and promised to stick with the tech school. I found myself feeling forced to cover for the diner owner just as I'd covered for my mother.

—

In addition to state assistance through JTPA, the tech school was accredited for state and federal aid. Because I had not lived on my own for two years, however, my mother would have to be involved in the application process, the financial aid officer told me. The JTPA program paid my tuition, but I was most likely eligible for financial aid to cover my living expenses.

"Nah, let's drop the idea. I'm not interested," I said, aware that my mother would never cooperate. I had been through this hassle at Penn State all for naught.

"I think you should apply anyway," the financial aid officer said. "If we can get her refusal to cooperate in writing, we can get your aid."

I thought he was misguided, but it turned out my mother's need to control and manipulate me actually worked to my advantage. When she received the information requests from the school, she probably relished the idea that she could hurt me by ignoring them. Her lack of response only prompted the financial aid officer to send her more forms and inquiries. I knew these would aggravate her to no end. The question was whether we could aggravate her so much that she wouldn't be able to hold back a nasty, written retort.

The answer, ultimately, was yes. The financial aid officer called to tell me that a form came back adorned with her very neat all-capitals printing. "There is no way in hell I'll ever help her get a grant to attend this school or any other," my mother wrote.

When the grant money finally came through, I felt like I had hit the lottery. I bought myself a winter coat and deposited the rest of the $1,500 check into a savings account, grateful to have this small safety net.

—

I made the leap to independence — getting an apartment — after securing a part-time job cleaning the school building after class. I would have barely a dime left over after expenses, but I could do it! I rented the apartment starting Sept. 1, thereby keeping my stay with Ken's family to one summer.

Shortly after I moved in — which was almost three months before I received my $1500 grant — the school relocated our classes to another campus and ended my job. I asked about a job cleaning at the new location, but they had full-time staff there to do it. I was devastated. How could I possibly survive?

"I know you have pride," Ken said, "but you do have an option."

"What?" I asked.

"Now, just hear me out," he said as if he was expecting an argument. "You could apply for welfare. I know that's not what you want to do, but I think you should consider it."

He would have continued his argument, but I cut him off. I would apply. It was ironic that he thought my pride would interfere, considering my living space. But Ken knew I once drove a

Corvette and that my mother drove a Mercedes. He'd been to my mother's house, and he saw the material lifestyle I'd known. From that perspective, it probably seemed inconceivable that I'd consider public assistance. But I knew deep down that I had no choice. I had no one to support me financially. Going back to Pittsburgh simply was not an option.

Holding my head high, I walked into the public assistance office and explained that I'd lost my job suddenly and that I had rent to pay. My father was dead, and my mother disowned me. I did have a lead on a part-time job at Sears Auto Center, but I still had to get through the next couple of weeks until that came through, assuming it would.

I'll never forget the reaction of the blonde middle-aged man who took my application. He'd jotted down notes while I talked. Then suddenly, he stopped, put down his pen, and lifted his head, looking me square in the eye. "You're the kind of person this system is supposed to help. It was designed to help people overcome hurdles, not to serve as a lifestyle."

I smiled and probably blushed.

"I'm proud of you for already exploring other options," he added, holding my gaze for a moment before looking back down at his forms.

I couldn't help but feel proud, too. And I was relieved to learn that I qualified for enough money to pay rent, plus food stamps and a medical card.

I did get my part-time job with Sears and started about a month later, making $4.20 an hour. I calculated my anticipated wages for the 20 hours a week I was available to work and compared them to what one was allowed to earn and retain public assistance. I discovered I'd lose the cash assistance and a portion of both my food stamps and medical coverage. The overall effect would be that my standard of living would actually decrease because of my job.

It was an interesting moment. The decision was easily made, however. I knew that I would have to take this step backward to get ahead in the future, and I did so without ever looking back.

—

Despite the financial difficulties, mechanics school was a fantastic experience. We started by rebuilding engines and I loved getting my first look inside one. It was great to be able to explore a topic that I'd chosen instead of one my mother had chosen for me.

Most of the students were rough-and-tumble types, many of whom were also scorned by their families for whatever reason. Here was a place where I fit in, despite being the only girl. Many of the guys struggled to make ends meet just as I did. I could relate to their cynicism because I felt it, too.

Instead of honing my professional image, I got a kick out of pushing the Fiat to its limit as if it were a go-cart on a little track. Being a small car, its speedometer pegged at only 85, and I was proud to peg it more than once. I learned to manipulate the gears and to make the tires "chirp" when shifting from first to second gear, something that most hot shots thought could be accomplished only with a larger, more powerful engine.

My fellow students introduced me to hard rock and heavy metal music, which had just begun to emerge as an art form at that time. The loud, crashing drums and screaming guitars spoke to the rebel in me who was struggling to break free from the role that had been thrust on me growing up. The music also spoke to the pain. I found the lyrics of bands such as Pink Floyd to be especially soothing. I could hear songs like Pink Floyd's "Mother" and pretend I'd written them about my pain. "Mama's gonna make all of your nightmares come true," the British band crooned. Indeed, mine had.

Pink Floyd's "Comfortably Numb" served as my theme song for several years, particularly because of a passage that mentions a child catching a glimpse of something but growing up and forgetting that dream. I came close to living a normal childhood in Middletown, but suddenly, it was ripped out from under me.

I found Pink Floyd's lyrics to be the most meaningful to my life, but it wasn't the only hard rock band I discovered. I found comfort in the music of Rush, Led Zeppelin, Def Leppard, AC/DC, and any other guitar-banging, society-slamming, loud, offensive band I could find. If the music was bound to bring a frown of disapproval to my mother and everyone like her, then it was for me. Even today, I still enjoy hard rock and heavy metal. Music serves as a source of comfort and a means of processing whatever emotions I'm feeling during the never-ending process of coming to terms with the past.

When mechanics school ended, I said my goodbyes and faced an uncertain future. I had landed the part-time job at Sears Auto Center, but I needed to find a second job. The search was difficult not only because of my lack of experience but also my size. Few people were willing to believe I was strong enough to work on the large diesel machinery on which I'd been trained. I never thought to tell them I'd been a collegiate athlete.

I finally did find a job, not that it really mattered. I was not a good mechanic. I suppose having learned about engines took away the mystery, leaving me disinterested. Still, I don't regret the time I spent in mechanics school or the time spent trying to be a mechanic. It was a worthwhile experience, if for no other reason than it was the first thing I ever tried on my own.

—

"Why did you get an apartment?" my mother asked. She called me in late November, about three months after I'd moved into my first apartment.

"No reason. I just wanted a place of my own," I said, figuring my mother's rather stupid question was her way of beginning to process the fact that I was asserting myself as an adult.

"How are you paying for it?"

"I have a job." At that time, I had only a part-time job and was actively looking for full-time work. But I wasn't about to reveal that I was struggling.

"Doing what?"

"I'm a mechanic." At the time, I was still working part-time at Sears Auto Center.

"What kind of mechanic?"

"Auto."

"Is this that school that you're going to — auto mechanics?"

"Yeah, I went for diesel but I didn't find a diesel job yet. I graduated school on the first."

She paused briefly and then said, "I bet your fingernails are beautiful."

"As a matter of fact, they are," I said with a chuckle.

Then she brought up the subject of my winter coats, which

remained at her townhouse in Pittsburgh, along with some of my other belongings. "What are you going to do about it?" she asked.

"I want to come get them, but I don't know when I'll have the money or the time off. Maybe Jeff would be able to get them for me," I suggested. Jeff was a college friend who lived in the Pittsburgh area, and my mother always approved of him.

After a moment of silence, I asked her for feedback on what I'd just said.

Following another silence which felt like it lasted eons, she said, "Don't go to any trouble." Her words came more rapidly than they had in her previous statements. It was like the calm and peaceful woman who'd been on the phone suddenly became possessed by another person whose whole attitude and manner of speech were different.

"Pardon me?" I said.

"Good-bye." She spoke the word rapidly, as if she were on speed, and immediately hung up the phone.

Although it sounded like she might be trying to renew our relationship, I suspected that she was digging for information that she might find useful in her quest for control. Plus, with Christmas only a month away, she wanted me to show up so she could keep appearances. I resented this even more because she'd ignored my 21st birthday only a few weeks before this phone call.

"I feel like getting away from there was a real load off my shoulders," I wrote in my journal that day. "Kinda like getting out of a pair of tight jeans after a long, tiring day and putting on a pair of comfortable shorts. I was also surprised that she was so nice and felt a little guilty for not feeling elated. I guess I exist now."

Ken and I discussed marriage and the fact that he wanted a "more permanent" relationship. Although Ken had been the first person to ever go out on a limb for me, ultimately, it would not work out for us.

I told him early that summer that I wanted to resume counseling. Neither of us had any idea that, ultimately, becoming a more secure and less angry person would mean first dealing with my overwhelming emotions.

"There was actually an end to the rage. I used to think there was never an end to it," I wrote in my journal in late December 1985 after Ken and I had a big fight. "The rage gave way to intense pain. I think maybe the pain was always there but covered up by all that rage, which was so overpowering that there wasn't a chance of feeling anything else."

Ken didn't know how to handle these intense feelings, and I believe he saw my anger and pain as proof he had failed me in some way. By the time I had moved into my apartment Ken had begun to balk at the idea of getting married. I knew he was hurting, but I didn't know why. He wouldn't open up about what was bothering him, and I saw both this and his hesitation about marriage as rejection.

It was a painful time for both of us. We broke up numerous times, only to get back together and then break up again. Although I had other boyfriends during our breakups, I probably would have married Ken in a heartbeat if he'd said the word. But he never did, and so, two years after I first moved to Tunkhannock, I bonded with the man I would eventually marry and finally got Ken out of my system.

- 21 -

FACING THE GHOSTS

Having both bucked my mother's control and faced her afterward, I felt ready to face bigger and more significant challenges by 1986.

When a friend from Middletown asked me to be a the photographer for her wedding, I accepted, unaware that I wouldn't be able to resist a compulsion to return to the house where I'd grown up.

I remembered the way, easily finding the correct exit from the interstate. The ramp brought traffic to a small highway, where I immediately saw two familiar landmarks. One was the Host Inn, a hotel where my family had gone for New Year's Day in 1975. Nicole, my mother, and I were having breakfast there when Nicole suddenly began shaking violently. In a state of panic, my mother held her and tried to comprehend what was happening. I could see by her wide eyes and open mouth that she was scared, as was I. Later, Nicole was diagnosed as being epileptic and put on medication to control her seizures.

Next door to the hotel was an abandoned Mobil gas station. The last time I'd been there was 10 years ago. It was still in business then, and gas was 48.9 cents a gallon. My dad seemed to know the people who ran it, as he seemed to know everyone. Whenever we stopped there, he would chat with the attendants while I listened to the conversation from the back seat. Mobil had been giving away Noah's ark play sets with plastic animals at that time, and my dad made a point of getting gas there as often as possible so I could complete my set.

But this time, instead of friendly faces, I saw only a desolate white building in the parking lot. The red horse was still flying over its roof, but the word "Mobil" was no longer underneath it. As I got out of the car and compulsively photographed the site, my heart felt as empty as the gas station lot. My defense mechanisms were working, keeping emotion at bay, allowing me to survive as they always had.

The short detour to my old neighborhood, located between these landmarks and my friend's house, seemed almost natural. I easily found my old house and stopped. I got out of the car and stood on the street in awe, looking at the house in the dim moonlight. It still looked the same in many respects but different in others. The trim, which had been white, had been painted brown, and a garage stood in front of where the carport had been. The in-ground pool was still there, but the fence was different. Instead of simply encircling the pool, it now went around the entire backyard.

Under the cover of the darkness, I slipped towards the house to get a closer look. No one was home, making it safe to climb the fence to have a look in the windows of my old bedroom. The cellar door, which created a ramp from the ground to one of two windows in the room, allowed me easy access to a window that would otherwise have been too high. I was surprised to see cane shutters but then I remembered those vaguely. My mother had hung them when she redecorated the room not long before we left.

Looking into my old room, I remembered my last weekend in the house, when I visited my dad and Puff. I recalled standing in the room, the shutters of the other window open, shining a flashlight onto the back porch of the next-door neighbor's house where several neighborhood boys were having a sleepover. I apparently woke them up, and they crept over to our yard like spies, shining their flashlights in my bedroom window and the windows to my parents' room and bathroom, all of which faced the neighbor's house. I darted from window to window, keeping them guessing from where I might shine my flashlight next. They finally caught me in my room, and I stood still, holding the light, expecting the embarrassing moment when I'd know I'd been caught. "All I see is hands," said one boy. Aha! By keeping the light shining and not running away, I had kept my identity a secret from their lights, even though I knew they had to know who I was.

The boy who had seen my hands was David, who I knew from school and the neighborhood. As I sneaked around my own house now, a decade later, I wondered if he would remember me. I didn't try to find him, though. I never intended to talk to anyone. Even though I didn't have any conscious understanding of what I was doing there, I felt that I had to be there alone. I didn't even discuss this part of my trip with my friend.

Breaking away from my reverie, I peered into a few more

windows. Quickly, silently, I moved about and discovered the carport was still there, hidden behind the garage. The door to the kitchen still had the 1960s style louvered windows. Since it was December, there was no way of knowing if my morning glories still bloomed on strings hung on the side of the carport shed or if the spring flowers still came up in what had been my garden underneath the dining room window. I did notice the mimosa tree that had grown next to my garden was gone, and I remembered my parents talking about its roots possibly damaging the house if it were allowed to stand. I wondered if this was why it was gone.

I darted up to the in-ground pool for a quick look. It was covered but otherwise looked much the same as it had when I lived there. I remembered how we celebrated with a lobster dinner when the pool was finally installed after endless construction delays. I also recalled inviting all of my classmates for a pool party at the end of fifth grade and how my parents' impending divorce derailed any such plans the following year.

I wanted to spend more time there, but I couldn't. I didn't want to be discovered, plus I didn't have much time. I left, but not before making plans to return the next day after the wedding.

The following afternoon, with my friend safely off on her honeymoon, I headed back to the house with my 35mm camera in hand. As I took a shot of the house from the front, I could more clearly see how the brown trim changed the look of it, highlighting the browns rather than the white in the brick.

I photographed the crimson king red maple in the front yard but noticed the white birch tree I used to climb was gone. Daylight offered little cover, but the front porch, a painted concrete slab hidden by shrubbery and wrought iron trim, seemed to be calling me closer. Perhaps it was because that was where, for the first time, I had lured Puff, who had become my beloved cat, into the house. I ventured through the yard, hoping to get a quick shot and then steal away undetected. But no sooner did I get to the porch and aim my camera when the door opened, and a woman peeked her head out. "May I help you?"

Uh oh. I'd been caught.

I was embarrassed, but I also wanted her to know I meant no harm in nosing about her property with a camera. So I told her the truth. "This might sound strange," I said, "But I used to live here. I was just taking some pictures of what the place looks like now."

"Oh, I thought you were a real estate agent," she said, sounding relieved. She and her husband were forever chasing away local realtors who were after them to sell the house, and she was actually glad I wasn't going to pitch a listing. "Would you like to come in?" she asked.

Astounded, I accepted her invitation, certain that a look inside would go far to satisfy my curiosity. I stepped into the foyer where Puff had climbed the wall and immediately burst out crying. The tears came quickly and without warning. I had not been feeling sad, nor had I been aware of any of the pain I felt living there. But once inside the foyer, my emotions ceased to be locked away, and gained control of my body.

"Oh, my," the woman soothed, taking me into her arms. "You were the one with the retarded sister."

Her acknowledgment of my painful past only made me cry harder. But it did provide me with a sense of relief. At least she knew I wasn't a total idiot. Oddly, I never thought to ask her how she knew about Nicole.

The woman introduced herself and her husband. They then proceeded to give me the grand tour. I don't remember much of what was said during my journey back in time, though I do remember that many things were familiar. The new homeowners still used many of the items that remained from our time there, such as the decorative wooden curtain rod in the dining room. Nicole's bedroom door still locked from the inside, and glued to the back of it was a set of wooden Raggedy Ann and Andy plaques that had been handmade by my mother. Although they were obviously significant, I barely remembered them.

The new owners of the house explained that they had bought the house seven years after we'd left but that a number of things had remained from our time because they were quality items. They were impressed with the fence around the pool, for example, even though it had eventually deteriorated to the point where it had to be replaced. They used the living room drapes my mother had made until they were just too old and outdated. The drapes in my parents' bedroom remained, however, as did the wallpaper we'd hung in the kitchen and my dad's bathroom. I asked about my birch tree and was told that it died and they had to have it cut down. But they were planning to replace it with another birch.

I told them tidbits about the house, like how Puff used to beat on the cellar door when she wanted to come upstairs. A quick rapping on the door provided a lively demonstration. I asked about the neighborhood and learned that most of the same people were still there.

The couple shared my journey to the past with quiet empathy.

They did not want me to remain stuck where I was — in a painful place where my estrangement from my mother seemed almost to be my life's focus. But they also seemed to understand that I had come from a difficult place and that seeing this house — their home — was of paramount importance to me.

After leaving the house, I took a quick spin through the neighborhood and photographed some of the houses where others I had known lived. But I didn't talk to anyone else.

Next, I went to visit my schools.

John C. Kunkel Elementary, where I had gone from kindergarten through third grade, looked the same. It was a white brick building constructed in an E shape. Colored circles hung in the windows, just as I had remembered. Green circles had meant recess was in progress. Red circles meant recess was over, and it was time to come in.

When I was about to start fourth grade, the kids in my neighborhood had been transferred to another school in town. My visit to Grandview, which had since been renamed Alice Demey, affected me more profoundly, perhaps because I was older when I went there. The building was open and I tiptoed through the halls looking for familiar names on the classroom doors but found only one, that of a fifth- or sixth-grade English teacher.

I went outside and walked around the playground. The melancholy patch of gray pavement seemed the perfect place to be on a gray day. The gray even paled the red brick. I felt the most connection to the school and my past while standing in the corner created by the L-shaped building. Leaves were blowing around in circles, creating the mini-tornadoes I always remembered. I could visualize kids playing and almost hear their voices, echoing from the past, like when hearing something in the night and then thinking you only imagined it.

Going home that night, the emotions rose to the surface and overflowed. I found myself feeling things that I had been unable to let myself feel when I left Middletown nearly a decade earlier. I finally began to grieve the loss of my dad, my sister, my dog, and my cat, as well as the intact family I had once known.

I also grieved for what never was. What would my life be like if we had stayed? Surely, my father would be alive since he would not have been in Pittsburgh and, therefore, not on the highway at the same time as the drunk driver. Maybe my mother would still have been abusive, but my dad would have been able to run interference.

What ifs also came from outside the house. I remembered a sixth-grade school dance we'd had to celebrate, moving on to junior high. Seven different boys had asked me to dance, and most of them took me totally by surprise. I had a wonderful time with a number of female friends in my class, too. The possibilities seemed endless, but they were tempered by the sadness of knowing I would not be able to stay to pursue them.

And now, there I was a decade later, unable to look back on my childhood with typical adult nostalgia, instead mourning 10-year-old losses and what might have been. I felt somewhat angry and cheated but mostly sad and alone. Little did I know, however, that as bad as I felt, what I had done — facing the ghosts of Middletown — was one of the most important things I would ever do.

—

One summer about 15 years later, I would make another journey, this time to face the ghosts of New Bethlehem.

My longtime friend Cheryl rode along with me. The town looked quite a bit different. The grocery store where we'd shopped was gone. So was the local bank. Most of the other businesses were either gone or had changed enough to be unrecognizable.

The road through town is shaped like a T. You come up Route 66 and enter the town as if you're coming across the top of the T. In the center of town, you can turn left, down the vertical part of the T, or continue straight as if you're still going across the top. We turned left onto Wood Street and drove up past my old house, which was just a few blocks from the intersection.

It looked the same, with white vinyl siding and a wrought iron railing surrounding the front porch. An alley ran from the main road between the house and the brick wall that marked the neighbor's property. A pull-off parking area was located behind the house, where steps led down from a sliding glass door with a large deck to the right. It was just as I remembered it.

The alley continued past the end of the property to the parking area of the elementary school where I had last seen Mark. Cheryl and I drove up and down the alley several times. I wasn't sure if anyone was home and I didn't want to knock on the door or even take photos as I'd done in Middletown. My time in Middletown was mostly happy. My time in New Bethlehem was anything but, and I had no desire to take photos or preserve this experience in any way.

On some level, it might have been cathartic to go inside the house, where my mother had beaten me, called me names, and where the sexual assaults had taken place. I think, however, I knew I could handle only so many ghosts at one time.

Cheryl and I drove around, and I tried to find where Mark had lived. I was unsuccessful, though I'd come close. I recognized the roads; I just couldn't figure out which house it was since I had been there only once or twice, when my mother had driven him home after a supervised date and before she broke us up.

Though there were ghosts at my house, I knew I would find some rather formidable ones at Redbank Valley High School. Still, I wasn't afraid to enter the school and have a look around.

It hadn't changed a bit. Shaped like an L, you entered the front door and could go straight down the hall where high school classes had been held. If you turned left, a much longer hall went past the office, past other high school classrooms, and onto classrooms for seventh and eighth grades. I had been there only for ninth and tenth grade, so I had not spent any real-time at the far end of the longer hall.

Cheryl and I had walked through town and did a little shopping. I remember being surprised that the people in town were nice. In retrospect, it's not really surprising. It's just that my memories were so clouded with pain that I could not remember a single kindness from when I lived there.

During the visit, I really didn't remember much of my time in New Bethlehem. I dug out my diaries and read them. Some of it came back. But I still felt a sense of disconnect between the information contained in my diaries and a real memory. Going to New Bethlehem, I hoped, would provide the visuals necessary to make me connect emotionally to what I wrote in my diaries and to remember those events beyond basic reading comprehension.

I found the visuals I needed went beyond buildings and the landscape. I needed to see faces.

Cheryl and I went back to the school and talked to the superintendent, who was in the building that day. I told him I was a former student and that I didn't have any yearbooks. He gave Cheryl and me permission to get the yearbooks out of the school library and have the school office staff photocopy pages from them.

Things started to click as I looked through the yearbooks and asked for photocopies of pages that included photos of Mark, me, the vulgar track coach, the English teacher who ignored my cries for help written in a journal, and others. I even got copies of pages that included photos of the few people I had considered friends — other outcasts who were nice to me because they were bullied, too. Wow.

The clerk was perplexed.

"What are you doing?" she kept asking.

"Trying to remember," I would say each time she asked. She didn't ask who I was, but, at one point, Cheryl used my first name, so it's possible she figured it out later. If she remembered right there and then, she didn't show it.

One of the copies I'd asked for showed photos of the principal and vice principal from the time I had gone to school there. The clerk spoke fondly of the principal, saying she worked in the office when he was there.

The dates of the yearbooks I was looking through told her

which years I'd been there. She asked me if I remembered her daughter and showed me her picture along with that of her boyfriend. She told me they'd gotten married. I told her the truth. I did not remember them.

Later, back at the hotel, while Cheryl and I were looking through the photocopies, visions of my past there suddenly started coming back to me. The mockery, name-calling, pushing, shoving, pranks, and the fact that I had no place to run, no place to find safety, except on the sly with Mark — off school property. As the memories came flooding back, I realized I knew who the school office clerk's daughter and boyfriend were. They were the leaders of my gang of tormentors.

No wonder I never had a chance against the bullies. They had an ally in the administration office, and their ally had the principal's ear. Realizing that made it all come together like the pieces to a sad puzzle.

I think bullying is as much a school institution as reading and math. Everyone knows who the bullies are. The kids know. The teachers know. The principals know. The parents know. These days the schools run programs aimed at deterring bullying. The kids come for an assembly and watch a film or see a presentation on how bullying isn't nice. Nothing seems to be done directly to make bullies take responsibility for their actions, however. Sometimes, parents will intervene and make their kids apologize in an attempt to teach them how to behave. School officials do this on occasion, too. But far too often, everyone just lets it go. Back in my day, it was even worse. They would make excuses about how kids will be kids or say that kids need to learn to get along on their own. Sometimes, they would even lie to us and say the bullies only picked on kids they liked. Oh, so we were supposed to be happy to be bullied?

When I was in school, if a fight broke out, everyone was punished, or no one was punished — except at Redbank Valley, where I was punished or ignored. No one ever looked into the causes of fights, and if they did, they acted like it was just kids' stuff and nothing worth fighting about. When people are throwing stuff at you, tripping you in the halls, or stealing from you, and no one in authority gives a damn, fighting is the only way to get it to stop.

By the time I started running, my confidence — and strength — increased to the point where I was finally successful in using the only tool available to me to stop the bullies — my fists, along with a couple of swift kicks. I'm sure my punches and kicks were fueled by the anger I carried against New Bethlehem and Redbank Valley, much as I did the anger I felt toward my mother. No one ever helped me, so I quit trying to solve the problem by following the rules. If I wanted to stop them, I had to do it myself. For better or worse, this strategy worked, and it was the only strategy that ever did.

—

Into adulthood, I struggled with the fact that people see anger as a negative emotion. Counselors will tell you emotions aren't positive or negative. You aren't obligated to feel any certain way. Anger is a normal human emotion.

A chance encounter in December 2019 helped me reconcile the anger I felt over my two years in New Bethlehem. At that time, I was in Maine working as a reporter for the *Ellsworth American*.

Every week, each reporter was to ask someone a question and get the person's answer and a snapshot, which were compiled and published.

I was having lunch at my favorite cafe, scanning the room to find someone I could approach to ask that week's question when I spied a woman eating alone. It's easier to find willing participants when they're alone than when they're with a group, so I approached her. I got her answer to the question and her photo. Somehow, we got to chatting, probably because I also ate alone, and the question of what brought us to Maine came up. In the course of the conversation, she mentioned she had been a teacher in a small school in a small town in Pennsylvania, one I'd probably never heard of. "Try me," I said, adding I had moved around a lot within Pennsylvania. Still, I did not expect her answer.

"Redbank Valley," she said.

I was stunned. I'm not sure if it showed on my face or if I managed to hide it. I told her I had actually been a student there.

Sadly, I remember very little else about the conversation. I think she said she ran the school musical. I don't think I had her for class, though I do remember sitting in a room where she was the teacher. It might have been a study hall, though. After some conversation, she said she remembered who I was.

I didn't tell her those two years at Redbank Valley were the worst years of my life. In fact, when it came up that circumstances would find her spending Christmas alone, I invited her to spend at least part of the day with us.

She graciously declined, "I don't mind spending Christmas alone," she said. I offered a couple of times and even gave her my card in case she decided she wanted company.

When our conversation was over, I left the restaurant feeling confused. Wasn't Redbank Valley and everything connected to it the epitome of evil? I found someone who had been there when I was and yet she didn't have horns or carry a pitchfork.

The experience of that encounter swirled around in my head for days. It filled me with an unexpected sense of peace. I still wondered why she never helped me. Did she not know what was going on? Had she not heard the rumors? When my mother and I left town, one neighbor asked — in all seriousness — if we were leaving because I was pregnant. So I knew there were rumors.

In the end, however, none of that mattered. I had found peace with it.

- 22 -

THE FINAL BETRAYAL

My mother developed a strange relationship with a coworker when we moved back to Pittsburgh in 1980. I was still in high school at the time, and Hazel, who I believe was actually my mother's subordinate, seemed normal enough. When they started getting together outside of work, I saw it as a good thing. My mother needed a friend, and she hadn't had any strong local friendships since we'd left Middletown.

Slowly, however, things got weird.

It seemed to me that Hazel was more enamored with my mother than my mother was with her. While I was home on college break during my freshman year in late 1982, Hazel showed up at the house and walked in without knocking. Then, she and my mother stayed up all night in the den on the first floor of the three-story townhouse. The main topic of conversation seemed to be estrangement from family. Hazel whined that her siblings were no good. She had lived with her parents, and after they died, even they became the subject of her whining. My mother, of course, had plenty of her own sad stories regarding her family. Sometimes they complained about work. The only happy thing they ever seemed to talk about was their pride in being Italian. I'd met Hazel's parents, and they didn't strike me as being Italian. Their last name didn't sound even remotely Italian. Perhaps Hazel had just invented an Italian heritage so that she could bond with my mother over something they supposedly had in common. I don't know.

The next time I came home, my mother kept the front door of the townhouse locked. Hazel didn't take the hint. She would stand out on the porch, ringing the doorbell repeatedly. When that didn't work, she might go away for a while but would return later to start the whole process over again. My mother told me not to open the door or even look out the window. Nor was I to answer the phone because Hazel often called after ringing the doorbell didn't work. If Hazel knew my mother was home, she would never go away.

I honestly never really knew the score between them. While my mother would pretend not to be home so she could avoid letting Hazel in, the two of them went on trips together. This doesn't sound to me like how you handle someone you don't like. I think some of it was a control issue. My mother didn't like someone else walking into her house without knocking — and, seriously, who would? — or having another person dictate when they would get together and how much time they would spend together. But this was my mother, so who knows?

At any rate, I didn't give it much thought. I had my own issues to worry about.

―

Sean and I tried to foster a reconciliation with my mother by moving to the Pittsburgh area in early 1988 before we got married. At first, it seemed to be working. My mother was involved in planning our wedding. In fact, I encouraged it. She relished the role and was surprisingly respectful, running ideas by me and asking questions. She was thrilled when I said I trusted her to handle it. I knew she had good taste and that everything would be exquisite, at least as far as a tiny wedding could be.

Another part of the reason I let her run with it was that I wanted to be married, but I really didn't want to plan the wedding. The whole process, from what to wear to keeping the guest list manageable, was just not my thing. Other brides may revel in planning the biggest party of their lives. Sean and I would have been happy finding a justice of the peace and getting married alone in the woods somewhere.

We wound up having a private ceremony followed by a small reception. It was a nice party, with great food. Generally, my mother behaved herself, and there were no major problems or arguments.

When it was time for Sean and me to leave, I said goodbye to everyone and then to my mother.

"I was wondering when you'd get to me," she said.

"I was saving the best for last," I replied.

"Be happy," she said.

She was a little wistful as we embraced, but she seemed generally happy for me.

It didn't take long for the shenanigans to start, however.

Sean and I got married the Friday before Memorial Day in 1988. We didn't have a real honeymoon. We spent three nights at a hotel in Monroeville, home of a large shopping district in the suburbs of Pittsburgh. The hotel had a water slide and mini golf, so we felt like we were living large.

That Monday morning, we left the hotel and stopped at my mother's house to get a few of my things. My mother whined because we weren't planning to spend the day at her house. I tried to explain we had a lot to do and we both had to go back to work the next day.

"If you loved me, you'd stay," she said.

I sighed softly but otherwise ignored the comment. Sean and I got what we needed and left.

The next several weeks were filled with more of the same. She called one day, furious because her car had broken down the day before and I wasn't there for her. I asked how I was supposed to know she needed me if she didn't call. I didn't get an answer.

Another time, we were in the car with her on a short trip that required traveling one exit on the Pennsylvania Turnpike. She asked if we had 40 cents for the toll. When we didn't have exact change and tried to give her $1, she flipped out, calling us "assholes" for not being willing to spare 40 cents. We even told her she could keep the change, but that just made her angrier.

The last straw came in mid-summer. Sean, who had a degree in engineering, had a seasonal landscaping job but wanted full-time year-round work in his field. He came home from the landscaping job one Saturday while I was out, checked messages, and, seeing none, went out to get a Sunday paper. In those days, the Sunday papers had the best employment ads, and they hit the stands on Saturday evenings. While he was gone, my mother called and left a message and we didn't see the blinking light on the answering machine until the next day.

We played the message, and I felt that all-too-familiar fear that I did not yet understand. My mother had called to invite us over for dinner the previous night. I called back as soon as we listened to the message but it wasn't soon enough. She told us she had made spaghetti, and it all went to waste because of our selfishness. I tried to explain what happened and she accused Sean of withholding messages from me. I told her I would not tolerate her trying to pit my husband and me against each other. She screamed insults and called me names before hanging up on me.

A couple of days later, she called again. This was long before caller ID, so I answered without knowing who was on the other end of the line.

"YOU HAVE MAIL HERE!" my mother screamed and then abruptly hung up.

There was no reasoning with her from that time forward. I got my mail and another argument. It was enough for me to realize that permanent reconciliation wasn't possible unless I was willing to put up with her unpredictable fits of rage. As a minor, I had been forced to put up with it. But I was no longer dependent on her. Although Sean and I didn't have enough money left over at the end of the month for a pizza, we had enough to get by, and I had no reason to submit to any more abuse.

Months passed without another word from my mother. I didn't even get a birthday card. As winter neared, Sean was facing a layoff from the landscaping company. He had an engineering job offer at a company in the Philadelphia suburbs. So we moved in November 1988. I sent my mother my change of address and, sometime the following year, I wrote her a letter laying everything out for her. I wanted her in my life, but I would not accept name-calling, accusations or manipulation. If she wanted us to have a relationship, I was willing. But it had to be a two-way street. What happened from there was her call. She could ignore me or she could reach out. I told her I loved her no matter what her decision. I never heard from her again.

—

In the summer of 1989, not long after we left Pittsburgh, Sean and I bought a house. I sent my mother a note telling her so and providing the new address and phone number. She did not respond.

Eventually, Sean and I settled into our daily lives as homeowners. In 1990, I had a job working for *The Reporter*, a daily newspaper in the suburban Philadelphia area. We weren't rich by any means, but we finally could afford the occasional pizza. Then, on the morning of Sept. 22, 1990, one of my mother's sisters called to tell me my mother had shot herself. She said Hazel had found my mother and didn't want anyone to call me. My aunt called over Hazel's objections.

It was a Saturday. I was 25 years old.

—

The next several days are a blur. I remember calling off work for the following week and driving from our home in eastern Pennsylvania to Allegheny General Hospital in Pittsburgh. We arrived around 10 p.m. My mother's sister greeted us and accompanied Sean and me into my mother's room. She was unconscious and breathing with the aid of a respirator. Her chest rose and fell in time to the noise made by the machine.

"It's going to be alright," my mother's sister said loudly, as if she thought yelling would help her message get through.

I was silent for a moment. Then, I placed a corner of my Bankie against my mother's skin. I told her that if I were ever seriously injured or in a coma, I had instructed Sean to touch me with my Bankie. I wanted to do the same for her.

Medical personnel told me that while my mother could survive, it wasn't likely. If she did, she would not be the same. The bullet entered her right temple and exited on the left side. Brain damage was inevitable. It was really only a matter of time until she passed.

At some point during the night, I found myself in a room with my mother's relatives and a man discussing organ donation. When the presenter asked if anyone had any questions, I said both of my parents had discussed donating their bodies to science in hopes that it might help answer questions about Nicole. At that point, my mother's relatives started screeching. They clearly did not like this option. The presenter told them all to hush because it was my decision. I didn't look at them or acknowledge them as the presenter spoke. He said I could either donate her organs or donate her body to science, but not both. I chose to donate her organs. My mother's relatives never said another word to me in that room or even later on.

Sean and I were at the hospital until Sunday morning. At some point during the night, Hazel showed up. She spoke as if she was in a blood feud with my mother's relatives over the estate, and she was the righteous one. I just let her talk. I hadn't gone to Pittsburgh to get my mother's things and hadn't even thought about how the estate would be settled.

As dawn approached, I took advantage of a counselor who was on duty to assist people dealing with tragedy and death. She asked me how I felt and what I wanted to say to my mother. I briefly told her our history and said I was angry because my mother apparently would rather die than reach out to me.

"So tell her," the counselor said.

"I can't," I said, adding that it just did not seem to be appropriate while my mother lay dying.

"Why not?" the counselor asked. "Shouldn't she know the truth?"

I decided she was right and went back to my mother's room where, without the presence of others, I could speak freely. I told my mother she destroyed hope. She could have had a relationship with me if she chose to make an effort. It was not unreasonable for me to expect her not to hit me or call me names. But she couldn't even do that for me, and that was on her.

I have no regrets over what I said.

We left the hospital around 6:30 or 7 a.m. Sunday and went to the police station. At some point, Hazel, my mother's sister, and her husband showed up. The police report was already completed. None of the police officers interviewed me or asked me any questions. The only one they had talked to was Hazel, who told them my mother was distraught over losing her husband and Nicole and that I had abandoned her. The cops didn't even confirm any of this with me. They were actually rather hostile.

Hazel said my mother had called her the day she shot herself and told her to come over. She arrived to find a note on the door that said not to come in but rather to call 911.

Hazel invited Sean and me to come over to her house, which had been nearly empty in anticipation of getting my mother's furniture. She said she wanted me to know what my mother left her and produced a typed letter. It said Hazel was to get everything except the car, which was to go to one of my mother's brothers, and the washer and dryer, which was to go to the sister who had called me.

The letter went on to say that I was to get the Lladro porcelain figurines I had ordered from Spain for her but only if I "got in touch," though what exactly that meant was never explained.

My mother's letter concluded by saying, "If you love me, take care of my cats."

Apparently Hazel didn't love her, at least not that much. Nor did my mother's siblings. The cats had been taken to the pound. Though we had already been up all night, Sean and I went over to my mother's house to get the cat litter boxes, dishes, and other cat supplies in anticipation of adopting her cats. While inside, we heard pounding and went downstairs to see the front door as it was being smashed right off the frame. My mother's entryway was a split level, with a landing in front of the door and a few steps leading both up and down from there. One of my mother's brothers — the one with whom I had lived when I started seventh grade — charged up the steps from the landing, his one arm drawn back, his hand in a fist, a posture that was intended to be threatening. Several of my mother's siblings came in behind him, shouting.

"No!"

"No!"

"No!"

"Don't hit her! She can sue!"

I didn't flinch. My mother's assaults taught me not to show fear, and I didn't. By the time they were all inside the door, I was already on the phone, dialing 911, and I held my position at the top of the stairs without moving.

Before the cop came, my mother's relatives began hauling things out of the house, prompting a neighbor to offer me his garage to store whatever I could take out. I took him up on his offer mostly because I saw what my mother's relatives were doing as theft.

When the officer arrived, he told my mother's relatives I was the heir and that they had no legal right to be on the property or to take things without my permission. But, he suggested to me that I not file charges because it would require returning to Pittsburgh from my home six hours away. And besides, he said, this was family. If only he knew what kind of family this was!

At the time, all I could think about was the difficulty of having to return to Pittsburgh later and the issues it might create with my job, as well as the expense, so it made sense not to press charges. In retrospect, I wish I had pressed charges, but I didn't come to that conclusion quickly enough.

Unfortunately, this was only the beginning of the nightmare, and what was to come was not their handiwork but rather that of Hazel.

The next day, Sean's parents arrived in Pittsburgh to offer support. They said they thought the material things weren't worth the fight and suggested I let it all go. I told Sean I wanted to rent a truck and empty the house right then and there. He was willing, but I knew that once we got home, we wouldn't have had any place to put it. So, we filled the pickup truck we had driven to Pittsburgh with whatever items from my mother's house would fit. His parents filled their pickup, too, and we left the rest behind. As we headed for the highway, I vowed I would not return to Pittsburgh again. Ever. I planned to let Hazel and my mother's relatives fight over her things.

I changed my mind, however, after Hazel hired an attorney. Starting about a month after my mother's death, he called repeatedly, telling me I needed to sign paperwork making Hazel the administrator of the estate and threatening to have me held in contempt of court if I didn't.

Eventually I met with a local lawyer who suggested I hire someone from the Pittsburgh area to represent me. He saw a copy of the letter Hazel had given me and said it was not a legal will. In addition, it appeared to have been signed with a stamp of her signature rather than by her hand.

Initially, Sean wasn't on board with the idea of returning to Pittsburgh. But I convinced him I needed to do this. We set up an appointment with a lawyer who we knew was at least a casual friend of my mother's and met with him in December, about two months after my mother's death. He advised me to go to the courthouse and get sworn in as the administrator of the estate.

In addition to her letter, Hazel produced another document saying she was the beneficiary of my mother's $10,000 life insurance policy. I had been the beneficiary until just a couple of weeks before her death. At the suggestion of my attorney, I contacted my mother's insurance agent, who advised me to contest the change in beneficiary, which I did.

The bank that held the mortgage on my mother's house had padlocked the door but agreed to let Sean and me in. We found a literal mess. The place had been looted. Most of the furniture was gone. Light fixtures had been pulled out, leaving behind holes in the walls and ceilings with bare wires sticking out. Trash was strewn about. It appeared that Hazel and my mother's relatives actually had, literally, fought over her stuff.

I found a few things, like a music box I remembered my dad had given to my mother, lying around on the floor with the trash. Nicole's and my baby books were still there, so I took those. Mostly, I remembered feeling numb. I was naive enough to be surprised that Hazel and my mother's relatives had resorted to looting.

While we were there, my mother's next-door neighbor invited us in. She told me my mother's sister had a key to the house and had taken all of my mother's jewelry before my mother was even dead. I was angry and appalled by the idea that, apparently, they knew ahead of time what my mother had planned and had done nothing to stop her suicide.

Before my mother shot herself, she gave the neighbor a pair of 14K gold and opal earrings. The neighbor wasn't sure why she had done that. When I asked if I could see them, she seemed relieved and said I should take them. I did, but I've never worn them.

I told my attorney that, in addition to the proceeds of the life insurance policy, I wanted my mother's birth certificate, two Raggedy Ann music boxes that had been Nicole's, and two rings my mother wore regularly. After nearly three years of legal posturing and wrangling, Hazel agreed to return these items if I agreed to split the insurance proceeds. However, once she got the insurance money, she never returned any of the personal items. I didn't pursue it. Legal remedies are inaccessible to those without money. I could have spent the insurance proceeds fighting it, but by that time, I was ready to close this chapter of my life. It was time to turn my back on the whole ugly group of people and the whole ugly mess they created.

—

Carol once asked me how I felt about all that transpired, and I always responded with anger. She would tell me that the things I experienced, both good and bad, shaped me into the kind, compassionate, and empathetic person I am. If I hadn't gone through these things, I wouldn't have turned out the same.

"Yes, but no one should have to go through that," I once told her.

She let it be for the moment, but we often came back to it.

"Would you change anything from your past if you could?" she would ask.

Of course I would! Who would choose to live through the things I did? I didn't want my parents to split up. I didn't want my dad to die. I didn't want to lose my sister. I didn't want to be the pawn in a battle between Hazel and my mother's relatives over her estate. I didn't want a lot of bad things that happened anyway.

"But they did happen," Carol would say. "And they molded you into the person you are today."

That was a nice sentiment. But I didn't really understand. I felt anger over not just what happened but also what people did specifically in order to hurt me, control me, or just get me out of the way. It's difficult to deal with anger, especially in a world that tends to add unnecessary negative moral implications to it. It's not wrong to be angry but people often act like it is. Still, I knew I needed to let go of my anger so that it didn't interfere with good things in my life.

This issue of forgiveness has also been a stumbling block for me. I don't see forgiveness as a task to cross off your to-do list, nor do I see it as a moral obligation or a sign of character. Forgiveness is a process that starts with acknowledging your anger. You're allowed to be sad, too, and to wonder why and wish it hadn't happened. People argue you shouldn't wallow in your pain. Instead, they say, you should be positive. Find a good lesson in your struggles.

There is some truth in that, but it's not the whole truth. Forgiveness is not linear. You aren't one step closer to forgiveness with each passing day. And it's not an all-consuming and nothing-else-matters-until-it's-done proposition.

I think the term "forgiveness" is misleading. You forgive someone after an argument or a misunderstanding. In the process, you patch up your relationship. With severe trauma, it's different. You don't work it out with, say, a rapist, a murderer or an abuser. There simply is no working it out with some people.

What you really want to achieve, in my opinion, is not forgiveness so much as acceptance. The bad things happened. You can't change that. Nothing can. You aim to get past feeling cheated because of what you went through, to stop wishing for a different outcome, and to no longer be overwhelmed or sidetracked by the sadness, loss, and pain. When you can do that and just live each day with whatever you have, you've achieved acceptance. Your past is no longer positive or negative but rather just simply what was.

I don't condone what Hazel or my mother's relatives have done. Nor will I ever. But I've reached a point where I can live with it. Part of the reason is all the work I did facing and accepting my emotions. Of equal importance, however, is the fact that I've forged new and better relationships with people who are, frankly, of a higher caliber.

I didn't get there quickly. And before I did, I had to face yet another big hurdle.

- 23 -
THE CRASH

In 2014, our house in Pennsylvania was done. We bought it new in 1995, with no lawn, only generic fixtures and floor coverings, and a wide-open basement with garage doors on one end and stairs to the main level on the other end. Over the course of the 20 years we lived there, we planted a lawn, and Sean built beautiful Japanese gardens, stone walls, ponds, and even created a raspberry patch. Indoors, he built walls separating the basement into a garage, laundry room, and two other rooms that served various purposes over the years, including a bedroom, guest room, office, and cat foster room.

While we lived there, we painted, ripped out the generic carpeting and installed laminate flooring, built an addition, built a deck and then a sunroom, put in a new front door and replaced generic light fixtures with nicer ones. After 20 years, there was nothing else to do except maintenance.

Sean's just not a maintenance man.

His energy and enthusiasm come from creating new things

and planning projects. He was bored with mowing the grass once a week from April to October, hauling mulch in for the garden beds in the spring, and just keeping up with painting, trimming, pruning trees, weeding gardens, and raking leaves away from the garage doors in the fall and again in the spring.

Still, the house was a small paradise that included a hot tub. I loved that house. I loved our daily four-mile walks down the winding back roads past cow pastures and horse barns.

But I love it here in Maine more.

When we bought our place on the Maine coast, we had been looking for something move-in ready. What we got was technically move-in ready. Everything worked. But, it needed updated cosmetics. And, since it was a hoarder house, it needed to be cleaned out. And nothing motivates Sean and me like a big project.

The first floor of the house was cluttered. You could move through, but space was tight. Upstairs, however, stuff was piled shoulder-high from one end of the room to the other. You could walk, maybe, three feet from the top of the stairs before encountering the piles of random objects. It was impossible to get through. In fact, we bought the house not really knowing what was on the second floor.

It had been a summer place for the former owner, who had not been there in at least two years. Dishes were still in the dish drainer. The end tables and shelves were full of candles, books, knick-knacks, and even pieces of flooring. Upstairs, there were eight or nine TVs, several old toaster ovens, an exercise bike, books, boxes of paper, wood boards in all sizes, an old rooftop TV antenna, linens, clothes, and bags full of purchases that had never been opened. Some items were new in the box and still had their hang tags. Other items, almost identical to the new ones, were held together with duct tape, and some of these were stuck back inside their original boxes.

The first step was a literal clean-out. We filled a 30-cubic-yard dumpster — that's a container the size of a tractor-trailer — with 2.89 tons of trash. That project took us a full week.

We hauled tons of stuff back to Pennsylvania to sell at yard sales. We found new dishes still in the box, a brand new Bissell cleaner still in the box, kerosene and electrical heaters still in the box, decorations, souvenirs, craft supplies, and even about $25 in change. We hauled a truckload of books to the local library, a truckload of boxes, plastic jugs, and glass bottles to the recycling center, and at least two truckloads of clothing, shoes, towels, sheets, and linens to the Goodwill.

Perhaps the best find was an old wooden steamer trunk, which we still have. And, underneath all that trash upstairs was a beautiful old four-poster bedroom set.

Some of the finds were just funny, though. I found a pair of glasses with the lenses held into the frames with electrical tape. To this day, I regret that I never took a photo of those glasses.

After the clean-out, the projects were endless — painting, new trim, finishing the floor (using loose pieces of flooring that we'd found), installing new windows, a new roof, new rugs, new siding, and, with the proceeds of the sale of the Pennsylvania house, we had a two-car garage built that included a workshop about the size of another half bay.

Then there was the sunroom, Sean's best project. We started by having a contractor put a roof over the front door and installing a cement pad in front of it. Gradually, as we had money, we built walls, mostly made of sliding glass doors, and finished the inside. It's a cozy little extra room from where we could watch the snow falling in the winter and the wildlife in the summer.

We had a great time working on all these projects together. Sean is one of those talented people who can do virtually anything from installing windows to hanging new siding. I'm not so talented, but I helped with a variety of tasks, from installing insulation to helping Sean move furniture so he could work.

It was a joyful time of bonding and working together on all these projects. Sean swore he wouldn't do any landscaping since he didn't want to get stuck having to maintain it. Still, he built a walkway with some small flower gardens and a fire pit for campfires. When all the projects were finally done, the walkway and small flower beds proved not to be a hassle to maintain.

—

Of course, the image of the happy little couple fixing up their house and walking into the sunset isn't entirely accurate.

It started to be. But then it was interrupted by the Great Bipolar Incident.

We were still living in Pennsylvania when I began to falter, but we already owned the house in Maine. We'd filled the dumpster and had it hauled away by the time I crashed in early 2014. After my family doctor advised me to take my first two weeks of medical leave, Sean thought the best thing for me would be a trip to Maine. And so, we set out for a visit to the house, which was then our getaway cabin.

Sean had been able to determine that when I reached my

lowest points, talking about the cabin and our plans for its future would pull me up. It wasn't exactly a cure, but it did provide hope by giving me something to focus on besides my misery. I might stop crying or lashing out, at least for brief moments.

Unfortunately, the trip didn't go so well.

We'd planned to work on the house, but we also wanted to go on some winter hikes. One such hike followed a trail at a nearby nature preserve.

Partway through, I decided I wanted to freeze to death.

I'd become frustrated over minor things — the wind kept blowing off my hood, and the icy terrain made walking difficult — but my mental state would not allow me to meet these challenges rationally.

We'd gone about a mile on the trail when, in a huff, I whirled around and headed back toward the car. My gloves were first to hit the ground, followed by my hat, scarf, coat, and even the sweatshirt I'd been wearing underneath. My husband hurried behind me, picking up my discarded insulation like a seagull picking up leftover picnic food. By the time we reached the car, I was wearing just a long-sleeved shirt and jeans. I barely noticed the temperature — 15 degrees, with wind chills hovering around zero.

"I'm walking home," I announced when I reached the car, having decided to head for our cabin, which was about a mile away from the parking lot.

As I stepped away from the car, my husband dropped the clothing he had collected and leaped from the side of the car to grab me from behind and haul me toward the car door.

I would have fought him — I usually do — but I was too exhausted to do so, perhaps from the cold, perhaps from frustration. I yelled, and my legs flailed above the ground until he set me down. But when he put me in the car, I didn't fight him.

I would not put my coat back on, however. As we rode back to the cabin, I sat silently, my hands folded in my lap, trying not to think about how mad I was, how much I was hurting, or how much I felt life was a cruel joke not worth living.

Although I never actually made plans to take my own life, I felt despair to the point where I wanted to die. If I could have just caused myself to stop breathing painlessly, I would have done so on this day and several times during the following month.

When we got home to the cabin, I climbed into bed, grabbed ahold of my Bankie, and cried. As I lay in bed, I had Bankie in a wad under my head, like a pillow. As I felt his familiar texture on my face and smelled his familiar scent, I gradually began to calm down.

Because improvement projects had created positive experiences in the past, Sean thought we ought to try something simple and paint the downstairs living area. A few months before, such a project would have been cause for joy, anticipation, and boundless energy. Instead, I collapsed into a heap of tears when droplets of paint hit the floor where I did not want them to be. Although a person with a clear head can see problems with paint droplets as normal, I saw them as a sign that I was inept and that my attempts to paint would only ruin the cabin.

I threw off the old clothing I was wearing along with my shoes and lay down in bed in a heap. Sean told me he experienced some of the same frustrations with paint droplets and that it was normal. But my mind would not compute. I was a failure. I wanted to die. At last, Sean convinced me to just take a nap with my Bankie. We agreed he would get me in a half hour, and we could decide what to do based on how I felt.

When Sean came to get me, I was able to handle the droplets. We finished painting and put the house back together without further issues. But this wasn't the last problem.

One of the worst meltdowns of the trip occurred after a twig snagged my Bankie. We were on our way out of the house, which meant walking a short distance to the car. Heavy snow had caused a small birch tree to bend down across the driveway. As I walked under the tree, a twig caught an open stitch in the blanket and pulled a thread out about two feet.

Once I realized what had happened, I screamed and dropped everything I was carrying, even Bankie. Although I have been able to fix many snags over the years, I didn't think I would be able to fix this one. As with every frustration I faced in this state, I felt like giving up.

Sean tried to reassure me, saying the snag could be repaired. But I knew he did not know how to do it himself. If it were to be fixed, I would have to do it. I'd been having problems with simple things like putting my shoes on and finding my gloves. How was I going to fix this very large snag?

I went back inside, where I just stood by the stove in the kitchen, holding Bankie, staring at that long snag and sobbing. Although I felt I could not fix the snag, ironically, holding my snagged Bankie did bring me comfort and calmed me down. Eventually, I felt good enough to begin trying to work on it. It got the yarn pulled back into its proper place, though I did so slowly, crying the whole time.

But even this was not the last raging fit of depression and

despair. Others came at random and from nowhere. Maybe I couldn't find something. Or I didn't like how my clothes fit. Whatever it was would send me into a crying rage — throwing things, crying, swearing. At one point, I even kicked in the storm door at the cabin.

—

About halfway through that week, I started keeping a journal. I began with a diatribe about how bipolar disorder is potentially fatal. I had faced adversity over and over while growing up and into early adulthood. Yet, I'd always managed to beat it, or so I had thought. I had been functioning in a good marriage, in the workplace, and society. Then, suddenly, I was not. I've had a diagnosis of depression since 1993. Once I got on medication, I coped reasonably well and believed that medication, attitude, and determination could overcome it. After my bipolar diagnosis, I had thought that I would get a prescription for a different medication, and then I would be fixed. When that didn't happen, it was like my life had been turned upside down, broken apart, shaken, and then scattered about like dust removed from a vacuum cleaner bag that had been caught in the wind. I had to figure out how to survive before I could figure out how to manage the disease and beat it. I wasn't sure I could do either.

—

During the fall of 2013, when all this first started, Sean had looked tirelessly for a psychiatrist, any psychiatrist, who would see me. Most had wait lists of at least three months. But I was in crisis now, Sean would explain. No one could help.

Finally, he was able to connect with one. I met him briefly when we were introduced during my first or second appointment. My care was actually handled by a physician's assistant, who extended my medical leave and prescribed an antipsychotic medication. It was new to the market at that time and designed to treat bipolar disorder, among other things. I was told that I should not take antidepressants again because they could actually make bipolar disorder worse.

When the new medication had little to no effect, the psychiatrist's office increased the dose and extended my medical leave by another two weeks. The increases — and medical leave extensions — continued. I wouldn't say the increased dosages made me feel any better. All the medication did was dull everything until I was too numb to feel any emotion at all. At the higher doses, my excessive frustration and outbursts stopped, but the medication interfered with my ability to walk and use my hands. Sean and I enjoyed hiking, but I found myself unable to handle any kind of uneven terrain. I could walk without falling, only on flat paved surfaces.

The physician's assistant then lowered the dose. It reduced the tremors that interfered with my coordination, but it brought back the depressive feelings.

His next step was to combine the new medication with … drum roll, please .. the antidepressants I had been taking before all this started. I objected, reminding him he had told me not to take antidepressants. But he insisted this would be ok. For better or worse, he was right. I began to feel better. The antidepressants took away the debilitating depression, but the antipsychotic medication still had me in a stupor.

All this monkeying around with medications and doses covered nearly all of the six months I was off work. I hated being home. I was bored. But I couldn't concentrate on anything beyond simple tasks. At one point, I did latch hook to pass the time. I didn't want to give up on being able to do at least a little something productive. So, I began working on my photo files, transferring them onto CDs for storage and organizing them better in the process. It sounds simple, and when I'm in a healthy mental state, it is. However, the drugs interfered with my normal reasoning process, leaving me confused and frustrated. Do I need to copy a particular batch of photos onto a CD? Or had I done that already?

As I felt my aggravation level rising, I would often stop and do something else. Sometimes, it worked, at least for the moment. But, the constant need to switch tasks due to frustration wore me down. The things I did while on medical leave should have been simple. The fact that I couldn't do them made me feel like a failure.

Finally, one day, I had had enough. I don't even remember what I was doing, but whatever it was, it wasn't working. It had something to do with the computer, and I couldn't seem to figure out how to complete the task I had intended to do.

I emailed Sean, who was at work and asked questions. When the answers didn't make sense or yield the results I wanted, my frustration grew. Suddenly, without thinking, I responded to his email, saying all this was a waste of time. "I'm going to go drive my car off a bridge," I wrote and then logged off the computer.

I stormed down the hall to the dining room, shedding clothing along the way. I had no idea why I needed to be naked to drive the car off the bridge, but apparently, I thought I did. As I reached the dining room, wearing only my bra and underpants, the realization of what I was doing hit me.

This was suicide.

I'm not sure whether I really didn't want to die or if I just didn't want to do the same thing my mother did. But I stopped myself from getting the car keys and continuing on my mission. Instead, I turned, leaned on the table and screamed. I forced every bit of air from my lungs to make the scream as loud as possible. And then I did it again. And again. I fell into a sobbing heap as I realized I could not handle this myself. I crawled into bed and called my friend Cheryl, who lived several hours away. I told her what I wanted to do, and her calming reassurance got me through the darkness. I must have gone back and looked at the computer because I saw a message from Sean saying he was leaving immediately to come home. I told Cheryl I needed her to stay on the phone with me until he got there. When Sean arrived, I told Cheryl I was no longer alone, and we ended the call.

—

For reasons I don't understand, things began to get better from that point. The physician's assistant at the psychiatrist's office had begun increasing the dose of antidepressants until I was on the same dose I had been before this all started. The only difference was I was also taking the antipsychotic. It doesn't make sense that I wound up on the same medication I had previously discontinued — a medication I was told was not appropriate for my diagnosis — along with a new medication supposedly designed to treat bipolar disorder. But, if nothing else, taking the two medications together brought me back to a place where I could function.

When I finally went back to work, I was stabilized, but I would not say I was well. I went through the motions. I knew my job so well that I was able to do it without thinking much about it. But there was no joy. I missed the thrill of the high I used to get from creative pursuits but I told myself this was just my new reality and I'd have to get used to it.

—

A few months after I had returned to work, a friend who knew how much I loved Maine sent me a link to the job ad for the *Bangor Daily News*. Considering this possibility brought a touch of happiness into an otherwise dull, gray life. Sean and I agreed I should go ahead with my application, and then we made plans to move.

I was still living in a medicated stupor when I began my new job in Maine. I had actually been a little nervous about the move due to my mental state. I feared I might not be able to do the job because I felt I was no longer as sharp as I used to be. Now, I understand my fears were not irrational.

Despite the difficulties of doing that job, however, moving to Maine helped me embark on this healing journey, one that would take me farther than any previous healing I'd done.

—

It was about a year after I left the BDN that I questioned whether I actually had bipolar disorder. Weaning off the antipsychotic worked, though it wasn't quick. I reduced the dose incrementally, staying at each new, lower level for at least two weeks. Once I was comfortable at that level, I would lower the dose again. In the end, I was able to go off the antipsychotic medication with no difficulties whatsoever. In fact, I felt a lot better than I had for about two years. Carol and my Maine psychiatrist had been right. I never had bipolar disorder.

- 24 -
RISING FROM THE ASHES

My crash had actually been caused by a combination of physical changes from surgery, issues from withdrawing from medications too quickly, and PTSD. Recent literature even refers to a condition known as complex PTSD, which arises from chronic or prolonged trauma. Some experts give it other names, but whatever the name, it fits me.

It turns out that what I believed were my character flaws were just normal reactions to triggers. No one else understood that. I didn't even understand it, at least not until after I moved to Maine.

During our sessions, I asked Carol many questions about how people are supposed to respond to the things that triggered me. It was apparent to me that I frequently missed social cues about what was appropriate. Understanding what is normal has been another step in my healing process.

So many of my habits came from my mother. I discovered, for example, that the reason it always makes me nervous when other drivers follow too closely is because I've been programmed to please others. My mother would tell me that if someone was following that closely, it was because I wasn't driving fast enough. Whatever happened, she made it my fault, not allowing for the fact that other people make mistakes, too.

These are things I have had to think about. Thinking isn't enough, however. I need to reach a point where I recognize that what I'm feeling is due to a trigger and not because of actual danger. Eventually, I will get to the point where these things no longer trigger me. While I can't say I have reached that point with no exceptions, I have reached the point where many of them no longer bother me. This has been freeing! Most importantly, now that my whole psyche isn't geared toward danger, past or present, I'm free to devote my energy to other ways of thinking.

I've been able to let go of the things I originally thought would give my life meaning, like becoming a great runner. I used to wistfully think about what might have been. What if I had been at North Allegheny in ninth grade and was able to run in the high school for four years before jumping to the collegiate level? What if my mother had died instead of my dad? What if Nicole didn't have Rett Syndrome? I created some amazing fantasy worlds imagining those things. But, what might have been never was. And it never will be. All I have now is what's real in this world. That has to be enough.

It's simple to say but harder to put into practice. During the Great Bipolar Incident, I remember a program on athletes competing in the Winter Olympics that surprisingly filled me with anger. It's the same story, no matter what sport or who the athlete is. They reach that level out of hard work and the support of family. No matter how hard I worked, there was no familial support. I did not have the money required to hire elite coaches or even train on a regular track. Carol was the only one to acknowledge that not reaching my goals in track was a real loss that I needed to grieve.

I often expressed regret that I didn't accept the track scholarships I'd been offered. It could have made a big difference in my running career.

But Carol pointed out, too, that had I not gone to Penn State to run as a walk-on, I would not have met Sean.

"You wouldn't trade that, would you?" Carol often asked.

"Not in a heartbeat," I replied. I finally understood she was right. I've reached a place where I can not only accept it but also embrace it.

—

Having learned to tease apart the fears of the past from the current situation, has actually been joyful. If you've never experienced fear on a daily basis, it's hard to explain how wonderful it is to not be afraid. Many everyday situations that used to cause me anxiety no longer do.

I was driving home a couple of years ago, listening to the song "Forgiven" by a Dutch band called Within Temptation. As I listened to the words, I realized I had reached the point where I could forgive my mother, at least for some things. Maybe someday I will forgive her for all of it. Some things she did may just be unforgivable. But I've been able to release at least some of my anger toward her because I understand how her past played a role in some of her behavior.

And it's not just about her. I have accepted my past, with

all the good, the bad, and the mediocre. Honestly, I think I've had more trauma in my past than most. But, as the saying goes, it is what it is. I can't change it. Accepting it has allowed me to more easily embrace the good that I've experienced as an adult. I no longer carry resentment about my past, and I no longer feel cheated.

In my youth, I thought I needed to make a big difference in the world in order to give meaning to my pain. I thought that if I could just use my experience to change the world, my suffering would be worth something. Now I realize that just getting through it and being able to come out smiling is enough. What I bring to the world is insignificant on a global level, but the smiles, jokes, relationships, kind words, or even just holding the door for a stranger can have an important impact. I don't need to change the world for everyone. I changed the world for myself, and I believe that has created positive energy that reaches others. So, I've made a difference. It's just not huge and flashy like I originally thought it would be.

—

In addition to all that good stuff, I have concluded I have a guardian angel.

Five or six years after moving to Maine, I remember waking up from a nap and, in that surreal state between being completely asleep and completely awake, I saw my sister.

She was as tiny as ever but showed no signs of her corporeal disabilities. Her hands were not clasped. Her arms hung by her side naturally. She was wearing a dark green jacket, a matching skirt, and beige, open-toed sandals. Her dark hair was bobbed, and she was looking down at me. As my mind entered the fully conscious state, she disappeared. But I'm sure of what I saw.

A couple of years later, when Sean and I were out celebrating his birthday at a local restaurant, the topic of Nicole's birthday came up because, ironically, she was born two days after Sean. It was a Thursday night, and we chatted about the fact that her birthday would be on Saturday.

At that moment, I felt a very strong sense of her presence, which enveloped me as if she were hugging me. Sean and I had had a difficult week, and the hug meant even more to me that night than it would have at any other, more ordinary time. I could not hold back the tears. I wasn't sad, just overly emotional — and appreciative.

I'm sure she has visited me many times. And I hope now and then, she will let me know she's there.

—

Throughout this process my attitudes toward Pennsylvania also have changed. I thought moving was as much about escaping Pennsylvania as it was about wanting to be in Maine. These days, however, I recognize Pennsylvania is where my roots are. Though I was only in Middletown for a few years, I consider it my hometown. I moved around a lot, but that puts me in the unique position of having ties to almost all of Pennsylvania.

In celebration of my love of two states, I am planning to get two tattoos. One will be the outline of the shape of Pennsylvania, with the Russian word for "love." The other will be the outline of the state of Maine with the Russian word "hope." I chose to use these words in Russian because my mother studied the language in her youth, and I did the same, only later in life. Maine is where I found hope. But Pennsylvania is where I found love — from my sister, from Cheryl, from Sean, from many cats, and, perhaps, even a tiny bit from my mother.

—

What surprised me the most about the healing process was finally being able to feel the love.

I used to think that love was pleasing others, that it was something to be earned, as my mother taught me. Then, when I broke away from her, my thinking changed. If my mother abused and hurt me, and I rejected that version of love, then the real version of love must be the absence of pain. If someone loves me, I reasoned, that means they will never hurt me. That's not true either, however.

So what is love, then?

I've come to understand that love is what breaks through when the fog finally clears; it's what rises to the top, pushing aside what Carol called the big four — anger, pain, sadness, and fear. Once you find it within you, it shines like a lighthouse beacon along a dark, stormy shore. I believe that love has always been there, under the surface, even when all I could feel was anger, sadness, pain, and fear.

I believe every significant relationship, including mine, comes with some pain. Although we don't intend to, we do hurt the ones we love. And those I love have hurt me. But I've reached the point where the pain no longer overshadows the love. I have fallen more deeply in love with my husband than ever before. I realize he stood by me for better and, most definitely, for worse.

I appreciate that more than I can say. Of course, I also wonder if it's not that I love him more than ever before but rather that I am more able to feel the love now because much of that other stuff is out of the way. In any event, it's a wonderful feeling.

I've also come to better appreciate my friendships. Though I'll always be somewhat of a homebody who enjoys solitude, I know I have people in my life who will be there for me when I need them. In fact, a couple of years ago, I went through a rough patch with depression and took a chance by telling several of my Maine friends that I needed them to check on me while Sean traveled for work. And guess what? They were there for me. I shouldn't find that surprising, but after a lifetime of having my cries for help fall on deaf ears, I can't help it.

But it's not only knowing they are there. It's also the joy of being together and sharing. I'm part of a group of friends who call ourselves the "Junk Angels" because we find and share many found objects with each other for projects and art. Periodically, we get together and swap these items. Writing and photography are my art, and I don't need supplies to do those things. Still, I love the swaps. I have drawers and boxes full of what Sean lovingly calls "little shit." My friends are a great source of little shit. And little shit makes me happy. That, and the bond of being with like-minded people, is what it's all about. And the members of that group aren't my only Maine friends. I consider myself lucky to have so many. And I love them all.

I feel the same deepened appreciation and love for Cheryl, who has been my friend since 1985. I've known her since before Sean and I were married. And I will never forget how she saved my life one day in April 2014, when I thought my best bet was to drive my car off a bridge.

Healing has meant a deeper appreciation for people who have been positive forces in my life, like my North Allegheny High School track coaches. Plus, I'm aware of the love of others whose contributions were more subtle. When I was in 10th grade, my mother told me my dad's brother and his wife had suggested taking me in. She asked if I wanted to live with them. I said no, of course, because that was the only safe answer.

Long after I was married, I asked my aunt if it was true that they had considered getting custody of me. She said it was. I don't know and didn't ask if they made any formal attempts through the courts or just asked my mother what she thought. I don't think I understood until long after I moved to Maine just how wonderful a gesture that was. Back then, my aunt and uncle had me over for at least one weekend visit, and I remember my aunt noticing that I looked at the ground when I walked. She was concerned because it was a sign of depression. Now I realize how much she cared. My aunt and uncle aren't particularly demonstrative, but I do think they tried to help me. It may not have worked out, but I deeply appreciate it nonetheless. I love them, too.

And then there's my parents-in-law. We've had our bumps, but now, the main thing that comes to mind when I think of them is that I love them.

I loved my parents, too, even my mother. It was because I loved her that I tried so hard to please her and earn her love. I now know it was impossible. And, in her case, there are still some of the big four emotions left to clear. But I can occasionally feel the love peeking through.

I'd like to say that everything is good now, that I no longer get triggered, and that I no longer have emotional meltdowns. But I'd be lying. The truth is I've fallen apart in Maine more times than I fell apart in Pennsylvania. There were times when I questioned whether this meant I made a mistake moving to Maine. How could this be the great positive healing place in my life if I still feel miserable?

Looking back, however, I now understand I fell apart so often because I finally felt safe enough to do so. I knew I wouldn't end up dead because I'd come to see the world differently. I still see all its flaws but I also see the good. It isn't just Maine's beauty or superficial friendliness but also real relationships with Sean and others.

I have friends who have seen me at my worst, and, like Sean, they love me anyway. One of the hardest things I ever did was ask for help. But it was a great thing because it allowed me to discover someone does care — quite a few someones. What a wonderful feeling to know I don't have to live up to some arbitrary standard.

Now that I no longer have to try so hard to survive, I've been able to figure out the real meaning of love. That's the best part of all of this.

TIMELINE

1960 — My parents marry and move to the Harrisburg area.

1964 — My birth.

1966 — Nicole is born.

1969 — My parents buy a house in Middletown.

1973 — We adopt Puff.

1973 — I give up the original Bankie in exchange for the orange one.

1974 — Nicole joins gatherings for handicapped children in Harrisburg known as the Aurora Club.

1975 — Nicole and other handicapped children are allowed to attend school.

June 1976 — My parents split up, and my mother and I moved in with her mother in the Pittsburgh area. My parents place Nicole in a nursing home. My mother takes our dog to the pound.

August 1976 — I am sent to live with an uncle so I can start seventh grade in the Norwin School District.

October 1976 — I visit Middletown for the last time. My dad has to give up Puff.

November 1976 — My mother gets a job and an apartment but I must switch to a different junior high within the Norwin School District.

Summer 1978 — We move to New Bethlehem.

August 1978 — I start ninth grade at Redbank Valley High School in New Bethlehem.

February 1979 — I meet Mark.

April 1979 — My mother decides Mark and I must stop seeing each other, and she begins taunting me.

August 1979 — I visit my dad for two weeks and come home to find my cat and her kittens are gone.

September 1979 — Mark and I are suspended from school and my mother threatens to have Mark arrested.

October 1979 — My 15th birthday passes without an acknowledgement from my mother.

Nov. 9, 1979 — My dad is killed by a drunk driver. Over the next year, my mother received $65,000 in insurance and death benefits, which she told everyone is to pay for my college.

January 1980 — I flip out at school, and child welfare services are called. The investigator tells me my problems are my fault.

June 1980 — I break up with Mark.

Summer 1980 — My mother and I move back to Pittsburgh.

August 1980 — I start 11th grade at North Allegheny High School.

January 1981 — I start winter workouts in preparation for the spring track season.

May 1981 — I complete my first season of track, having gone from being a sprinter to being a distance runner.

Summer 1981 — My mother buys a customized Corvette from my uncle.

November 1981 — I complete my first and only season of high school cross country.

Winter 1982 — Claiming she doesn't have money to send me to college, my mother tries to get me to enroll in college early so she can continue to receive Social Security death benefits.

May 1982 — I complete my second season of track and am noticed by a college track recruiter. But my mother pressures me to get academic, not athletic, scholarships.

June 1982 — I graduate high school.

August 1982 — I begin my first year at Penn State and join the track team as a walk-on. My tuition is unpaid because my mother won't cooperate with the financial aid process.

April 1983 — I meet Ken.

May 1983 — My mother is hours late picking me up from the Penn State dorms and finds fault with me, causing me to realize I must find a way to become independent.

Summer 1983 — I block my mother's punches and stop her physical abuse.

August 1983 — I begin my sophomore year at Penn State with my tuition still unpaid.

Fall 1983 — My German language teacher notices I seem depressed and suggests counseling.

May 1984 — I end my sophomore year at Penn State with a D average.

August 1984 — My junior year at Penn State begins. Midway through, I change my major to secondary education with a specialty in foreign language.

May 1985 — I drop out of college and move in with Ken's family.

September 1985 — I get my first apartment. I adopt Big Zepp.

1985-1987 — I attend counseling sessions with Jack.

Summer 1985 — I enroll in diesel mechanics school. Cheryl and I become friends.

November 1985 — I complete mechanics school.

Early 1986 — I get my first newspaper job and a better apartment. I'm introduced to photography. I return to Middletown to explore my past. I return to my mother's house to get the rest of my belongings.

Aug. 1, 1986 — I meet Sean.

1987 — I move to New York State in search of a better job. I adopt Wee-Cat.

May 28, 1988 — Sean and I get married.

1990 — Sean and I take our first trip to Maine.

Sept. 23, 1990 — My mother dies by suicide.

December 1990 — I reestablish contact with Nicole.

1998 — I attend counseling sessions with Mim.

1999 — Wee-Cat dies.

April 30, 1999 — Kira Kat is born.

September 2000 — Big Zepp dies.

2005 — Nicole visits my house. I face the ghosts of New Bethlehem.

Summer 2009 — Sean and I adopt Lily.

July 2013 — Sean and I buy a house on the Maine coast.

Fall 2013 — I feel like my antidepressants aren't working and seek medical help.

2014 — After being diagnosed as bipolar, I take six months off work, returning to my job in the summer.

December 2014 — I apply for a job at the *Bangor Daily News*.

Jan. 26, 2015 — Kira Kat dies.

February 2015 — I move to Maine. Sean follows after our house in Pennsylvania is sold.

March 2015 — I start a job as a reporter with the *Bangor Daily News*.

September 2015 — I start counseling sessions with Carol.

Summer 2016 — I leave the *Bangor Daily News*.

Sept. 7, 2016 — Nicole dies.

October 2016 — We adopt Pash.

2019 — I start working at the *Ellsworth American*.

December 2019 — While on assignment for the *Ellsworth American*, I meet a woman from Redbank Valley High School.

July 2020 — We move from the Maine coast to the Moosehead Lake area.

December 2020 — We buy a shuttered antique shop.

June 1, 2021 — We open our antique shop as The Lily Cat: North Woods Antiques and Buttons.

www.ingramcontent.com/pod-product-compliance
Lightning Source LLC
Chambersburg PA
CBHW020048170426
43199CB00009B/203